STUDENT-CENTERED
PHYSICAL EDUCATION

Middle ... Skills

**HUMAN
KINETICS**

Library of Congress Cataloging-in-Publication Data

Smith, Timothy K., 1953-
    Student-centered physical education : strategies for developing
middle school fitness and skills / Timothy K. Smith, Nicholas G.
Cestaro.
        p. cm.
    Includes bibliographical references (p.) and index.
    ISBN 0-88011-590-4
    1. Physical education and training--Study and teaching (Middle
school)--United States.   I. Cestaro, Nicholas G., 1949-   .
    II. Title.
GV365.S55   1998
796'.071'273--dc21   97-36681
                                                                 CIP

ISBN: 0-88011-590-4

Acquisitions Editor: Scott Wikgren; **Developmental Editor:** Kirby Mittelmeier; **Managing Editor:** Jennifer Stallard; **Editorial Assistants:** Jenn Hemphill, Laura Seversen; **Copyeditor:** Alan Gooch; **Proofreader:** Erin Cler; **Graphic Designer:** Stuart Cartwright; **Graphic Artist:** Kathleen Boudreau-Fuoss; **Photo Editor:** Boyd LaFoon; **Cover Designer:** Jack Davis; **Cover Photo:** Human Kinetics/Tom Roberts; **Photographer (interior):** Lorraine J. Raffa Photography; **Photo Shoot Models:** Amanda Esposito, Fetima Fields, Erin Elizabeth Kelly, Rensmay Lam, and Benjamin A. Moore; **Illustrator:** Timothy J. Shedelbower; **Printer:** United Graphics

Printed in the United States of America

10 9 8 7 6 5 4 3 2 1

Human Kinetics
Web site: http://www.humankinetics.com/

United States: Human Kinetics, P.O. Box 5076, Champaign, IL 61825-5076
1-800-747-4457
e-mail: humank@hkusa.com

Canada: Human Kinetics, Box 24040, Windsor, ON N8Y 4Y9
1-800-465-7301 (in Canada only)
e-mail: humank@hkcanada.com

Europe: Human Kinetics, P.O. Box IW14, Leeds LS16 6TR, United Kingdom
(44) 1132 781708
e-mail: humank@hkeurope.com

Australia: Human Kinetics, 57A Price Avenue, Lower Mitcham, South Australia 5062
(088) 277 1555
e-mail: humank@hkaustralia.com

New Zealand: Human Kinetics, P.O. Box 105-231, Auckland 1
(09) 523 3462
e-mail: humank@hknewz.com

contents

key to diagrams

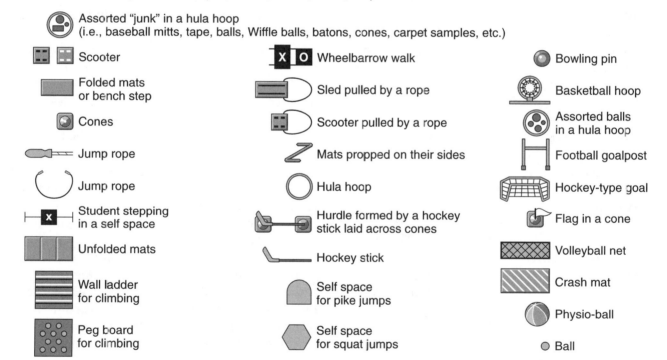

X **x** **O** **o** **A** **B** **C** **D**   Students

→   Student movement (i.e., running, walking, hopping, stepping, jumping, etc.) and/or directional arrow

--→   Ball or object in motion (i.e., thrown, kicked, rolled, etc.)

  Assorted "junk" in a hula hoop
(i.e., baseball mitts, tape, balls, Wiffle balls, batons, cones, carpet samples, etc.)

Scooter	Wheelbarrow walk	Bowling pin
Folded mats or bench step	Sled pulled by a rope	Basketball hoop
Cones	Scooter pulled by a rope	Assorted balls in a hula hoop
Jump rope	Mats propped on their sides	Football goalpost
Jump rope	Hula hoop	Hockey-type goal
Student stepping in a self space	Hurdle formed by a hockey stick laid across cones	Flag in a cone
Unfolded mats	Hockey stick	Volleyball net
Wall ladder for climbing	Self space for pike jumps	Crash mat
Peg board for climbing	Self space for squat jumps	Physio-ball
		Ball

preface

We believe that the ultimate goal of physical education should be to help all students acquire the knowledge, skills, and appreciation for living a physically active, healthy life. We further believe that "force-feeding" students a steady diet of football, basketball, and softball, or drilling them in the same old boring calisthenics every day, does not help students accomplish this goal. In fact, outdated, *subject-driven* programs often turn off the majority of children to physical education and physical activity in general.

Therefore, we have developed a *student-centered*, integrated modular approach to teaching middle school physical education that challenges exclusivity, boredom, and gender bias. In this book, we share what we have learned by developing a program to center on the child rather than on sports or calisthenics. This book serves as a creative and practical resource for physical education teachers because it is filled with simple activities that go a long way in building a foundation for a lifetime of physical fitness.

All the fun, physical activities we share have been tried and proven to promote student fitness and skill development. We have developed the approach outlined in this book by drawing upon our combined 50-plus years of diverse experiences in education, as well as our innumerable interactions with other physical educators from across the country and in our own backyard. Both new and veteran teachers will find this book a useful and practical resource—the type of book you would refer back to for years to come.

To make this book easy to use, we have arranged it into two parts: *Student-Centered Modular Approach*, that will help you to develop and organize your classes, and *Teaching Modules*, that provide you with practical, easy-to-follow, step-by-step directions for more than 150 fitness-related activities using warm-up, skill drills, team, individual, and paired games. Ten detailed health-fitness modules are provided to help you present and reinforce key lifestyle concepts in addition to the "physical" components of physical education.

We feel that this book will prove valuable in providing you with ideas, strategies, and activities that will make physical education relevant to your students, helping them to become more successful in their quest for fitness-oriented lives, both in and after school. Along the way, both you and the students will become more motivated about physical education and have fun doing so! Enjoy!

acknowledgments

As with any worthwhile endeavor, this book is the culmination of the efforts and experience of many people. Our ideas and strategies put forth in this book have been shaped by years of experience, by personal interaction with other teachers and our students, and with help from our colleagues and friends. Activities have evolved over time through trial and error, discussions, presentations, and readings, and for these opportunities and the individuals involved, we are grateful.

We would like to especially thank two individuals at Human Kinetics Academic Division: Scott Wikgren, acquisitions editor, for his vision, patience, and guidance in making this book a reality; and to Kirby Mittelmeier, developmental editor, for his early involvement in the writing process and his invaluable insight and suggestions that served to make this book stronger. Additionally, the administration at East Syracuse-Minoa, where we teach, has always been supportive of us as educators, particularly Carolyne Pfeiffer, our principal. Jane Allen, Nancy Ames, Gary Becker, Hank Collins, Jim Gorney, Doug Hartman, Jean Huss, Mark Powell, and Leslie Reitano have all contributed to our being better teachers through their ideas, expertise, and teaching styles. We are fortunate to have them as colleagues.

Finally, we give a very special thank you to the countless students who make it a point to come back and tell us how rewarding and fun our classes were. It is for you and future generations that we have written this book.

To our parents, James and Kathryn Smith and Carmine and Felicia Cestaro,
who encouraged us to be active from day one

To our beloved wives, Roseann Smith and Beeje Cestaro,
for their devotion, patience, and support

To our children, Drew Smith and Gina and Jared Cestaro,
for their understanding and pride

To our students, who make teaching worthwhile

credits

Table 3.1 on page 18 is adapted with permission from T.K. Smith and N.G. Cestaro, 1995, "Teaching health/fitness concepts to elementary students—a modular strategy," *Journal of Physical Education, Recreation & Dance* 66 (4): 70.

Diagram 4.1 on page 29 is adapted by permission from C.J. Hopple, 1995, *Teaching for Outcomes in Elementary Physical Education* (Champaign, IL: Human Kinetics Publishers), 12.

Table 4.1 on page 30 is adapted from M. Franck, G. Graham, H. Lawson, T. Loughrey, R. Ritson, M. Sandborn, and V. Seefeldt. *Outcomes of Quality Physical Education Programs* (1992) by permission from the National Association for Sport and Physical Education (NASPE) 1900 Association Drive, Reston, VA, 20191-1599.

Table 4.3 on page 33 is reprinted with permission from T.K. Smith, 1997, "Authentic assessment: using a portfolio card in physical education," *Journal of Physical Education, Recreation & Dance* 68 (4): 50.

Table 4.4 and 4.5 on pages 34–35 are reprinted from M. Franck, G. Graham, H. Lawson, T. Loughrey, R. Ritson, M. Sanborn, and V. Seefeldt, *Outcomes of Quality Physical Education Programs* (1992) by permission from the National Association for Sport and Physical Education (NASPE) 1900 Association Drive, Reston, VA 20191-1599.

Portions of chapter 4 are reprinted in part by permission from T.K. Smith, 1997, "Authentic assessment: using a portfolio card in physical education," *Journal of Physical Education, Recreation & Dance* 68 (4): 46-52.

Diagram 5.19 on page 67 is reprinted by permission from T.K. Smith, 1996, "Off-season vertical jump training for junior high volleyball players," *Strength and Conditioning* 18 (1): 27.

Diagram 5.27 on page 79 is adapted by permission from T.K. Smith, M. Powell, and P. Belodoff, 1992, "Control the line, control the game!" *National Strength and Conditioning Association Journal* 14 (6): 67.

Table 6.2 on page 85 is reprinted by permission from T.K. Smith and N.G. Cestaro, 1995, "Teaching health/fitness concepts to elementary students—a modular strategy," *Journal of Physical Education, Recreation & Dance* 66 (4): 71.

part 1

A STUDENT-CENTERED MODULAR APPROACH

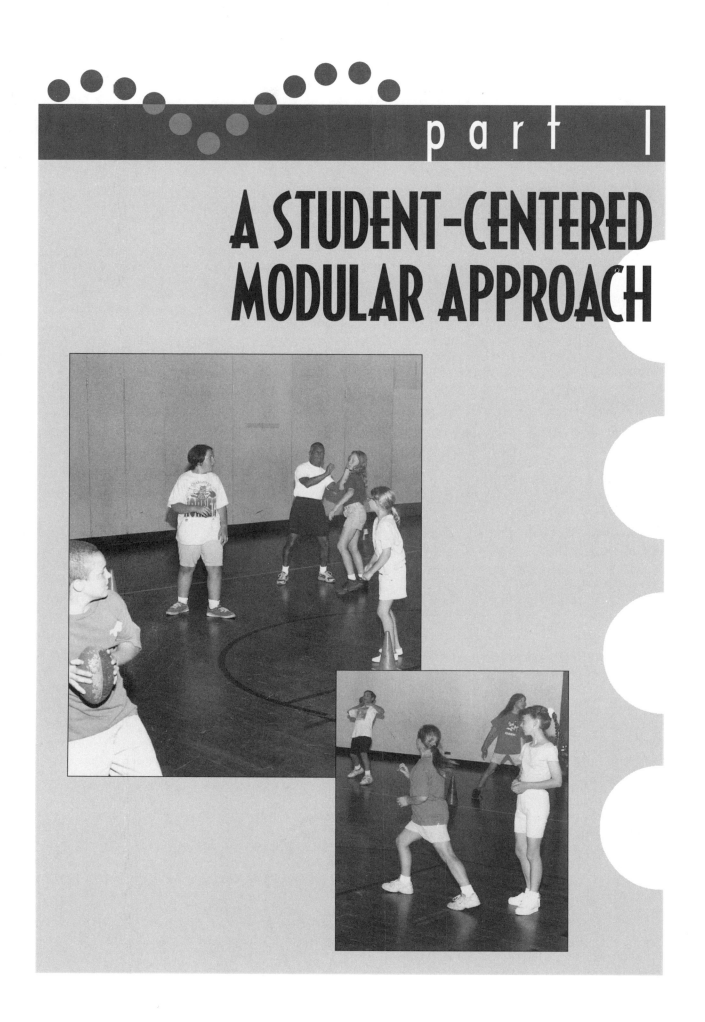

chapter 1

Student-Centered Physical Education

For years, the traditionalists in physical education have taught their classes in three-week units that focus on acquiring and applying skills. For many students, this teaching technique has meant three weeks of frustration. The education of the high achievers (the good athletes) suffers because of the inability of their lesser-talented classmates to function at as high a level. The lesser-talented students in a particular unit cannot improve their skills because of limited opportunities for contact with balls or other objects—thus limiting their opportunities for success—during traditional games. Students who dislike a particular unit often just tune out, not helping themselves, their classmates, or their teachers.

This book breaks from tradition by offering a curriculum that focuses instead on the student. Rather than focusing on winning games, perfecting skill execution, and promoting competition, our suggested curriculum focuses on keeping students moving with fun, progressively challenging tasks (warm-ups, skill drills, and games) that allow them to compete, suc-

ceed, and refine their skills within their own levels of comfort. Because the curriculum is centered on the needs and behaviors of the preadolescent child, it minimizes or eliminates the pitfalls common to the traditional format of teaching in unit blocks.

In student-centered physical education, sport skills are used as a means to an end instead of being targeted as the end themselves. Preparing students for a healthy, fitness-oriented lifestyle is our overall goal. Through participation in warm-ups, skill drills, and games, and through group discussions centered on the *health-related fitness modules* and resultant self-discovery and awareness, students gain a firsthand feeling for, and understanding of, the benefits of a fitness-oriented lifestyle. Although the choice to follow such a lifestyle is ultimately theirs, we have at least presented a strong case for such a lifestyle, showed students that it can indeed be fun and relatively easy to achieve, and, most importantly, given them the basic tools for building such a lifestyle.

DEFINING THE STUDENT-CENTERED APPROACH

We have developed our program around three frequently observed student behaviors and needs:

- Every child wants a chance at success in the classroom, in the gym, and in life. Being successful breeds more positive behaviors.
- Preadolescents have short attention spans. Changing the focus and activities within a class period captures and maintains their interest.
- Students who expect to move and participate, and have fun doing so, will be more motivated to move and participate actively.

Central to the student-centered theme of this book are maintaining program relevance for each student and providing numerous opportunities for each student to experience success. By relevance we mean that students can relate to the material being presented daily in class and can connect with it. The material is pertinent to them, serving a purpose that meets their needs whether that be physical, intellectual, or social. To attain student relevance, we mix and match individual, pair, and team activities, whether they be warm-up, skill-related, or game-oriented tasks. Relevance motivates students, and success leads to more positive educational behavior.

> Ways to build relevance into your curriculum:
>
> - Hold discussions with your students as to their goals.
> - Hold similar discussions with their parents.
> - Keep up with current trends (e.g., step aerobics, cross-training, etc.).
> - Use contemporary music in your classes.
> - Discuss lifetime health concepts.
> - Use short, quick statements ("sound bites") to disseminate information during activity.

The suggestions and strategies in this book will require many physical education teachers to break from their current 40-week "sports"-focused curriculum and switch to a more modular "skill"-focused curriculum (perhaps even playing certain sport activities out of season and several times throughout the year). Such a change will allow you as a teacher to be much more flexible in meeting the needs of your students by choosing warm-up, skill-development, and game modules that address the level of your students on a class-by-class basis without extra work and planning. These changes can be easily made through subtle module substitutions within the class format as outlined in chapters 2 and 3.

Four major concepts will help make your curriculum more student centered by increasing students' opportunities for success and reducing negative pressure, thereby increasing motivation.

MAXIMIZING MODIFIED GAMES

The first concept is to *maximize modified games while minimizing traditional games*. Consider, for instance, the perspective of an insecure and overweight seventh-grade student in a traditional setting. How relevant is a three-week football unit in his life? A child who has probably struggled with physical activity—and sports in particular—all his life knows that he will be relegated to the task of blocking another overweight child for 30 minutes, three times per week, for three weeks.

Consider this from your perspective as an educator: How motivated will this child be in your class? The answer, of course, is *minimally.*

A more student-centered solution is to have students participate in modified football-related activities, whereby they not only learn and use the skills of football, but they also experience varied levels of success and have fun doing so. By playing such games as Pass-Over or Punt-Over (refer to chapter 8), each child will repeatedly touch a ball and have a chance at success 50 to 100 times in a given class

Bob and Alicia do not fit the stereotype of the "jock"-like student. They are less coordinated than many of their peers and relatively weak for their body sizes. If we present traditional games in class with one ball, they will hardly ever touch it or fail when they do, either of which will cause them to withdraw, disrupt, or distract from the game and class environment. By using modified games with multiple balls, they will function at their own levels of competence and get repetitive chances at success. Other students will be too busy to notice Bob's or Alicia's level of play, and the whole class in general will be more enthusiastic, positive, and productive.

session (see photo 1.1). Spread over three weeks throughout the school year, this activity would provide between 450 and 900 opportunities (three weeks times three classes per week) for success and fun. When doing the activity, students' heart rates elevate, promoting cardiovascular wellness. Calories are used for expending energy, thus stimulating weight loss.

In the worse-case scenario, even if the child only catches five passes or punts and throws or kicks for six points in a period, this is 11 successful experiences he would not have enjoyed if he were blocking for the other, more-talented students.

Also, students who participate successfully in modified games become so active, and the games so fast paced, that they have little if any time to notice the triumphs or struggles of others. The spotlight is therefore removed from individual performances, and with it, negative pressure. Yet, everyone's success, as small or large as it may be, contributes favorably to the total team effort and achievement. Because of the repetition of skills in various drills and modified-game activities throughout the school year, all children, including those with special needs, can achieve high standards and success through your classes. Many students with special needs have an affinity for "special-area" subjects, especially physical activity. For these students, physical education class may be the only successful spot in a long and trying school day.

Photo 1.1 Activities like "Pass-Over" provide expanded opportunities for students to experience success.

Students are going to perceive the physical education class that emphasizes modified games as more relevant, more motivational, less threatening, and, ultimately, more positive as compared with the traditional curriculum, in which the football unit forces most students to spend the period walking repeatedly from the huddle to the line of scrimmage.

ROTATING ACTIVITIES WEEKLY

Your curriculum will also become more student centered—and more motivational to students—if the 40-week program creates more opportunities for student success.

Experience tells us that we all (students and teachers alike) learn at different rates. Consider the child who really struggles with passing or setting a volleyball early in the school year. Perhaps the student has a problem "reacting to" or "moving to" any type of ball or has a fear of the hard "volleyball" itself. Regardless, this child will experience limited success in striking tasks during either modified or traditional games (although she will have more opportunity for success, with less pressure, in modified games, particularly if modified balls are used as well). In a traditional three-week unit, there is little hope for weeks two and three being different from week one, thus frustrating the student and limiting skill acquisition.

Instead, let's say you do volleyball for one week. The student, knowing you change your curriculum weekly, endures the volleyball week and continues to come to your class enthusiastically during subsequent weeks as you rotate through a variety of other activities and experiences. During that one "volleyball week," you may even choose to use two different activities to create diversity while targeting the same skills of passing and setting, further motivating students. This is also an ideal time to use individualized warm-up activities and individual/paired skill drills, allowing students to work at their own comfort and skill levels for a portion of the period before becoming part of a "team" concept during game activity.

During the next eight weeks, you might want to challenge your students with a number of other ballhandling activities: Platform Basketball, Goal Ball, End-Line Soccer, Boxball, and Pillo Polo, to name but a few. By using this approach, you will see students improve their catching, throwing, and striking skills as all the repetitive ballhandling drills and opportunities pay off. When you once again return to volleyball, say in January, you will find that the student has probably made tremendous progress in her ability to pass, set, and serve a volleyball, much to your pleasure and the pleasure of the student as well. Repeat this process, and in the spring, even greater successes will be apparent. Perhaps you will have so much success that the following fall the student will be playing in intramural volleyball or on the school team.

As an end result of this focus on varied activities, you will find that success in traditional games is a natural outgrowth of success at skills developed in modified activities.

FOCUSING ON SKILL THEMES

Structure your program so it focuses on movement and fitness skills as opposed to specific sports. For example, rather than teaching three weeks of soccer, three weeks of field hockey, and three weeks of football every fall, try rotating through a week of striking, a week of catching/throwing, and a week of kicking each month. By shifting from the more traditional physical education focus of "sport" to teaching "movement and fitness skills," you will find that learning is best facilitated through a year-long process.

The traditional concept of trying to create a physical education curriculum as a "feeder program for sport" is not logical. A true sports curriculum only reaches approximately 8 percent to 10 percent of the student population, an elite group. The modular skills-based approach targets 100 percent of the student population, making it valuable to students, parents, and administrators.

The basic skills of striking, catching, throwing, and kicking should be supplemented by skills associated with weight transfer, rolling and balance (gymnastics), body space awareness, effort and relationships (wrestling/self-defense), and running, jumping, and landing (track and field). These are skills used in a variety of athletic games and recreational activities, and as such, a variety of sport-type games and modified activities can be used to teach, reinforce, and refine these skills.

MAKING STUDENTS AWARE OF YOUR GOALS AND EXPECTATIONS

Students, like most adults, respond to expected behavior and goals by doing what is required of them. In chapter 2 we will discuss "Objectives Within Physical Education," and it is reasonable to discuss these goals and objectives with students at the beginning of the year, making them partners with you in their own education. You may even wish to go so far as to have students write down their own expectations and goals of their physical education experience. By sharing goals and expectations, you as the teacher and your students can more clearly define expected outcomes from your course. If students have a clear idea of where they are headed, they will more likely be focused on tasks as you progress toward that end. The portfolio card presented in chapter 4 provides a viable assessment tool for students to rate their progress throughout the year while allowing for you, as their teacher, to provide constructive feedback as well. By working together, both you and the student should share

> The task of addressing expectations of students and teachers is made easier if we enter into a personal, verbal contract with our students that is based on mutual respect. We promise them well-planned, exciting, student-centered lessons to help them learn in an energetic, fun environment. In return they promise us that they will give 100 percent to every class, knowing that they will like some classes better than others and knowing that they will do better in some classes as compared with others. The overall purpose of our contract is to join together in full commitment toward creating the best possible environment for learning.

a more productive, positive educational experience. By using the modular lesson plans and teaching strategies outlined in chapter 3 to prepare for your classes, by exhibiting enthusiasm, and by setting high expectations for your class, you will find that the majority of students will be motivated and will respond in kind, meeting your predetermined goals and objectives.

INDIVIDUALIZING PHYSICAL EDUCATION FOR TODAY'S STUDENT

By using nontraditional one-week units, with varied warm-ups and modified activities to develop skills, you will help all students more fully develop sport and lifetime skills. The modular curriculum detailed in later chapters allows students to learn at their own pace, experiencing personal success while functioning at their own levels of competence. This teaching technique follows current educational trends and benefits the less-talented student as much as the elite, since it essentially creates *small groups* of students with *similar talent levels* within the larger class setting.

In the modular curriculum setting, students either in skill drills or within the framework of many of the modified game activities work with students of equal abilities, much as would occur in elementary school reading groups. Conversely, it is not uncommon to see students of different abilities pair up if the students are friends or if the more-talented student is compassionate and mature, serving as a mentor to the less-talented student. Both situations provide for a positive learning environment.

It's important to realize that not all your students are team or socially oriented. For some students, the team-oriented game activities are the least enjoyable segment of the class. Most students will work independently, however, and this is why so many of the warm-up and skill activities presented in chapters 5 and 7 are so effective as teaching strategies.

In a student-centered approach, every child has time to be an individual and showcase talent so that neither low- nor high-functioning students experience the frustrations of the traditional class setting of mixed skill levels. Enjoyment and success motivate students to maximize learning regardless of skill level, which over time will elevate competency levels within each individual student and your class as a whole.

The innovative modular approaches outlined in chapters 2 and 3 will help you develop your student-centered "physical education" curriculum, preparing students for a healthy, fitness-oriented lifestyle. By building upon each previous level of the curriculum, and by modifying team games and introducing lifetime activities, you will promote social, physical, and intellectual growth while creating more individualized, personalized, and meaningful classes.

Adults in our society need variety to stay on task and motivated—why not young adults?

Motivated students not only are more on task, but they also acquire more knowledge and skill and are less of a disruptive force to their classmates and your class, making education more positive for all involved. With the materials in this book, a teacher can change something about her lesson every day while still maintaining the continuity of focusing on a particular skill. Surprise and anticipation of something new breeds excitement as opposed to predictability, that often creates boredom.

It is these ever-changing experiences that our students tell us they enjoy and want more of, creating a cycle whereby we deal with more highly motivated students, that in turn enhances our ability to focus on the needs of students and truly educate them. We hope that the materials in this book will help you to do the same.

chapter 2

MODULAR APPROACH TO PHYSICAL EDUCATION INSTRUCTION

Effective instruction requires a well-planned system of delivery, using a variety of learning styles to present information. By using interchangeable modules within the lesson format (how to do this is detailed in chapter 3), you can maximize the needs of students by mixing individual, partner, and group experiences for students, developing both fitness and sport skills at the same time. The modular approach also allows physical educators to better address interdisciplinary education while focusing on global and more specific physical-activity objectives.

DEFINING MODULAR INSTRUCTION

The *modular approach* to instruction is an organizational tool that can best be described as a "menu" of sorts. Each day, you the teacher have the flexibility to select activities and experiences within a designated lesson to best present your goals and meet the needs of your students based on relevance, progression, integration, and, ultimately, outcome objectives. Modular planning requires that you move away from

unit plan designs in which sport is the focus; instead, you will be focusing on the needs of your students and using a variety of skills and learning styles to maximize student outcomes.

The various modular areas (warm-ups, health-related fitness concepts, skill development, and game activities) use printed word, graphic display, real object (sports equipment), and human encounter to help you smoothly and effectively deliver your objectives (Smith and Cestaro 1992; Smith 1994). This modular teaching system provides you with greater *flexibility* in designing your classes because you can mix and match modules to extend time spent on one modular area while moving ahead more rapidly in another, much as a classroom teacher does. For example, perhaps you feel your classes' fitness levels are low, yet their striking, catching/throwing, and kicking skills are high. You may choose to change warm-up modules slowly, repeating and using *fitness circuits* as warm-up activities (chapter 5) for several months. At the same time, however, you might challenge your students' skill development by changing skill focuses (striking, catching/throwing, and kicking) weekly and activities

When students ask us, "What are we doing in PE today?" our favorite answer is, "Come down and be surprised." Adults and children alike enjoy surprises because they are different, exciting, out of the ordinary. Our students can bank on the fact that some aspect of the class will be different from their previous classes. It might be a new warm-up, a different skill drill, or a new modified game that ties everything together for them. The element of surprise is a great *child-centered* idea!

within a particular skill area daily. The beauty of the modular approach is that it allows for this flexibility in class-by-class design.

The modular approach also allows you to keep your classes *relevant* with respect to student interests and learning styles. For instance, when spring training opens for major league baseball and you're sitting under three feet of snow, you can play targetball, a "striking" baseball-type game indoors. During Super Bowl time in January, why not play arena football indoors as a "kicking" game? During college basketball's "March Madness," you could set up your own tournament using "catching/throwing" skills applied to a basketball-type game. Mixing modules and drills that use individual, partner, and small-group tasks will provide a variety of learning styles within your class, reaching both the conformist and the nonconformist student and further stimulating students through relevance. Relevance need not only be seasonal with respect to "pro" sports. You may wish to present a volleyball theme the week before school volleyball tryouts, a gymnastics theme just before gymnastics tryouts, or a dance theme just before the first school dance. Try to appeal to a student's sense of relevance both in and out of the school environment.

The modular approach also allows you to manipulate, interchange, or rotate modular selections to *progressively* present concepts based on student outcomes, as opposed to the limitations associated with traditional unit planning, because you are not locked into three-week, seasonal blocks. Even within a for-

mal unit, the games and activities presented in this text allow for greater student involvement and success than do the more traditional games because of their modified nature; you will be able to change activities period by period within a day based on various class needs. As an example, a normal striking progression might be hand hockey, Pillo Polo, and floor hockey, but if you are dealing with an advanced class, you may wish to play floor hockey all three times during the year. Conversely, if a class is struggling with striking skills and positioning on a court from a team perspective, you may instead wish to stay with Pillo Polo, skipping the more advanced game of floor hockey. You as a teacher can best *integrate* your needs (objectives) with the needs of students (outcomes) and with other subject areas as well.

To be successful, a student's educational program should incorporate cognitive, affective, and psychomotor aspects of learning (McSwegin, Pemberton, Petray, and Going 1989). Some children, particularly those of average to below-average intelligence or those with special needs, have a tendency to learn certain academic skills and concepts better through a medium of physical activity than through more traditional classroom approaches (Humphrey 1990). When you consider that "play" and "activity" make up a large part of the experiences through which children learn, the importance of physical education in the overall school curriculum becomes obvious (Miller, Cheffers, and Whitcomb 1974). Using the modular approach enhances the physical education experience.

INTERDISCIPLINARY INTEGRATION

The need to integrate interdisciplinary concepts into the physical education setting is necessary if we, as physical educators, are to be viewed as a vital part of a student's education (Heitmann and Kneer 1976). The results of the "National Children and Youth Fitness Study" of the 1980s pointed out that inadequate time was spent teaching lifetime sports skills needed for active lifestyles out of school and as adults.

This created a renewed focus on the improved teaching of life skills (Pate, Ross, Dotson, and Gilbert 1985; Ross and Gilbert 1985), that is exactly what the modular approach targets. Physical education should, therefore, include activities to meet not only physical education objectives but also the objectives students encounter through their total school and life endeavors, particularly health and fitness concepts (Smith 1985).

Corbin (1987) suggests that to be fit for a lifetime, individuals must set objectives and be taught skills that enable them to assess their own fitness, interpret their own results, and develop personal fitness programs by finding solutions to their own personal fitness problems. This, of course, involves developing problem-solving skills—skills that are developed in academic areas as well.

One of the easiest, and most effective, ways to integrate "classroom" concepts into your lessons is through the choice of language you use during your discussions and descriptions of goals, drills, and games. The comments you make and discussions you have are an excellent way to incorporate or highlight key social, mathematical, and scientific concepts into your lessons. The potential to provide or relate information is limitless if you think about the many interdisciplinary principles that apply to physical-activity, game, and sport performance. Nowhere is this concept more obvious than in

Bert is a student with special needs who is included in one of our sixth-grade classes. Upstairs in the classroom, Bert struggles both academically and with anger control. In physical education class, he is the "star." He can process information and execute tasks correctly. We were discussing different angles used in mathematics during one lesson (obtuse, acute, right), and Bert got to apply this information in a "hands-on" fashion during a team handball game. He was quite successful both at the game and at explaining after class how the angles played a role in the game. Bert's ability to successfully process and integrate information from different sources illustrates the role interdisciplinary integration plays in the classroom.

team-oriented activities (chapter 8). Children in these activities are required to take information in, determine solutions, and execute within seconds while cooperating and working toward a shared goal.

Table 2.1 highlights some examples of interdisciplinary concepts that easily integrate with physical education, but it is in no way meant to be complete. Integrating these concepts into your daily lesson plan modules through verbal or graphic means will help your students realize many of the overlapping concepts between participation in physical activity and the academic setting.

Every Olympic year, the physical education staff and other "specials" join the sixth-grade classroom teachers to integrate on a large grade-level project. Each student researches a different country and formulates a report on her findings using the school's computer and library resources. Flags of these countries are made in art class, and songs from a variety of countries are presented in music class. One day is devoted to sport, and we organize the running of a "symbolic torch" through the neighborhood, ending at the track in our stadium at the school, kicking off a day of sporting events whereby students are grouped by continents. As a culminating experience for the project, the cafeteria (with help from the Parent Teacher Organization) prepares lunch one day in a buffet style, presenting various foods from around the world.

MULTILEVEL PLANNING

By using the modules presented in part II of this book, you can logically develop progressive goals and expectations to challenge students as they journey through their middle school years, whether that be grades six through eight or seven through nine in your district. Although the primary goals will remain the same for each year of middle school, the expected outcomes of knowledge and skills should increase with each grade level.

Table 2.1 A Sample of Social/Educational Concepts Easily Integrated Into PE	
Social	**Basic Sciences (physics/biology)**
cooperation	energy synthesis
patience	momentum
problem solving	friction
non-violent solutions	trajectory
respect	gravity
Math	**Anatomy/Physiology**
angles	cardiac anatomy
counting	respiration
linearity	antagonistic muscle function
prediction equations	nutrition and performance

Table 2.2 presents a suggested yearly curriculum of skill themes by grade level. Let's take a look at some examples to see how the curriculum is organized progressively.

During the ninth week—which focuses on dance—you will see that in the first year of middle school, the students are challenged with line dances. Line dancing alleviates the need for dancing with a partner, which many students of this age group find to be an awkward experience. In the second year, when students do feel more comfortable about themselves and about interacting with members of the opposite sex, "mixers" are introduced so that students not only are dancing but are mixing with members of the opposite gender without being locked into a specific partner. At the third and most advanced stage of middle school, square dances and reels are taught, requiring a greater interaction with one partner.

As another example, look at week number 25. Hand hockey is suggested as a logical Level I game, so students receive tremendous repetitive striking practice using a short lever arm and multiple, relatively large balls. At Level II, the same skills are challenged while lengthening the lever arm (Pillo Polo stick) and reducing the size of the ball. During Level III, more individualized responsibilities are placed on students through the increased strategies of floor hockey, use of a smaller goal, increased

lever length (hockey stick), and one, smaller ball.

The same concept of changing levels within a module to challenge students holds true for the *warm-up* and *health-related fitness modules* presented in chapters 5 and 6.

OBJECTIVES WITHIN PHYSICAL EDUCATION

A rather global goal of education is to stimulate and develop the full potential of each child. More specifically, this goal can be broken down into *global objectives* (communication, social, cognitive, and affective) and *physical-activity objectives* (psychomotor, cognitive, and affective). The modular approach of teaching promotes these global goals because it promotes teaching styles that target physical-activity skills and student outcomes. It focuses on the student as opposed to course material in the same way a classroom teacher might do.

For example, while classroom teachers could have the luxury of grouping children of similar skill levels into reading and math groups, physical educators may be scheduled with 25 to 40 students of varying abilities and be asked to accommodate each of their needs. Our modular plan allows students to progress at

Week	Level I	Level II	Level III
Table 2.2	**A Sample Yearly Curriculum for Three Levels of Instruction**		
1	Review school rules, program orientation, and cooperative warm-up activity.		
2	Hand Hockey	Pillo Polo	Garbage-Can Baseball
3	Partner Kickball	Punt-Over	Speedball
4	Hooper	Ultimate Football	Goal Ball
5	Fitness Assessment	Fitness Assessment	Fitness Assessment
6	Sock-Over	Punch Ball	Paddle Tennis
7	Amoeba Soccer	Multicone Soccer	Indoor Soccer
8	Pass-Over	Ultimate Football	Arena Football
9	Line Dances	Circles and Mixers	Squares and Reels
10	Beach Volleyball	Quadrant Volleyball	Volleyball
11	Elephant Ball	Obstacle Kickball	End-line Soccer
12	Team Handball	Quadrant Football	Three on Three Basketball
13	Gymnastics/Tumbling	Gymnastics/Tumbling	Gymnastics/Tumbling
14	Gymnastics/Tumbling	Gymnastics/Tumbling	Gymnastics/Tumbling
15	Gymnastics/Tumbling	Gymnastics/Tumbling	Gymnastics/Tumbling
16	Obstacle Course	Obstacle Course	Obstacle Course
17	End-line Hockey	Four-Corner Hockey	Floor Hockey
18	Two Base-Alley Kickball	Six Player Soccer	Indoor Soccer
19	Beat "Michael Jordan"	Platform Basketball	Three on Three Basketball
20	Targetball	Modified Cricket	Garbage-Can Baseball
21	Punt-Over	Obstacle Kickball	Speedball
22	Team Handball	Reaction Ball	Goal Ball
23	Wrestling	Wrestling	Wrestling
24	Wrestling	Wrestling	Wrestling
25	Hand Hockey	Pillo Polo	Floor Hockey
26	End-line Soccer	Multicone Soccer	Indoor Soccer
27	Hot Shots	Basket-A-Rama	Full-Court Basketball
28	Sock-Over	Three-Court Volleyball	Walleyball
29	Partner Kickball	Sticks and Kicks	Ultimate Rugby
30	Team Handball	Three-Base Basketball/Football	Transitional Lacrosse
31	Track & Field	Track & Field	Track & Field
32	Track & Field	Track & Field	Track & Field
33	Fitness Re-Assessment	Fitness Re-Assessment	Fitness Re-Assessment
34	Captain and Crew	Scotch Foursome	Medal Play
35	Reaction Ball	Goal Ball	Transitional Lacrosse
36	Amoeba Soccer	Speedball	Ultimate Rugby
37	Targetball	Repeat Baseball	Softball
38	Review yearly accomplishments, record keeping, and cooperative warm-up activity.		
39	Final Exams	Final Exams	Final Exams

their own developmental rates by spreading and repeating skills over the course of the school year. Instead of one concentrated unit, the child visits and revisits the same skill in progressively more complex drills and modified games. Through observation and assessment, physical education teachers can group students of similar abilities within a class, much like classroom teachers do with reading groups, assuring each student a more successful experience.

The development of a child's potential is an ongoing, evolutionary process helped along by a number of educational and life experiences. The "physical" orientation of physical education makes for a unique contribution to the educational process by providing opportunities for skill development, formulation of positive attitudes, and application of knowledge in ways not possible within the classroom setting. The gymnasium becomes a movement and decision-making laboratory. Social and academic objectives (as illustrated in table 2.1) can be enhanced and reinforced in a student-oriented physical education setting through individual, partner, small-group, and team problem-solving activities.

On the following pages are global and physical-activity objectives that pertain to middle school students (State Education Department 1986; State Education Department 1991).

GLOBAL OBJECTIVES

Global objectives within physical education focus on how students communicate, interact, and learn and on the value they place on physical activity in their lives.

Communication

Students will master communication skills by

- listening to directions,
- solving problems with peers, and
- cooperating with others in team activity.

Social

Students will learn to respect and accept differences among people and skill levels by

- abiding by rules and working within them,
- developing trust and respect through cooperative efforts and experiences, and
- accepting responsibility and delegating the same amount of responsibility in group efforts toward accomplishing a task.

Cognitive

Students will gain and apply interdisciplinary concepts by

- refining social skills in group activity,
- using computation skills in scoring,
- applying physics concepts in performance,
- using geometry concepts in team sports, and
- questioning physiological changes through self-awareness.

Affective

Students will be provided with opportunities that promote and offer the development of

- positive self-esteem,
- improved health, fitness, and mental outlook, and
- decision-making options that avoid the harmful effects of alcohol, drugs, and other negative health behaviors.

Students will develop the skills and understanding necessary to enjoy a lifetime of physical activity.

PHYSICAL-ACTIVITY OBJECTIVES

Physical-activity objectives have three basic forms: what students can do (psychomotor), what students know (cognitive), and what students value (affective).

Psychomotor

Sixth and seventh grades:

- Students will demonstrate the ability to perform motor skills that apply to a variety of game and sport activities (catching/ throwing, kicking, and striking).

Eighth and ninth grades:

- Students will demonstrate proficiency in basic skills during game and sport activities (basketball, football, hockey, kickball, lacrosse, racket activities, soccer, softball/baseball, team handball/speedball, track and field, volleyball, and wrestling/self-defense).

Cognitive

Sixth and seventh grades:

- Students will identify the similarities of and differences between various game and sport activities.
- Students will recognize the contributions that game and sport activities make to physical fitness.
- Students will demonstrate familiarity with terminology, rules, and criteria of specific game and sport activities.

Eighth and ninth grades:

- Students will identify scientific principles and concepts involved in game and sport activities (see table 2.1).

Affective

Sixth, seventh, eighth, and ninth grades:

- Students will participate actively with understanding during game and sport activities.
- Students will appreciate the need for and follow the rules of game and sport activities.
- Students will respect and accept individual variations in performance.

Look at the big picture when structuring your multilevel yearly curriculum. Interchange the modules to best suit your needs, integrating with other disciplines in the overall academic experiences shared by students, and enjoy the success of your students right along with them.

MODULAR LESSON PLANNING

This chapter will help you design a modular lesson through step-by-step planning and includes an example of a complete modular lesson that we actually use. In addition to detailing modular components, this chapter also offers successful teaching strategies that target diverse learning styles. By substituting the modular activities provided in part II of this book into the components outlined in this chapter, coupled with the teaching strategies, you will be able to run your classes smoothly and effectively.

TEACHING A MODULAR LESSON

The student-centered lesson format presented in table 3.1 will help guide you as each segment of the modular lesson is developed throughout this chapter. The table is based on a 40-minute class period with students having 33 minutes of physical activity and 7 minutes of instruction related to fitness and skill development. In some middle schools, students have to change clothes during this 40-minute time span, so the actual time in activity may be slightly less. But the proportionate time allotments of approximately 80 percent activity to 20 percent instruction should be held constant.

We will describe how the parts of a modular lesson plan work and then walk you through a sample lesson detailing each segment presented in table 3.1 as it relates to a "striking" class using *hand hockey* as the game activity.

CLASS OVERVIEW (30 SECONDS)

The *class overview* segment gives students a brief overview of the day's lesson. The teacher can explain the objectives to students when they arrive for class, or, if the students change clothes for class, the teacher can announce the objectives in the locker room or post them on a bulletin board for the students to read. For example, an overview might be as simple as, "Welcome folks. Here is where we are headed today. We will start class by warming up with a fitness circuit, then discuss heart function and pulse rate, practice striking skills, and finish class with a striking game. The result for each of you is improved fitness, a better

Time	Activity
0:00:00–0:00:30	Class Overview (30 seconds)
0:00:30–0:02:30	Entry (2 minutes)
0:02:30–0:05:30	Warm-Up Module (3 minutes)
0:05:30–0:08:00	Health-Related Fitness Concept Module (2:30 minutes)
0:08:00–0:21:00	Skill Development via Selected Drills (13 minutes)
0:21:00–0:23:00	Transition Period (2 minutes)
0:23:00–0:38:00	Team Game or Individual/Partner Activity Module (15 minutes)
0:38:00–0:40:00	Closure (2 minutes)

Table 3.1   Anatomy Of A Modular Lesson

This table is adapted with permission from the *Journal of Physical Education, Recreation & Dance*, April, 1995, page 70. The *Journal* is a publication of the American Alliance for Health, Physical Education, Recreation and Dance, 1900 Association Drive, Reston, VA 20191.

understanding of your heart's function, improved skill levels, and a fun time."

ENTRY (2 MINUTES)

Next, students enter the gym, and they are moving from the moment they do so. No wasting time: They are expected to move . . . they know it . . . they do it! The purpose of this part of the lesson plan is twofold. First, they equate the gym with movement, and second, it starts the warm-up process. Students could jog, skip for height, or move in any number of ways to incorporate large muscle activity in a rhythmic manner.

Be creative in varying what your students do each day upon entering the gym, just as you vary other aspects of your lessons. Use music to vary tempos—slower-paced music for walking and faster-paced for running. Since students at this age often equate running, skipping, and sliding with "work," use the music and variety to disguise how much exercise the students are doing, focusing their attention instead on creative movement while verbally talking about the physiological changes and benefits resulting from their "warm-up entry."

This is an ideal time to take attendance by counting students and easily observing who is absent or unprepared, as opposed to the more traditional, and time-consuming, method of sitting the students down and working your

way through cards or a book. The entry segment needs only two minutes.

WARM-UP MODULES (3 MINUTES)

The entry segment is followed by the *warm-up module*. The purpose of the module can vary. You may wish to use a circuit that is consistent with the activity lying ahead. For example, you could use a lower-body strength circuit for a volleyball-type game activity because volleyball requires lower-body agility and power. Conversely, you may wish to use an aerobic warm-up circuit because volleyball is a more anaerobic-type activity. Or, because volleyball requires leg strength and agility, you may wish to use a warm-up circuit that develops upper-body strength, giving students a more complete body workout during the overall class period. Furthermore, you may wish to use one of the "cooperative" warm-up activities to promote teamwork with your class. These are decisions you will have to make based on your individual program philosophy and goals.

The warm-up modules will allow each child, regardless of skill level, fitness capacity, or body size, to achieve success at a level relative to himself in keeping with the overall program premise and goals. The warm-up segment also allows each child to be an individual. This caters to the nonconformists in your class, as well as to the enriched, both of whom do not like to depend on the actions or help of others. Such a circuit appeals to their independent nature.

Warm-up modules may also be easily interchanged within the class format as presented in table 3.1. Chapter 5 presents a number of interchangeable warm-up circuits and activities that can be used at various levels within the middle school program.

HEALTH-RELATED FITNESS CONCEPT MODULES (2:30 MINUTES)

Having expended energy for five minutes (entry plus warm-up), the students will welcome a short rest break, providing you with an opportune time to briefly impart health-related information to them during the *health-related fitness module*.

These modules are designed to help students better understand, and relate to, the effect exercise and lifestyle behaviors have on their bodies. Today, we are teaching a more "remote controlled" type of child with a short attention span. Information should come in short "sound bites" with lots of creativity and variety to capture children's interest, keeping them on task, or else they will just tune us out. Over a 10-month period, cardiovascular, pulmonary, muscular, nutritional, and fitness concepts are explored through concise, direct, weekly focuses.

Suggestions for *health-related fitness modules* are provided in chapter 6.

SKILL-DEVELOPMENT MODULES (13 MINUTES)

Skill drills should be based on the lesson objectives for that day (catching/throwing, kicking, or striking). This period allows students of all levels to work on skill development at their own pace and capacity, without the added pressure of game-type demands. This segment of the lesson format is meant to serve as the "traditional" teaching time within a class, using drills, relays, and instructional techniques classically put forth in "methods" classes and "coaching" texts.

Skill-development ideas are presented in chapter 7 by skill and activity.

TRANSITION TIME (2 MINUTES)

Put simply, transition time is a two-minute window of time for students to move from skill development to activity participation. Equipment is relocated if necessary, game rules and objectives are reviewed, and teams are formed.

While some students like to work in pairs or small groups, others prefer to work alone. As teachers, we need to create drills that appeal to all types of *learning styles*. As an example, during volleyball you may wish to:

- designate one section of the gymnasium for students to practice passing and setting in a *small-group* circular formation, counting how many times they can successfully volley the ball, keeping it in the air;
- designate another area for *pairs* to work on their passing and setting; and
- let *individuals* in yet another section work on wall volleys or passing and setting in succession to themselves.

In our sample lesson on page 21, we might say something like: "OK . . . everybody put your balls away and sit on the center circle. Today's game is *hand hockey,* and here are the rules." As we are describing the rules, we would be setting up cones to mark the end zones or have two students do it. After describing the game and rules, we would quickly divide students into three teams by birthdays (January through April, May through August, and September through December), shirt colors (whites; blues, greens, and blacks; and everyone else), or some other random method. Students would then be set into position, and we would start the game activity, repeating the directions as play is initiated.

GAME-ACTIVITY MODULES (15 MINUTES)

The "fitness-oriented" *game activities* will challenge your students with fun, action-packed games. Modified and traditional activities, based on student level and desired skills, are presented in chapters 8 and 9. Their design and rules will help all students make meaningful contributions to the activity, regardless of developmental level. All students thus will experience more numerous opportunities at success within a game format as compared with the most traditional of games in which a select few play at the "skilled" positions. As game activities progress, a variety of cues (auditory, visual, tactile, and kinesthetic) will create an environment in which all learning styles will thrive.

The total class population will be more active and thus receive more physical-fitness benefits from your class. Students will display a higher level of interest in the class. In general, they will contribute to and learn from the class experience rather than shy away from it or detract from it with negative behaviors, as is common in many traditional settings.

> **Y**ears ago I had a heavyset, not-very-athletic student named Mark in one of my seventh-grade classes. Many of our modified game activities presented in chapter 8 involve goalkeeping skills with numerous objects being played at once. Mark loved the challenge of stopping balls from scoring. His eye/hand coordination improved, as did his self-confidence. I would "pump" Mark up in class with verbal praise and talked him into managing my modified boy's lacrosse team. At practice I would work him out with the goalkeepers. By eighth grade, Mark did not want to manage, he wanted to play. He went on to become a goalkeeper for our varsity lacrosse team and is now a prominent law-yer—his self-confidence still intact!

CLOSURE (2 MINUTES)

End class by reviewing daily objectives with students. Reinforce the numerous opportunities they had to succeed, the interest they showed toward activity, and the high-energy enthusiasm they displayed toward the overall class experience. Closure is also an appropri-ate time to review any questions students may have.

We might say: "Everyone have a seat right here in front of me. I saw a lot of good things in class today. . . . I saw people use teamwork to move the ball. . . . I saw people change body shapes to get high and low balls. . . . I saw great cooperation." While talking, make eye contact with appropriate students to further reinforce these positive behaviors. Query the students about the class and have them raise their hands as you ask questions such as: "Did you get your exercise today? . . . Did you score any goals? . . . Did you have fun?"

Most students will raise their hands for all three questions. Follow up with: "Well then, that was a great class. Look how successful you were. Now, find your pulse . . . and . . . count." After 10 seconds, say, "Stop . . . and multiply your number by six. Raise your hand if your pulse rate was higher than at rest. . . . Raise your hand if your rate was higher during exercise. . . ." Briefly explain again why, wish the class a good day, and watch them *calmly* exit the gym having been relaxed at the end of class. They could even be stretching while you have your *closure* discussion.

Don't be surprised at how fast the class goes by; time flies when a class is "clicking." By using the modular lesson format presented in table 3.1 and substituting in appropriate warm-ups, health-related fitness concepts, skill-development drills, and game activities to meet your daily class objectives, you should have highly productive, highly successful classes. In a word, your physical education program should become more "positive" for all involved.

> **S**ample Modular Lesson: Hand Hockey
>
> Class Overview
>
> - Greet class and provide an overview of the day's lesson.
>
> Entry
>
> - Students enter the gymnasium using rhythmic, large-muscle activities (running, skipping, etc.) to stimulate muscular and cardiovascular blood flow.

Warm-Up Module

- For our sample lesson, we have chosen a fitness circuit of push-ups, crunches, side-to-side jumps, and lunges. We chose this warm-up circuit because *hand hockey* is a lesson we do early in the year, and we are trying to focus on improving fitness at this time, too. Also, because *hand hockey* uses striking and upper-body exercise, our circuit uses two lower-body stations (jumping and lunges) to help students exercise their whole bodies throughout the entire day's lesson.

Health-Related Fitness Concept Module

- In our sample lesson, we would use this time block to sit students in front of a bulletin board and briefly discuss the following:

  - Function of the heart—"to pump blood with oxygen throughout the body, especially to those muscles involved in exercise"

  - Measurement of heart rate—"you can measure your pulse rate at two spots on your body: at the carotid artery in your neck and at your radial pulse on your wrist"

- Demonstrate the proper technique for measuring at these two sites, and have students count their resting pulse. Discuss the differences between resting and exercise heart rates.

- Later, during the activity portion of your class, stop students and have them count an "active" heart rate. Using a question-and-answer format works well for this concept:

  - "What happens to your heart rate when you're scared?"

  - "When you take a test...?"

  - "When you're late getting home...?"

  - "How does music affect heart rate; why does a dentist play soft music and a pep band loud music?"

- Be sure to continue having students take their pulse rates throughout the year in a variety of situations (aerobic activities, anaerobic, at rest, etc.) and make comparisons along the way. Reinforce previously taught physiological concepts and add the concepts of an *age-related target heart rate zone*.

Skill-Development Module

- In our sample *hand hockey* lesson, we would give each student a ball and

  - discuss biomechanical considerations for striking:

    stability,

    levers/leverage, and

    extension.

  - discuss and demonstrate striking techniques:

    eyes focused on the ball,

    changing body shape based on ball position (high versus low versus waist high),

    control versus power (open hand versus fist), and

  - strokes:

    forehand,

    backhand,

    overhand, and

    underhand.

  - Provide individual practice for students:

    Give each student a ball and let him experiment with different striking techniques based on verbal cues (forehand, backhand, etc.).

  - Provide a partner activity such as volleying back and forth with a partner.

- Students of like ability will gravitate toward one another, forming groupings of similar abilities common to academic settings.

Transition Time

- Use this time to relocate equipment, explain game concepts and rules, and form teams.

Game-Activity Module

- Play the selected "fitness-oriented" game activity, in this case *hand hockey*.

Closure

- Review daily objectives, answer student questions and, reinforce positive concepts of the day.

TEACHING STRATEGIES

A number of teaching strategies can enhance your daily classroom presentations for students and increase the effectiveness of your modular lessons. The following strategies keep students motivated and on task, increase their understanding of difficult concepts, and help promote a positive health and fitness philosophy.

BE A ROLE MODEL

One of the most effective yet simplest techniques that you can use to have a favorable impact on students is to be a positive role model. This doesn't mean you have to become a Michael Jordan, Gail Devers, or Arnold Schwarzenegger; it simply means living a fitness-oriented lifestyle. Embrace it, enjoy it, and share your enthusiasm and experiences with students. Discuss your workouts, recreational experiences, and fitness-related activities with them. If students see you living the lifestyle you profess, not just talking about it, they will have much more respect for you and take you more seriously. Forget the adage, "Do as I say, not as I do!" Lead by example.

Do not let students see you smoke. Do not let them see you abuse alcohol or drugs. Maintain an ideal weight, have an even temper, and

project an image of health that is achieved through moderation in eating behaviors, exercise regimen, and general lifestyle. No motivation is stronger than the respect a student has for his or her teacher, and thus a teacher has tremendous influence on a young person. We take this responsibility seriously and wish all physical education teachers did so.

ENTHUSIASM

In the class situation, use fitness-focused language. Be a sportscaster in class by calling the play-by-play action, but point out physiological changes and occurrences as well as good plays. Discuss changing heart rates, why a rest break is needed, and why students sweat more in June than in January by relating these issues to health and biology concepts. Discuss angles, leverage, and momentum by relating students' movement experiences to math and physics concepts. As undergraduate physical education majors, we all took these and other science courses, so why not apply these experiences and help our students better integrate the varied knowledge they are now acquiring through enthusiastic, ongoing commentary (refer to table 2.1).

Teaching does not end when you give directions. For example, you may say, "Only two minutes left. You are now using fats for energy . . . think of your Krebs cycle from biology . . . you're using oxygen to create energy . . . you're working aerobically."

Or you might say, "Matt, good pass off the wall to Maria . . . way to figure the angle and use the wall as a teammate. Hey . . . did everybody see the way Matt formed a triangle using the wall, Maria, and himself? Good job Matt!"

Use fast-paced drills and games to maintain enthusiasm with your students. Vary sport-related games while developing spatial awareness and locomotor skills. Team concepts that apply to a number of sports will be refined. For example, hockey, basketball, and lacrosse use the fast break. The objective is to move the ball or puck up ice, court, or field as quickly as possible while filling lanes to the left, center, and right of the goal. Students who play these games, while learning specific athletic skills, will make the proper associated adjustments to a fast break even when introduced to a new game such as soccer.

Strive to provide each student with the opportunity for both individual and team success by using end-line games and end-zone games that have students competing 3-on-3, or 2-on-2, for brief periods of time but that involve the majority of students throughout the game. The beauty of end-line games is that they keep all the students in a class involved in the game as either goalies or "fielders" throughout the whole class. Although students' roles vary throughout the class period, students are nonetheless always active and contributing to their team's success. Mass games like ultimate football tend to cloud individual achievements but allow for team-oriented achievements. Modified games allow more students to be involved at once, touching the ball more often during a given physical education period and, ultimately, having more opportunity for experiencing success, higher-energy levels, and a more positive class environment.

COMMUNICATION

Good communication techniques are among life's most important skills for successfully dealing with others, yet developing such techniques is an area that many of today's students need to improve on most. We feel so strongly about improving communication skills between students that we start and finish each year with activities that require sharing, teamwork, cooperative effort, and communication. New teachers often struggle in communicating clearly with students as well. The following techniques and materials may be useful to both new and experienced teachers.

Verbal

We have found that many students have difficulty remembering long, tedious directions. In part, this is due to poor listening skills on the part of students but is also due to the increasing number of students with special needs we have

mixed into our daily classes. To help all students better understand material, teach in short, concise units. For example, if you are teaching End-Line Soccer (see diagram 8.15) you may want to

- divide the students into three teams,
- place the students in their starting areas, and
- then give specific rules for the game activity.

Repeat the rules as the game progresses. Those who understood the rules at first will be reviewing them, while others may finally understand the rules the second or third time they hear them.

Printed Material

Bulletin boards can be used to present information and at the same time force students to read, a priority today in every school. Generate excitement for your program through creative displays in the halls. Use the cafeteria to display messages regarding healthy food choices and the role nutrition plays in either preventing or contributing to illness and performance. Display a new body system (e.g., circulatory or respiratory) or a "muscle of the month" in the gym as outlined in chapter 6 (see photo 3.1).

Graphic Display

You can become a visual display yourself! Wear shirts, leotards, or other types of clothing that depict muscles and body systems. As you move, students will see the muscles move as well, gaining a better understanding of their location, interrelationship with other muscles, and use with specific activities. Try painting your body (biceps red and triceps blue). Students will quickly learn about antagonistic groups and have fun watching you in the process.

If you open yourself up and are creative, students will respond in kind. Use stretch bands tied to your body at the points of origin and insertion to demonstrate concentric and eccentric contractions. Students will see the muscles' locations more clearly, learn anatomical terms in an applied format, and see angles lessen (flexion) or become larger (extension). Students

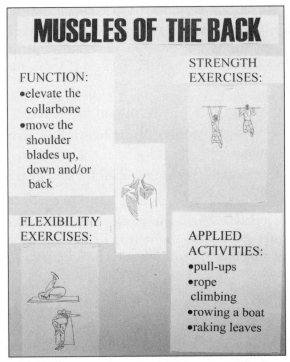

MUSCLES OF THE BACK

FUNCTION:
- elevate the collarbone
- move the shoulder blades up, down and/or back

STRENGTH EXERCISES:

FLEXIBILITY EXERCISES:

APPLIED ACTIVITIES:
- pull-ups
- rope climbing
- rowing a boat
- raking leaves

Photo 3.1 A sample *"muscle of the month"* display.

will retain concepts longer and with greater understanding than from merely hearing you talk or reading about them.

Audio

Different school settings will provide different opportunities for learning and integration. Perhaps the most direct and effective method for promoting fitness concepts is the public-address system. Make a "public service" announcement each week regarding a fitness- or health-related topic. Everyone in the school will be able to relate to it, teachers and students alike, helping the physical education department gain further recognition as an important team member in a student's education.

Video

We strongly feel that videos should never replace the role of a teacher. However, there are certain circumstances in which videos might be an appropriate teaching tool. Certain students respond well to visual cues with respect to learning styles, and, for these students in particular, videos will be a benefit. Watching instructional videos should only be one of several stations within a class period, limited to 5

to 10 minutes, leaving plenty of time for physical activity.

Another example of video use might be in a fitness unit in which the teacher may supervise half a class in a weight room, instructing on the use of resistance devices, while the remainder of the class "steps" or "aerobic dances" to an exercise video. Such an experience will help students see that they can exercise at home by renting or buying videos or by following the cable channel fitness shows available today.

INTEGRATION

If you integrate your teaching with other disciplines, you can develop experiences for your students that enhance fitness and provide an opportunity for educational exchange and discovery. At the middle school level, coordinate your activities with concepts being taught in biology, health, math, and other subject areas. Use the gymnasium as a "movement laboratory" for putting theory into practice. Cardiovascular fitness can directly and indirectly affect coronary heart disease risks; students learn about such risks in their middle school health curriculum. Lacrosse, hockey, basketball, and other team games are all related to spatial relativity using triangles and other mathematical concepts. What students eat and the effect that food has on weight control, performance, and endurance are related to food preparation and choices being made at lunch and at meals out of the school. Aerobic activity, energy production, and the Krebs cycle were mentioned earlier in this chapter.

Help students more clearly see the relationships between these varied curricula through displays and experiences that heighten their awareness and understanding of multidisciplinary concepts. An appropriate, well-placed comment will go a long way toward helping students consciously integrate key educational comments.

Over time, students will enjoy and appreciate the success they experience in a student-oriented, integrated, fitness-driven curriculum. Once out of school, they will continue to remember and appreciate their physical educa-

In a "hands-on" way of learning about respiration, we used our physical education class to experiment with vital capacity and anaerobic output. Although it was a simple-enough task that we asked the students to perform (with a minimum of direct science application), our little "experiment" certainly caught the attention of our students. We asked our students as they entered the gym to take the deepest breath they could possibly hold, then hold their breath and run as fast as possible around the perimeter of the gym, seeing how far they could go without taking another breath. The students had fun with this task, which led to discussions on vital capacity, respiration, the role of carbon dioxide in the respiratory process, ventilation, and maximal oxygen consumption relative to aerobic-type tasks. We integrated health and biology concepts with fitness performance while providing students with a firsthand experience—the type of experience they tend to remember!

tion program (and teachers) when they canoe, fish, play golf, jog, sail, ride horses, play tennis, or enjoy a host of other recreational activities (Smith and Cestaro 1992).

INCLUSION

The concept of *inclusion* provides students who have disabilities with meaningful opportunities within the educational system through interaction with their "nondisabled" peers. Obviously, in many activities, inclusion will require specially designed instruction and perhaps support services, special resources, personnel, and curricula (Block and Vogler 1994). When inclusion works, students develop positive relationships through their interactions that should carry through to adulthood. Inclusion is certainly not the answer for all persons with disabilities, nor is inclusion possible for all activities. Common sense, safety, student appropriateness, and teacher creativity and training all need to be considered when developing the inclusion process.

We follow a philosophy of *least restrictive environment* (LRE), placing students on a continuum of support services and alternatives and selecting experiences that are most appropriate for the student with disabilities. LRE objectives are accomplished while students with disabilities simultaneously interact with nondisabled students when appropriate, with the ultimate goal being that disabled students will enter the regular class environment (Sherrill 1994).

As an example, we have an adapted physical education class in our building one period that consists of seven students. Three of the students have Down's syndrome. Two of the students are mentally retarded, one is autistic, and one has cerebral palsy and uses a wheelchair. During weeks in which basketball is being taught in regular physical education, the adapted-class students are "pushed in" with the regular class. They mix well with the nondisabled students in dribbling and passing tasks, such as wall or partner drills, by modeling and through peer mentoring. The student who uses the wheelchair tosses a "soft-type" ball to herself and catches it instead of dribbling, while a teacher-aide wheels her through cones, down lines, or however else the drills are designed. During passing drills, the student passes and catches using the "soft-type" ball.

When the regular class moves to shooting drills or games, the adapted-class students remain at one basket while the regular-class students use the other five baskets in the gym. The student with cerebral palsy has a modified basket set up using a large garbage can placed against the wall. Using the wall as a backboard, the student shoots at a target that challenges her yet allows for success.

Conversely, during a soccer week that is outdoors in the fall, it is inappropriate for these seven students to mix with their nondisabled peers because of safety concerns and an inability to react to the faster-paced play of the regular-class students. Being outdoors, however, provides ample space for teaching stations, so the adapted-class students work at their own drills and play their own modified game alongside their regular-class peers. This allows the adapted class to stay on task with curriculum yet learn at a pace and level that is appropriate for it.

A large part of the success experienced by all the students (adapted and regular class) in these examples is the ability and willingness of the adapted-class teacher and regular-class teachers to communicate and cooperate while keeping the best interests of students as their focus. Laying a positive, clear foundation of inclusion purpose, objectives, and expectations is important for implementing successful inclusion strategies. Your presence and relationship as a professional in interacting with your fellow teachers is just as important as the contacts and equal-status opportunities you create for students.

CLASSROOM-MANAGEMENT TECHNIQUES

The system of modular sequencing put forth in this book will greatly aid you in better managing your classroom environment. The components were detailed earlier, but the manner in which they are presented (organization and transition) is the key to successful teaching.

Teaching in the modular format will require more planning on your part as a teacher. You will need to plan for materials and activities for the modules and for transitions between them. We present and outline the materials and activities in detail in part II of this book. Being organized by correctly "staging" the needed materials before class will allow you to execute smooth transitions from one module to the next. Doing so will minimize downtime in your class and, with it, disruptive behavior. Preparing for the next act needs to be a combination of preplanning and movement between modules while diverting student attention from the actual reorganization of gym materials.

Here are some simple management techniques we use to make class periods move smoothly:

- Warm-up students indoors; drill and play activities outdoors.

- If you have more than one gym available, use one for warm-up activities and one for game activity.

- Reset the warm-up materials immediately after each class so you are ready for the next one if you must use one gym and stay indoors.

- Lean folded mats against the walls after warm-ups; they will be ready to quickly knock down before your next class.

- Strategically place equipment in the gym to minimize walking for it and moving it between modules.

- While students are putting balls away after skill drills, place cones and materials into position for game activities. You will finish together.

- Have "enrichment-type" students help you move equipment. They can both do a task and listen to your directions at the same time. Have them help you reset for the next class as well. They will remember the general layout you had for warm-up activity.

- Anticipate each module, visualize it, and move quickly during transitions.

Although the *teaching strategies* presented in this chapter require some effort, the rewards are well worth it because your classes will flow better and your days will be more pleasant. Remember that the overall mission of this book is to help students enjoy and learn about physical activity so that they will continue to be active the rest of their lives. The outcomes will be tremendously positive for all of us as a society.

AUTHENTIC ASSESSMENT

The term *assessment*, most simply defined, means gathering information. Logically, this process leads to evaluation or the making of judgments based on assessment findings. In physical education and in teaching—as in many forms of instruction—assessment becomes part of the teaching and learning process instead of standing alone as a separate component. Assessment information is varied and might include

- redefining physical education goals and objectives,
- identifying student strengths and weaknesses,
- restructuring the physical educational curriculum and environment,
- motivating all participants in the educational process,
- modifying teaching strategies to include various learning styles, and
- clarifying communication among teachers, students, and parents.

Authentic assessment evaluates students through observation in "real life" situations.

For example, using a wall volley to evaluate basketball passing is one way to gather information, but to do it *authentically* the teacher would observe a student's passing abilities under game-like conditions. Authentic assessment has become the trend in education as teachers in other disciplines use projects, writing samples, and portfolios to evaluate how students apply basic skills.

MOVEMENT TOWARD OUTCOME ASSESSMENT

Although assessment and evaluative tools have existed for years in education, the movement in the past decade has been toward developing specific outcomes with respect to learning. Information gathering for evaluation is seen as "a way of designing, developing, delivering, and documenting instruction in terms of its intended goals and outcomes" (Spady 1988, 5). The concept asks all educators (kindergarten through 12th grade) to cooperatively work together, ultimately helping students meet and demonstrate broad exit-level *outcomes*, whether they be departmental, district, or state-generated goals. Four principles will help you smoothly integrate assessment and outcome items: clarity of focus, expanded opportunity, high expectations, and designing down (Brandt 1992; Spady 1988).

CLARITY OF FOCUS

All phases of the curriculum process—planning, instruction, and assessment—should *clearly focus* on exit-level outcomes expected of students. Essentially, these outcomes become the goals toward which we teach and assess. We feel that outcomes should be skill based, as opposed to sport based, and fitness based through movement. As an example, we wouldn't teach football for football's sake; we would use the activity of football as a means to teach catching/throwing, kicking/punting, teamwork, cooperation, and movement goals. Over the years, your curriculum should become more student oriented and student relevant, ultimately helping students.

EXPANDED OPPORTUNITY

In teaching for outcomes, you place less restrictive time constraints on a student to perform. A modular approach, whereby skills are revisited throughout the year, provides students with greater opportunities as compared with a more traditional program of teaching in

The concept of *expanded opportunities* fits nicely with the authentic-assessment philosophy presented in this chapter because it allows for the developmental and growth differences commonly found among middle school students. Students do not need to achieve a given benchmark by a given date (e.g., at the end of a three-week unit), but instead they can strive to achieve selected benchmarks over time (by the end of a given year), having several chances to prove themselves as skills are revisited.

three-week unit blocks. An *expanded opportunity* provides students ample time with multiple opportunities to learn, practice, and achieve expected outcomes. Students can learn at a varied pace, which provides multiple chances at achieving or mastering content. It is important, however, to assure that students demonstrate appropriate prerequisite skills before moving to higher levels. For example, a student would not attempt a dive roll until he has mastered a forward roll.

HIGH EXPECTATIONS

Students should be encouraged to *accomplish all expectations* that are within their grasp. You as the teacher are extremely valuable through your use of teaching strategies (chapter 3) that help students achieve their goals; you also serve a valuable role in motivating and supporting them in their quests. Students must know what expected outcomes are, and they must acknowledge that teacher support is available and must use that support to help themselves achieve outcomes.

The movement toward outcome assessment provides those of us in physical education with a golden opportunity to actively contribute to "whole-child education." Target the following three areas to maximize your department's contributions and visibility in educating today's students:

- List your *state* goals for physical education and cross-reference your curriculum to make sure you meet each and every expected outcome.

- Actively communicate with your local administration and fellow teachers by sitting on *standards* committees to ensure that your discipline is seen and heard and plays an integral part in the overall school curriculum. Such participation allows you to take your rightful place in contributing to student outcomes.

- Solicit and listen to your *students'* goals and help students meet their expected outcomes!

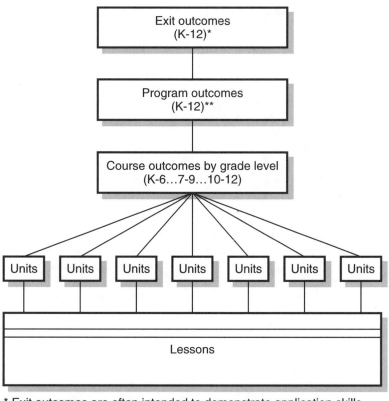

* Exit outcomes are often intended to demonstrate application skills and are generic to all content areas.

** Program outcomes refer to skills, knowledge, and behaviors of specific content areas.

Diagram 4.1 The designing down process. Adapted from C. J. Hopple 1995.

DESIGNING DOWN

The process of *designing down* means starting at the end and working back. By starting with graduation-level outcomes (grade 12) and working backward, your department can ensure that the outcomes at each level are on a continuum from basic toward final, more advanced outcomes. This process will also help you better understand what your "niche" is and what curriculum expectations are within the overall district program based on the grade level at which you teach. The "designing down" sequence, as described by Hopple (1995) is presented in diagram 4.1.

As physical educators, the movement toward *outcomes* provides us with an ideal opportunity to enhance communication within our own departments and with teachers in other disciplines. With communication, you can make physical education an integral part of "whole-

child education." In essence, it gives us a freer hand in structuring and implementing outcome-related programs. Even if your school or state does not promote an outcome-related model, the concepts presented in this chapter will help you in planning, instructing, and assessing your students, making your overall program stronger.

ASSESSING STUDENT OUTCOMES

The gathering of information in *"real-world"* situations is authentic assessment. This process works well for us as physical educators because much of our day is spent observing performance as students demonstrate competence by applying learned skills in game-like activities. Game-like activities require cooperation, teamwork, strategies, problem solving, and decision making—all facets of real-world life.

As a teacher, you should ask yourself several questions about establishing assessment criteria:

1. What are the skills I expect my students to perform (e.g., throwing or catching)?

2. What are the parameters or specific types of performance I expect from my students (e.g., throwing for accuracy and distance)?

3. What level of performance is

   • unacceptable (e.g., not reaching a partner 10 feet away or making the partner move to catch the thrown ball),

   • acceptable (e.g., throwing accurately to a stationary partner 10 feet away), or

   • exemplary (e.g., throwing to a partner running at full speed 20 feet away)?

The National Association for Sport and Physical Education (Franck et al. 1992) has established benchmark outcomes for varied grade levels that easily lend themselves to authentic assessment. These outcomes include cognitive (what a student knows), affective (what a student values), and psychomotor (what a student has, is, or does) performance outcomes. Examples of each for an eighth-grade level are presented in table 4.1. Documentation options

of the benchmarks include the use of *rubrics* and *portfolios*.

RUBRICS

Rubrics are carefully worded scoring systems with specific standards and criteria for judging a student's performance. A rubric defines quality criteria and/or standards by which performance will be developed and assessed, and it contains essential qualities necessary for acceptable performance. It is a scale (continuum) that explains in detail the possible levels of performance for either a portfolio or a performance task. The scale usually has from three to five levels.

Using throwing as an example, table 4.2 illustrates a scoring rubric for a benchmark outcome. Although this example uses "exemplary," "acceptable," and "needs improvement" to rate performance, you may feel more comfortable using other terms. *Level I*, *Level II*, and *Level III* may be more appropriate for a middle school situation to describe entry, intermediate/transitional, and exit-level performances as we will with gymnastics/tumbling in chapter 9. In describing interpersonal behaviors (works well with others, values differences and similarities in others, etc.) and intrapersonal behaviors (self-control, participates in activities, etc.) you may wish to use *A* (showing age appropriate development), *I* (improvement shown in this area), and *N*

Table 4.1 Sample Benchmark Outcomes for Eighth-Grade PE*

As a result of participating in a quality physical education program it is reasonable to expect that the student will be able to:

HAS	Combined skills competently to participate in modified versions of team and individual sports.
IS	Sustain an aerobic activity, maintaining a target heart rate, to achieve cardiovascular benefits.
DOES	Identify and follow rules while playing sports and games.
KNOWS	Describe personal and group conduct, including ethical behavior, appropriate for engaging in physical activity.
VALUES	Respect physical and performance limitations of self and others.

*These outcomes include cognitive (what a student knows), affective (what a student values), and psychomotor (what a student has, is, or does) performance outcomes. Adapted from Franck et al. 1992.

Table 4.2   An Example Of a Rubric Scale Using Throwing for Force and/or Distance as a Skill
Exemplary
• the student stepped in the direction of the target being thrown to with the *non-throwing* leg • the student visually focused on the target being thrown to • the student sequentially coordinated their musculature to maximize motor function relative to the throwing task • the student adjusted the force with which they threw to maximize both distance and accuracy
Acceptable
• the student stepped with the *non-throwing* leg • the student visually focused on the target being thrown to • the student used their entire body (legs, torso, and arm) in the throwing motion
Needs Improvement
• the student did not step when throwing (kept the feet planted) • the student used only the arm to throw

(needs improvement in this area) to define the quality criteria and/or standards by which performance is assessed for each of the specific performance outcomes. With respect to fitness testing, raw scores may be presented and interpreted as *A* (above national norms), *W* (within national norms), and *N* (needs improvement to reach national norms).

The actual scale used in a rubric is less important than the fact that you and your department establish benchmarks similar to those presented by the National Association for Sport and Physical Education (Franck et al. 1992), further define them in terms of criteria/standards, and use this information to better plan, instruct, and assess your students.

PORTFOLIOS

A *portfolio* is a collection, whether cumulative or representative, of a student's work. It should have several qualities to truly reflect the student's ability, capacity, or achievements with respect to performance outcomes. Also, the portfolio should cover the breadth and scope of the

student's curricular experiences, showcasing the process, not just the final result, and containing data tied to all units and themes used in the learning process (Fulmer 1994). Managing data for each student in the school district can, however, become an overwhelming challenge.

The most important issue is how to decide what goes into a student's portfolio. We have mentioned assessment information about inter- and intrapersonal behaviors, physical performance, and fitness outcomes, but what about reports, collages, special projects (science/ health fair), and other physical education related material?

To merely collect and record information, for recording sake, is pointless if the original intent of assessing—to help students learn—becomes lost in the "shuffling" of papers and projects. By combining a number of popular assessment tools, you can create a simple portfolio card that provides not only logical physical education documentation but also a manageable system of charting student growth through the middle school years as well.

PORTFOLIO CARDS: A VIABLE ASSESSMENT TOOL

A viable solution to the portfolio issue in physical education is to design a card that documents a student's performance for each grade level she achieves in school. An 8 1/2-by-11-inch heavy-bond card, color coded by grade, would be ideal for this purpose. The actual design of the card should meet the needs of your staff, students, and district, but the card should be divided into five sections: grade-level benchmarks, "self-concepts" assessment, fitness norms, extracurricular activities, and teacher comments. The benchmark outcomes will most likely take up one complete side of the card. The other four sections can be placed together as illustrated in table 4.3 (Smith 1997).

OUTCOME BENCHMARKS

To create this section of the portfolio card, you can use benchmarks from the National Association for Sport and Physical Education (Franck et al. 1992) or use ones that your staff develops. This section should change with each grade level as expectations become higher. Representative benchmark outcomes are provided by grade levels (six and eight) in tables 4.4 and 4.5. Using checklists that are periodically updated, in your attendance book for example, and then transferring this data to a more permanent card is one method for charting a student's progress. Teaching with a modular format of short, skill-focused (catching/throwing, kicking and/or striking) units that rotate weekly, as opposed to the traditional three-week units (Smith and Cestaro 1992; Smith and Cestaro 1995), provides ample opportunity for updating selected outcomes throughout the year, as you will most likely only have two to three dozen benchmarks per year that you use on a rubric scale.

SELF-CONCEPTS ASSESSMENT

A *self-concepts assessment* provides subjective inter- and intrapersonal criteria that students can check off along with the teacher, involving the two more closely in the assessment process. This assessment tool allows for interactive discussion; notice the differences in opinion between student and teacher in the sample "self-concepts assessment" presented in table 4.3.

FITNESS NORMS

The third section of the portfolio card presents raw scores for fitness testing and compares them with national norms on a rubric scale as described earlier. One commonly used assessment protocol is *The Prudential FITNESSGRAM* (Cooper Institute for Aerobics Research 1994), parts of which are listed in table 4.3. The test can be administered throughout the year with the best raw score in each category being recorded at the end of the school year. The establishment of personal fitness goals by students and the keeping of an exercise log, both of which can be handed in periodically for your review and feedback, might prove more motivational to students than the actual fitness norms they achieve. Notice that the last column in table 4.3 allows students to record their personal fitness goals. Keep in mind that assessing fitness, like assessing benchmarks, is a waste of time unless the results are used to further a student's education. Your curriculum should promote the assessment items, which part II of this book will help you to directly do. Fitness and skill assessment should also be used as a self-evaluation tool for you, as the teacher, to determine whether you are meeting the needs of your students and whether you should adjust your curriculum accordingly.

FITNESS COMPONENTS

Each of the subsequently discussed fitness components are *health related* in that they associate with a health risk (coronary heart disease, obesity, low back pain, etc.) Compare your assessment of individual students to *health-fitness standards*, not just normative data, to promote healthy, preventative lifestyles. Encourage students to *self-compare* as you focus on changing fitness levels through improved habits by

| Table 4.3 | A Sample of the Side of the *Portfolio Card* for "Self-Concepts" Assessment, Fitness Assessment, Listing of Extracurricular Activities, and Teacher Comments. |

+ an area of strength (promotes)   * meets expectations (demonstrates)   - improvement needed

	1st Semester		2nd Semester		3rd Semester		4th Semester	
Self-Concepts	Student	Teacher	Student	Teacher	Student	Teacher	Student	Teacher
Cooperation	+	+						
Peer Respect	*	−						
Adult Respect	+	+						
Shares/Teamwork	+	*						
Self Control	*	−						
Responsible	+	+						
Sportsmanship	*	−						
Attitude	*	−						
Motivation	+	+						
Participation	+	+						
Behavior	+	+						
Skill Growth	+	+						
Basic Knowledge	+	+						

Fitness Components	Raw Score	Standard Score by Age and Gender	Personal Goal
Aerobic endurance (1 mile run)			
Body composition (% fat)			
Flexibility (sit and reach)			
Muscular strength (pull-ups)			
Muscular endurance (curl-ups)			

Extracurricular activities related to physical education:

Teacher comments:

This table is reprinted with permission from the *Journal of Physical Education, Recreation & Dance*, April, 1997, page 50. The *Journal* is a publication of the American Alliance for Health, Physical Education, Recreation and Dance, 1900 Association Drive, Reston, VA 20191.

Table 4.4   Representative Benchmark Outcomes for Grade Level Six

HAS	6	1. Throw a variety of objects demonstrating both accuracy and distance (e.g., Frisbees, deck tennis rings, footballs).
HAS	6	2. Continuously strike a ball to a wall, or a partner, with a paddle using forehand and backhand strokes.
HAS	6	3. Consistently strike a ball, using a golf club or a hockey stick, so that it travels in an intended direction and height.
HAS	6	4. Design and perform gymnastics and dance sequences that combine traveling, rolling, balancing, and weight transfer into smooth, flowing sequences with intentional changes in direction, speed, and flow.
HAS	6	5. Hand dribble and foot dribble while preventing an opponent from stealing the ball.
HAS	6	6. In a small group keep an object continuously in the air without catching it (e.g., ball, foot bag).
HAS	6	7. Consistently throw and catch a ball while guarded by opponents.
HAS	6	8. Design and play small group games that involve cooperating with others to keep an object away from opponents (basic offensive and defensive strategy) (e.g., by throwing, kicking, and/or dribbling a ball).
HAS	6	9. Design and refine a routine, combining various jump rope movements to music, so that it can be repeated without error.
HAS	6	10. Leap, roll, balance, transfer weight, bat, volley, hand and foot dribble, and strike a ball with a paddle, using mature motor patterns.
HAS	6	11. Demonstrate proficiency in front, back, and side swimming strokes.
HAS	6	12. Participate in vigorous activity for a sustained period of time while maintaining a target heart rate.
IS	6	13. Recover from vigorous physical activity in an appropriate length of time.
IS	6	14. Monitor heart rate before, during, and after activity.
IS	6	15. Correctly demonstrate activities designed to improve and maintain muscular strength and endurance, flexibility, and cardiorespiratory functioning.
DOES	6	16. Participate in games, sports, dance, and outdoor pursuits, both in and outside of school, based on individual interests and capabilities.
KNOWS	6	17. Recognize that idealized images of the human body and performance, as presented by the media, may not be appropriate to imitate.
KNOWS	6	18. Recognize that time and effort are prerequisites for skill improvement and fitness benefits.
KNOWS	6	19. Recognize the role of games, sports, and dance in getting to know and understand others of like and different cultures.
KNOWS	6	20. Identify opportunities in the school and community for regular participation in physical activity.
KNOWS	6	21. Identify principles of training and conditioning for physical activity.
KNOWS	6	22. Identify proper warm-up, conditioning, and cool-down techniques and the reasons for using them.
KNOWS	6	23. Identify benefits resulting from participating in different forms of physical activity.
KNOWS	6	24. Detect, analyze, and correct errors in personal movement patterns.
KNOWS	6	25. Describe ways to use the body and movement activities to communicate ideas and feelings.

(continued)

Table 4.4	*(continued)*		
VALUES	6	26.	Accept and respect the decisions made by game officials, whether they are students, teachers, or officials outside of school.
VALUES	6	27.	Seek out, participate with, and show respect for persons of like and different skill levels.
VALUES	6	28.	Choose to exercise at home for personal enjoyment and benefit.

Reprinted from Franck et al 1992.

Table 4.5	Representative Benchmark Outcomes for Grade Level Eight		
HAS	8	1.	Explore introductory outdoor pursuit skills (e.g., backpacking, rock climbing, hiking, canoeing, cycling, ropes courses).
HAS	8	2.	Combine skills competently to participate in modifed versions of team and individual sports.
HAS	8	3.	Perform a variety of simple folk, country, and creative dances.
HAS	8	4.	Use basic offensive and defensive strategies while playing a modified version of a sport.
HAS	8	5.	Practice in ways that are appropriate for learning new skills or sports on his/her own.
IS	8	6.	Correctly demonstrate various weight training techniques.
IS	8	7.	Sustain an aerobic activity, maintaining a target heart rate, to achieve cardiovascular benefits.
IS	8	8.	Improve and maintain appropriate body composition.
IS	8	9.	Participate in an individualized fitness program.
DOES	8	10.	Identify and follow rules while playing sports and games.
KNOWS	8	11.	Recognize the effects of substance abuse on personal health and performance in physical activity.
KNOWS	8	12.	List long-term physiological, psychological, and cultural benefits that may result from regular participation in physical activity.
KNOWS	8	13.	Describe principles of training and conditioning for specific physical activities.
KNOWS	8	14.	Describe personal and group conduct, including ethical behavior, appropriate for engaging in physical activity.
KNOWS	8	15.	Analyze and catagorize activities and exercise according to potential fitness benefits.
KNOWS	8	16.	Analyze offensive and defensive strategies in games and sports.
KNOWS	8	17.	Evaluate the roles of exercise and other factors in weight control.
VALUES	8	18.	Feel satisfaction on days when engaging in physical activity.
VALUES	8	19.	Enjoy the aesthetic and creative aspects of performance.
VALUES	8	20.	Respect physical and performance limitations of self and others.
VALUES	8	21.	Desire to improve physical ability and performance.

Reprinted from Franck et al 1992.

helping students understand their results relative to health-fitness issues.

Health Issue: Aerobic Endurance

Coronary heart disease (CHD) is the number one cause of death in the United States, although the death rates for CHD and stroke have fallen significantly in recent years (American Heart Association 1994). Many risk factors are associated with heart disease, such as elevated blood lipids (fats), hypertension (high blood pressure), stress, smoking, the consumption of fat, and physical inactivity. Many of these risks are easily reduced through a physically active lifestyle that includes *aerobic activity*. The *aerobic endurance assessment* will help students assess their capacity relative to health-fitness standards and guide them in making appropriate lifestyle changes.

The more traditional *one mile run/walk* is still an excellent tool for determining a student's estimated VO_2max (i.e., aerobic capacity). We have found, however, that the newer *PACER* assessment, as described in *The Prudential FITNESSGRAM Test Administration Manual,* that is a multistage 20-meter shuttle run, is quite effective in motivating students and also offers us the latitude of assessing aerobic capacity in the smaller confines of our gymnasium. You may wish to choose one or both of these assessment tools to measure your students' aerobic endurance based on your school's facilities and the needs of your students.

Students performing at or above the health-fitness standard are considered to be at an acceptable level for aerobic endurance. They should be encouraged to maintain these levels through adolescence and into adulthood. Students below the acceptable level should be encouraged to improve, moving their scores into the health-fitness zone.

Health Issue: Body Composition

Total body weight can be broken down into two components. *Lean body weight* refers to the collective weight of muscle, bone, and internal organs. The remaining weight is *body fat*. The ratio of fat weight and lean weight to total body weight has health implications. An excessive accumulation of fat is referred to as obesity and is associated with a number of risk factors: CHD, stroke, and diabetes.

Diet and exercise habits can affect obesity. Students need to learn at an early age about developing self-responsibility with respect to eating low-fat, low-sugar diets, as well as not overeating. Also, aerobic exercise needs to become a regular part of their lives at an early age so that these behaviors are more likely to carry over into adulthood.

The optimal range for fat content varies between boys (10 percent to 20 percent) and girls (15 percent to 25 percent). These ranges are associated with little, if any, health risk. Students outside these ranges should be encouraged to move back into the suggested ranges, keeping in mind that there is a 3 percent to 5 percent error associated with estimating body fat via *skinfold techniques* as outlined in *The Prudential FITNESSGRAM Test Administration Manual* (Cooper Institute for Aerobics Research 1994).

Instead of using skinfold testing, you may wish to assess *body mass index (BMI)*. This procedure provides an indication of the appropriateness of a student's weight relative to height, determined by the following formula: weight (kg)/height (m)^2. The healthy fitness zone for boys and girls varies with age, ranging from 20 to 27.8 for boys and 21 to 27.3 for girls.

Students on the high side are encouraged to move their scores into the healthy fitness zone. Those students with low scores (below 8 percent fat or less than 13.1 to 17.0 *BMI* for boys and below 13 percent fat or less than 14.1 to 15.0 *BMI* for girls, based on age) should also be targeted to move toward the appropriate healthy fitness zone.

Of most concern are those students who exhibit *severe changes,* because such changes may signal potential health problems.

Health Issue: Flexibility

Throughout their lifetimes, most Americans will encounter some form of back discomfort, caused in large part by daily activities adding to the stress of weak muscles in the low back and hip flexors. Physical inactivity contributes to the risk for low back pain. Through regular physical activity that includes both stretching and maintaining an optimal body-fat range, many low back syndromes can be minimized or prevented.

The health-fitness standard for the *back saver sit and reach test* is administered to one side at a time as described in *The Prudential FITNESSGRAM Test Administration Manual* (Cooper Institute for Aerobics Research 1994). Health-fitness standards once again vary by gender and age (8 inches for boys and 9 to 12 inches for girls, based on age). Students who fall below the health-fitness standard level are at an increased risk of developing low back/hamstring disorders. They should be encouraged to participate in activities that will help to improve overall flexibility, whether that be in your classes or at home.

The *shoulder stretch* is a simple test used to assess upper-body flexibility. Furthermore, it may be useful in educating students that flexibility is important in all areas of the body, not just the hamstrings and lower back.

Health Issues: Muscular Strength and Endurance

Many basic activities of daily living require upper-body strength for lifting, carrying, and moving objects. An inability to meet these needs places the body at greater risk for injury. The *pull-up, modified pull-up,* and *push-up assessments* address this area.

Low back problems are associated with weak abdominal muscles and poor flexibility in the low back and hamstring muscles. Weak abdominals affect posture, resulting in a misalignment of the spine that places strain on the lower back muscles. The *curl-up assessment* targets these muscles.

A test of trunk extensor strength and flexibility (the *trunk lift*) addresses the musculoskeletal fitness of the abdominals, hamstrings, and back extensors as they work in concert to maintain posture and help prevent or control low back problems.

Students whose scores fall below the health-fitness standards in these areas should be encouraged to improve their scores through activities that improve general body strength, an area targeted by many of our warm-up activities (chapter 5).

EXTRACURRICULAR ACTIVITIES

Provide a blank section on the card to list a student's participation in extracurricular activities that are an extension to the physical education program (i.e., play days, intramurals, interscholastic participation, and indications of life applications such as family recreation, community sports, and dance recitals). This list will help document a student's extra effort, work above and beyond class expectations, and general interest in your total program offerings.

TEACHER COMMENTS

Also provide space for any individual comments you care to make. Your comments have added value in targeting students with developmental or behavioral problems and allow you to offer support to the student and parent by suggesting ways to improve on performance outcomes. These comments become particularly important for parental conferences or special-needs issues or when a student's work and behavior are "red flagged" either by you or by teachers in other disciplines. As an example, brief comments about benchmark-assessment outcomes or translation of the rubrics into summary notations would make more sense to people outside of physical education, such as parents, other teachers, and administrators. Exceptional and appropriate behaviors might also be recorded here. Most students do behave well, and exceptionally good behavior should be recorded also.

ASSESSING PROGRAM OUTCOMES

Let your overall goals, need for documentation, student enrollment, and district use of portfolio data guide you in designing a system to best meet your needs. The example we have provided is only a sample. The benchmarks suggested by the National Association for Sport and Physical Education (Franck et al. 1992), however, are a realistic starting point for defining the outcomes you are looking for at each level and developing *authentic assessments*. Use them to join your peers in shaping your districtwide assessment plan. In many states—such as Kentucky, Pennsylvania, New York, and Vermont to name but a few—outcome-based assessment plans are directly recommended from state education councils set up to deal in large part with educational accountabil-ity. The trend in education of moving toward rubric and portfolio assessment is real and growing, necessitating a reevaluation of teaching styles and a restructuring of curriculum content to help students move forward. Ultimately this will give your students greater challenges, resulting in greater outcome-based achievements.

Portions of this chapter are reprinted in part with permission from the *Journal of Physical Education, Recreation & Dance*, April, 1977, 46–52. The *Journal* is a publication of the American Alliance for Health, Physical Education, Recreation and Dance, 1900 Association Drive, Reston, VA 20191.

part II

TEACHING MODULES

chapter 5

WARM-UPS

The *warm-up module* prepares students for the skill development and game activities that lie ahead. In addition, this physical warm-up period is an ideal time for you to teach fitness-related topics such as the differences between anaerobic and aerobic activity, performance concepts such as speed, power, and agility, and social skills such as cooperation.

Unfortunately, the "warm-up" is one of the most ignored segments of a lesson plan, when in fact it can provide a valuable forum for a student to both enjoy and benefit from individualized movement. Because most physical education classes are heterogeneous, unlike reading and math groups in which students of equal ability can be grouped, the warm-up session allows students to work at individual capacity levels without detracting from the education of others. This focus on individuality sets a positive tone for class activity right from the start.

As was mentioned in chapter 3, the rationale you use in choosing a particular *warm-up module* will vary based on the goals of your class and needs of your students. Modules have been grouped by their primary focus:

The warm-up module can also be used to showcase individual talents. For instance, through verbal cues and praise, a student who is the best rope skipper or the best at cartwheels can become a "star," as opposed to always blending into a group. We have also found that the warm-up format we present works especially well for students with special needs.

fitness circuits; power, speed, and agility drills; cardiovascular and cooperative tasks; or jumping/landing activities. Within each grouping, activities progress from easiest to most difficult; sometimes these differences are admittedly subtle. For many of the warm-ups there are, of course, some overlap among the categorical groupings. Select daily modules based on your goals and needs, taking into account the skill development and game activity you will be using later in the day's lesson.

When using a module of "circuit" format, rotate students through the stations in 30- to 60-second time segments to maximize fitness benefits. Try using music (on to exercise, off to rotate) for motivation and to maintain student interest. Some of the modules have no stations, and the total activity time should take no longer than three to five minutes, perhaps slightly longer if students are playing some of the cooperative games or slightly less if they are playing a particularly active game.

Table 5.1 provides a listing of warm-up activities for each of the four groupings.

FITNESS CIRCUITS

The warm-up circuits presented in this section focus on improving the overall fitness of students. Some circuits focus on total fitness from a strength perspective (e.g., The Ultimate Body Circuit), some are more anaerobic in nature (e.g., Scooter Triathlon), and some target selected muscle groups (e.g., Upper-Body Strength Circuit). Purpose, materials, and procedures are outlined for each of the circuits.

Table 5.1 Warm-Up Activities by Grouping

Fitness Circuits		Power, Speed, and Agility Drills	
Scooter Triathlon	(page 43)	Pull or Push Your Own Weight	(page 55)
Upper-Body Strength Circuit	(page 44)	The Maze	(page 56)
Lower-Body Strength Circuit	(page 45)	Inside-Outside Relay	(page 57)
Chest, Back, and Leg Circuit	(page 46)	Orbiter	(page 58)
Leg, Chest, and Ab Circuit	(page 47)	Predator and Prey	(page 59)
Total Body Hula Hoop Circuit	(page 48)	Vertical Jump and Pull Circuit	(page 60)
Total Body Circuit 1	(page 49)	Speed Dynamics 1	(page 61)
Total Body Circuit 2	(page 49)	Speed Dynamics 2	(page 62)
Total Body Circuit 3	(page 50)	Power Agility Circuit 1	(page 63)
The Ultimate Body Circuit	(page 51)	Power Agility Circuit 2	(page 63)
Total Body Circuit With Partner	(page 53)	Power Agility Circuit 3	(page 64)
		Bounding Circuit 1	(page 64)
		Bounding Circuit 2	(page 65)
		Multidirectional Speed Circuit	(page 66)
Cardiovascular and Cooperative Tasks		**Jumping/Landing Activities**	
Cleanup	(page 68)	Safety Falls	(page 77)
Ship to Shore	(page 68)	Jump-Rope Activities	(page 78)
Rescue	(page 69)	Grid Drills	(page 79)
Amoeba	(page 70)	Basic Plyometric Jumps	(page 80)
Junkyard Relay	(page 71)		
Basketbowl	(page 73)		
Farmer	(page 75)		
Ball Thief	(page 76)		
Team Carry	(page 76)		

SCOOTER TRIATHLON (MAY BE USED AS TEAM OR INDIVIDUAL WARM-UP)

Purpose:

- To warm up via an aerobic exercise using both upper- and lower-body muscles

Materials:

- 4-6 scooters
- Large area of gym space
- 4-6 cones

Procedure:

- Divide the students into relay-like groups balanced by ability to assure success (see diagram 5.1):
    - If using a team format, make teams of three students each.
    - The teammates should cooperatively decide which event they will each perform.
    - If using an individual format, the three events should be performed consecutively.
- The first event is "swimming":
    - Instruct the students to lie prone on the scooters, using butterfly-like or crawl-like strokes to propel the scooters around the far cone (buoy) and back.
- The second event is "cycling":
    - Instruct the students to sit on the scooters and use their feet to propel the scooters around the far cone and back.
- The third event is "running":
    - Instruct the students to place both hands on the scooters, locking the elbows to support their weight.
    - Shoulders should be directly over the scooters for balance.
    - Students then run with the scooters on the floor around the far cone and back.

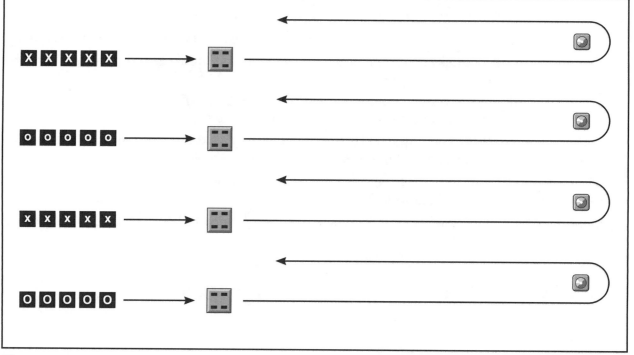

Diagram 5.1

The overriding objective in physical education is to help students experience and develop a love for a fitness-oriented lifestyle. The warm-ups we present can be modified to best suit the needs of various sizes and types of students in your classes. For example, in the Scooter Triathlon, some students, mainly the severely overweight or taller ones, have difficulty in the running event. Physically, they just can't bend over to assume the running position. Allow these students who struggle to put any combination of the three events together so they can experience success and meet the intended goal of fitness development (e.g., two swims and a cycle, or two cycles and a swim). This shows your students you both recognize and are sensitive to their needs. It also focuses attention on what is most important—movement!

UPPER-BODY STRENGTH CIRCUIT

Purpose:

- To warm up while developing back, shoulder, chest, and arm strength/endurance

Materials:

- Benches (or bottom step of bleachers)
- 4-6 folded mats
- Long rope
- 4-6 scooters

Procedure:

- Divide the class into five random groups of even numbers.
- Place the students at each of the five stations (see diagram 5.2):
  - Students work at their own pace and capacity within a given station (30 seconds per station).
- Station 1—Students lie prone on the bench/bleacher, then pull themselves the length of the bench/bleacher using their arms.
- Station 2—Students lie prone on a scooter and mimic a "butterfly" or "crawl" swim stroke, propelling the scooter around the cone and then back to the wall.
- Station 3—A length of rope is attached to the wall (bleachers or door). Students pull themselves "hand-over-hand" the length of the rope while lying on a scooter.
- Station 4—Using folded mats, students perform decline push-ups with either their feet or knees elevated by the mat and hands on the floor.
- Station 5—Using folded mats, students continually vault or cartwheel back and forth over the mat.

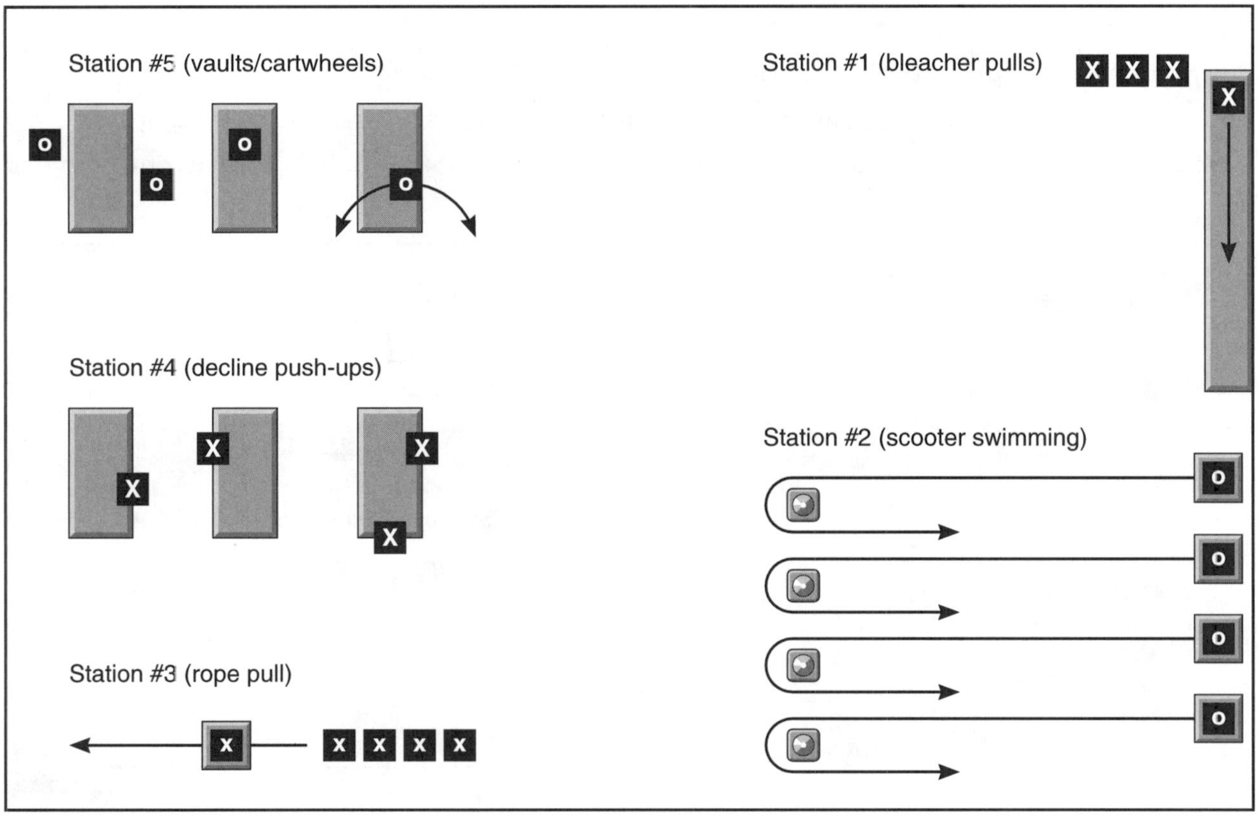

Diagram 5.2

LOWER-BODY STRENGTH CIRCUIT

Purpose:

- To warm up while developing cardiorespiratory fitness and muscular endurance of the quadriceps, hamstrings, and calf muscles

Materials:

- 4-6 jump ropes
- 4-6 scooters
- 4-6 folded mats
- Benches (or bottom step of bleachers)
- 6-8 lines on the floor

Procedure:

- Divide the class into six random groups of even numbers.
- Place students at each of the six stations (see diagram 5.3):
  - Students work at their own pace and capacity within a given station (30 seconds per station).
- Station 1—agility side steps: shuffle back and forth across three lines spaced approximately 4 feet apart (remind students to maintain a low center of gravity).
- Station 2—scooter bicycle: have students sit on the scooter and move away from the starting point a given distance using only their feet to *push* the scooters; then, using only their feet, have them *pull* their scooters back to the starting position.

- Station 3—jump rope (any style jumping)
- Station 4—ski jumps over a line (feet together, lateral bounding)
- Station 5—bench-step marches to a four count (use benches or first row of bleachers)
- Station 6—lateral bounds to and from an elevation (students laterally bound up onto a folded mat, then off the other side, and repeat)

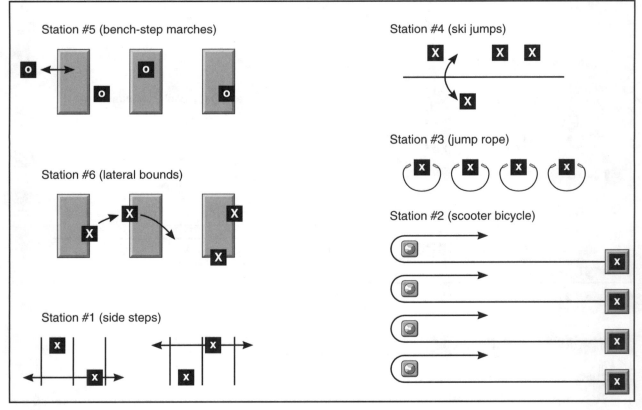

Diagram 5.3

CHEST, BACK, AND LEG CIRCUIT

Purpose:

- To warm up while focusing on the muscles of the back, chest, and legs

Materials:

- 1 long rope (approximately 12 feet long)
- 6 folded mats
- Benches (or bottom step of bleachers)
- 4-6 scooters

Procedure:

- Divide the class into five random groups of even numbers.
- Place the students at each of the five stations (see diagram 5.4):
  - Students work at their own pace and capacity within a given station (30 to 60 seconds per station).

- Station 1—Students lie prone on the benches and/or bleachers and pull their own weight the length of them.
- Station 2—Anchor the rope to the floor at one end and either you hold the other end or have a student hold the other end at waist level. Students jump side to side over the rope, progressing from the low end to the high end.
- Station 3—Students place their feet up on the folded mat while assuming a push-up position on the floor with their hands. Moving their hands, students walk (circle) around their mat, completing as many laps as possible.
- Station 4—Each student lies prone on a scooter and propels the scooter using a "swimming" motion with his arms.
- Station 5—Students jog up and down on the folded mats to a four count.

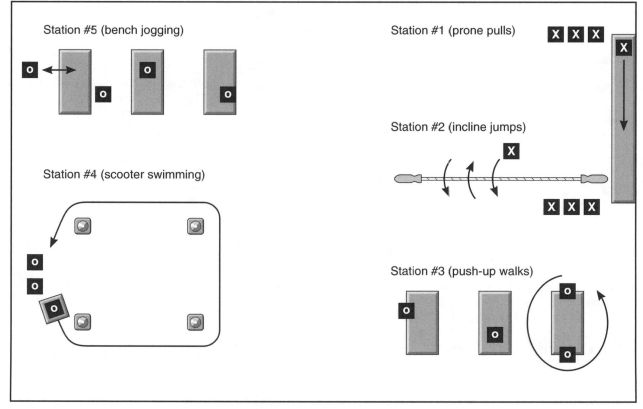

Diagram 5.4

LEG, CHEST, AND AB CIRCUIT

Purpose:

- To warm up using a low-level fitness circuit that also includes agility and coordination

Materials:

- 1 large exercise mat
- Lines on the floor
- Wall space

Procedure:

- Divide the class into four random, equal-sized groups.
- Place the students at each of the four stations (see diagram 5.5):
  - Students work at their own capacity within a given station (30 to 60 seconds per station).
- Station 1—push-ups off the wall
- Station 2—abdominal crunches (feet flat on floor)
- Station 3—lateral bounds, side to side over line
- Station 4—lunges, large steps with knee over ankle

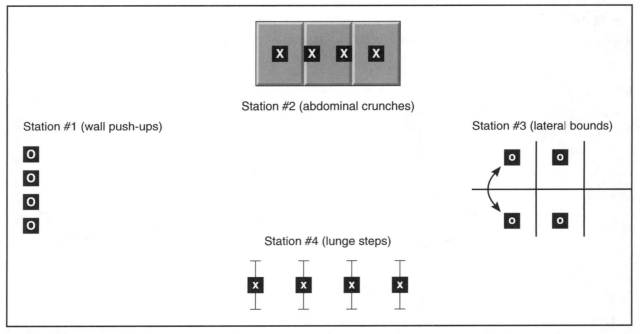

Diagram 5.5

TOTAL BODY HULA HOOP CIRCUIT

Purpose:

- To warm up while developing total body strength and endurance

Materials:

- 1 hula hoop for every student

Procedure:

- Give students hula hoops and have them find a separate space.
- Verbally cue students through the following circuit, spending 30 seconds on each task:
  - Jump in and out of the hoop landing on both feet.
  - Assume a push-up position, hands in the hoop, feet out. Spin in one direction for 5 seconds, then switch direction (repeat for 30 seconds).
  - Lie on your back in hoop and perform crunches.
  - Assume a push-up position, feet in the hoop, hands out. Walk your body around the hoop, pivoting on your feet. Switch direction every lap.

– Stand in the hoop on your right foot. Hop in and out of the hoop on your right foot only.

– Stand in the hoop on your left foot. Hop in and out of the hoop on your left foot only.

TOTAL BODY CIRCUIT 1

Purpose:

- To warm up while developing total body strength, endurance, and coordination

Materials:

- 6 large exercise mats
- 6-8 cones placed on their sides

Procedure:

- Divide the class into four random, equal-sized groups.
- Place the students at each of the four stations (see diagram 5.6):
  - Students work at their own capacity within a given station (30 to 60 seconds per station).
- Station 1—push-ups off the knees with back straight
- Station 2—abdominal crunches (knees over hips, feet elevated)
- Station 3—lateral bounds, side to side over cones
- Station 4—bench stepping up and down on folded mats

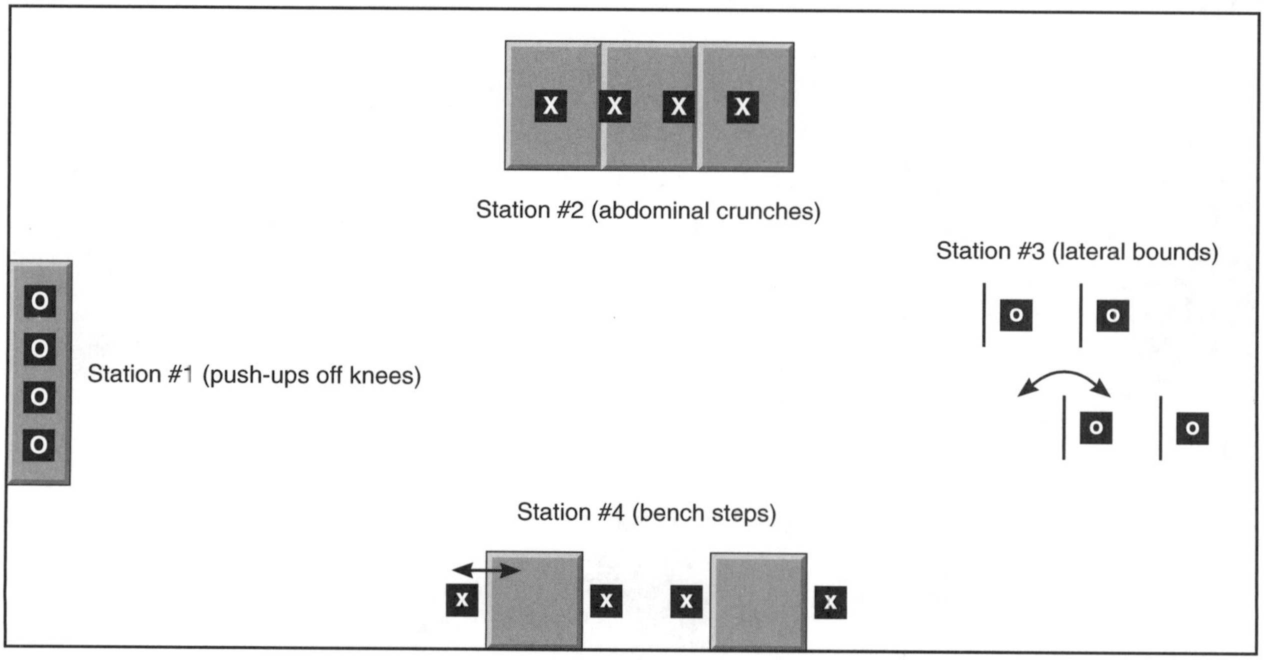

Station #2 (abdominal crunches)

Station #3 (lateral bounds)

Station #1 (push-ups off knees)

Station #4 (bench steps)

Diagram 5.6

TOTAL BODY CIRCUIT 2

Purpose:

- To warm up while developing total body strength, endurance, and coordination

Materials:

- 3 large exercise mats
- 1 long rope anchored to the floor at one end
- Vertical climb ladder

Procedure:

- Divide the class into four random, equal-sized groups.
- Place the students at each of the four stations (see diagram 5.7):
  - Students work at their own capacity within a given station (30 to 60 seconds per station).
- Station 1—push-ups off toes
- Station 2—lateral bounds, side to side over a rope that inclines from the floor to the teacher's waist
- Station 3—abdominal crunches (knees over hips, feet extended up toward ceiling)
- Station 4—vertical climb up a ladder mounted to wall

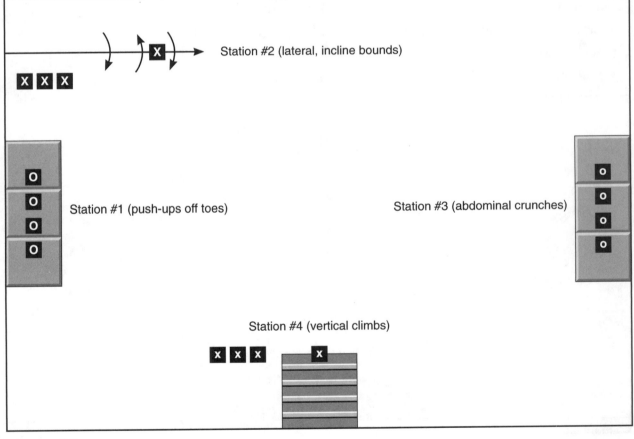

Diagram 5.7

TOTAL BODY CIRCUIT 3

Purpose:

- To warm up while developing total body strength, endurance, and coordination

Materials:

- Pegboard or vertical climb ladder
- 6 large exercise mats
- Floor space
- Wall space

Procedure:

- Divide the class into four random, equal-sized groups.
- Place the students at each of the four stations (see diagram 5.8):
  - Students work at their own capacity within a given station (30 to 60 seconds per station).
- Station 1—push-ups with the feet elevated on folded mats
- Station 2—abdominal crunches (knees over hips, feet pressed flat against a wall)
- Station 3—climbing up a peg board and/or vertical ladder
- Station 4—squat jumps

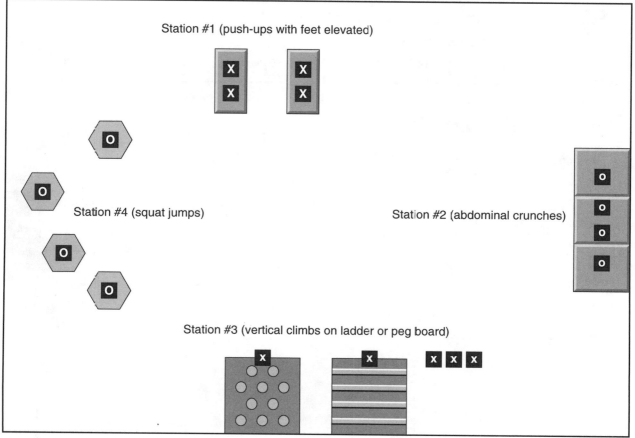

Station #1 (push-ups with feet elevated)

Station #4 (squat jumps)

Station #2 (abdominal crunches)

Station #3 (vertical climbs on ladder or peg board)

Diagram 5.8

THE ULTIMATE BODY CIRCUIT

Purpose:

- To warm up while developing total body strength, endurance, and coordination

Materials:

- 7 large exercise mats
- 1 long rope anchored to the floor at one end
- 3-4 scooters
- Wall space
- 6-8 jump ropes

Procedure:

- Divide the class into six random, equal-sized groups.
- Place the students at each of the six stations (see diagram 5.9):
  - Students work at their own capacity within a given station (30 to 60 seconds per station).
- Station 1—push-ups off toes
- Station 2—abdominal crunches (knees over hips, rotation with each crunch)
- Station 3—start from a push-up position with the feet on the wall; walk up the wall into a handstand, then back down to the starting position, and repeat
- Station 4—bench stepping onto and off of folded mats
- Station 5—rope skipping, any style
- Station 6—lie prone on a scooter and pull along a rope toward where the rope is anchored

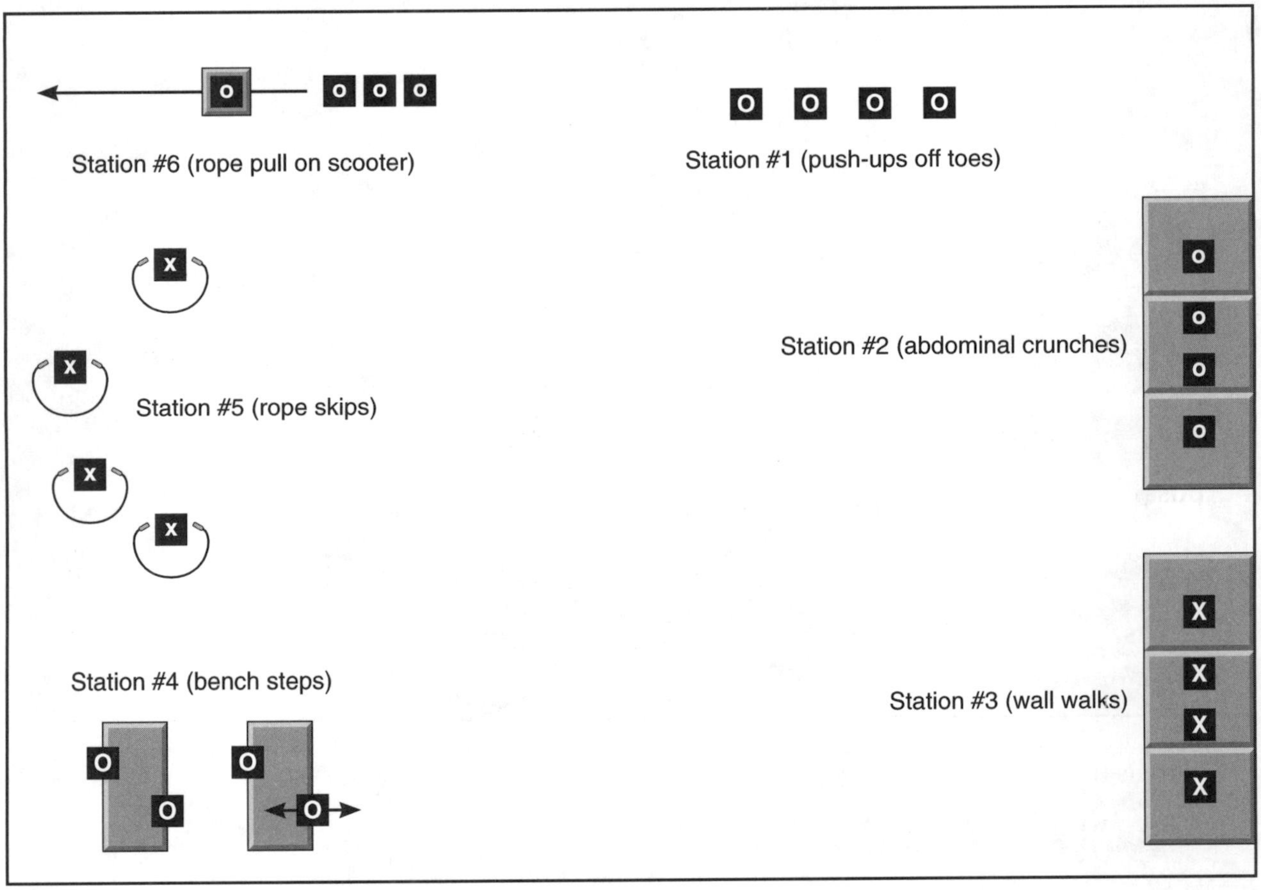

Diagram 5.9

Strength and conditioning circuits give you the chance to introduce the concept of strength training through the principles of *overload* and *progression*. Although these circuits serve as a good starting point, the use of free weights (barbells and dumbbells), Universal Gym, Nautilus, Cybex equipment, and the like will greatly add to the experiences you offer your students. If you are fortunate enough to have this equipment available, introduce its use through warm-up activities, and encourage students to train on it before or after school in intramural-type programs.

Although books could be written (and have been) about the principles of strength training, here are some simple guidelines to follow with the middle school age group:

- If using free weights, introduce students to *functional exercises* (i.e., exercises that incorporate many of the major muscles in a given exercise: squats, dead lift, bench press, incline bench press, and power clean).

- If using a strength training machine (Universal Gym, Nautilus, Cybex, etc.), introduce enough *isolation exercises* to target muscles fully and differently (i.e., exercises for the chest might include bench press, "pec deck" flys, and dips).

- Use a circuit format to keep students moving; pair students at each station, and use 30 seconds of exercise with 30 seconds of rest as your guide.

- Keep the students' repetitions from 8 to 12 for a given exercise. When they can perform 12 repetitions, add weight and start the process of *progression* over again with a heavier *overload*. Increases of 5 percent for upper-body exercises and 10 percent for lower-body exercises are reasonable. This range of repetitions will both increase strength and allow them to train safely.

TOTAL BODY CIRCUIT WITH PARTNER

Purpose:
- To warm up while developing total body strength and endurance, cooperation, and trust among partners

Materials:
- 7-8 large exercise mats
- 6-8 cones
- 3 balls (basketball, volleyball, soccer, etc.)

Procedure:
- Divide the class into four equal groups.
- Place the students at each of the four stations (see diagram 5.10):
  - Within each group, have the students find a partner to exercise with.
  - Students work at their own capacity and rotate through stations every 30 seconds.

- Station 1—bench steps onto and off of folded mats (one partner up, other partner off)
- Station 2—lateral bounds, side to side over cones set on their sides (partners face each other with hands resting on partner's shoulders)
- Station 3—wheelbarrow walks down the mat (one partner holds the other's feet; switch and return)
- Station 4—partner crunches with legs interlocked, handing off a ball on each repetition

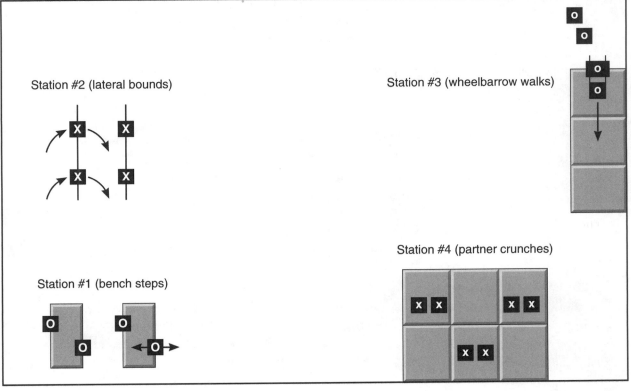

Diagram 5.10

It will help your students to learn by displaying posters of the muscle groups being developed at each exercise station, as well as diagrams of the exercises themselves. These displays will enhance the educational experience for those students who learn through "printed material" or "graphic displays."

POWER, SPEED, AND AGILITY DRILLS

This section of warm-ups presents activities designed to improve the power, speed, and agility of your students. Some of the warm-ups are partner activities (e.g., Pull or Push Your Own Weight), some are team oriented (e.g., Inside-Outside Relay), and some are plyometric (e.g., Bounding Circuit 2). All are challenging and provide a fun format through which students can train.

PULL OR PUSH YOUR OWN WEIGHT

Purpose:

- To warm up by providing resistance training for the quadriceps, hamstrings, and calf muscles, while developing power through anaerobic training

Materials:

- 10-12 jump ropes
- 6-8 carpet samples (2-by-3-foot rug)
- 10 scooters
- 5-8 plastic sleds (padded underneath)
- 4 cones

Procedure:

- Have the students pair off into partners using the concepts of "trust" and "body type" in their decisions.
- The students will perform three challenges and may do so in any order to maximize equipment and time use (see diagram 5.11).
- The first challenge is a "chariot race":
  - One student sits on a rug with her legs folded in front of her. This student holds the jump rope handles by wrapping them around her hands.
  - Her partner stands in front of the rug with the rope draped around the front of her waist. This student then proceeds to run, pulling the sitting student and rug around the four cones placed in the gym.
  - After passing all four cones, the students switch places.
- The second challenge is a "tractor-trailer push":
  - Each pair of students has two scooters.
  - One partner sits on a scooter while placing his feet on the other scooter.
  - The other partner stands behind the scooters and pushes his partner around the four-cone course.
  - Hands should be placed on the partner's shoulder blades for safety.
  - Communication and trust between partners relative to steering and speed is important.
  - After completing the course, partners switch.
- The third challenge is a "dogsled race":
  - This challenge, the most difficult of the three because of the greater friction involved, is similar to the "chariot race" except the passive student lies prone in a plastic sled while holding the rope handles.
  - After being pulled around the four-cone course, partners switch places and repeat.

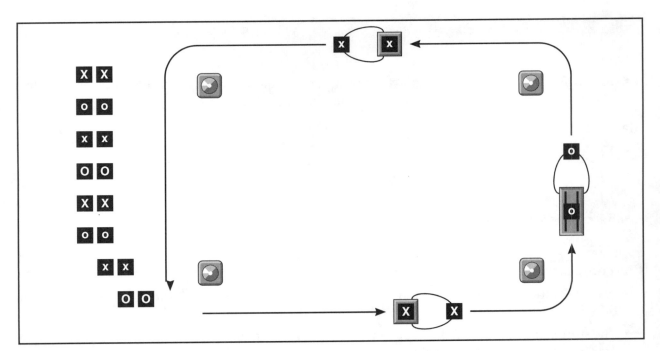

Diagram 5.11

THE MAZE

Purpose:

- To warm up while focusing on agility, foot speed, and eye/hand coordination

Materials:

- As many folding mats as you have
- 24 cones
- 6 hockey sticks
- 6-12 footballs

Procedure:

- Create maze walls as shown in diagram 5.12 by turning your mats on their side edges.
- Cones are used to create a slalom course, and hurdles are formed by placing a hockey stick across two cones.
- Have the students line up at the starting point and run through the maze at 5-second intervals.
- To develop eye/hand coordination, have students run through the maze with a football after taking a handoff or run pass patterns:
    - Square in; square out
    - Post; flag
    - Curl in; slant

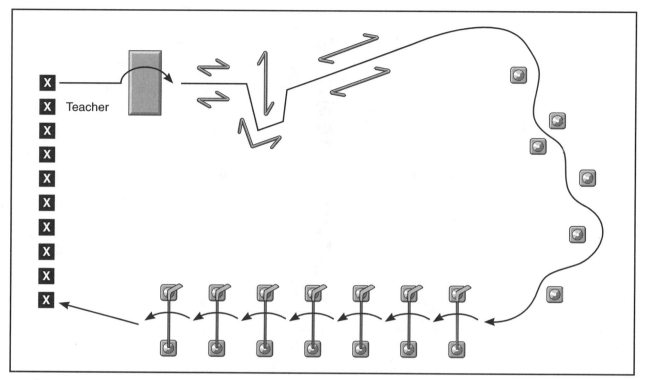

Diagram 5.12

INSIDE-OUTSIDE RELAY

Purpose:

- To warm up while developing anaerobic systems and refining track techniques

Materials:

- 8 cones (different colors work best)
- 4 mats (folded and placed on their sides)
- 2 relay batons
- 2 footballs
- 2 medicine balls

Procedure:

- Divide the class into four groups of even numbers.
- Place the students into relay lines as depicted in diagram 5.13:
  - Relay lines on the opposite sides of the rectangle are actually on the same team.
  - For variety, make all four relay lines separate teams.
- Explain, demonstrate, and/or review sprint and baton handoff techniques.
- On the command "Go," the two students start the race, running halfway around the gym, handing off to the line opposite them. The student receiving the baton in turn runs halfway around the gym and hands off accordingly:
  - Students start from inside the cones but run around the outside area of the cones and mats, that are folded on their sides.
  - For variety, use medicine balls or footballs.

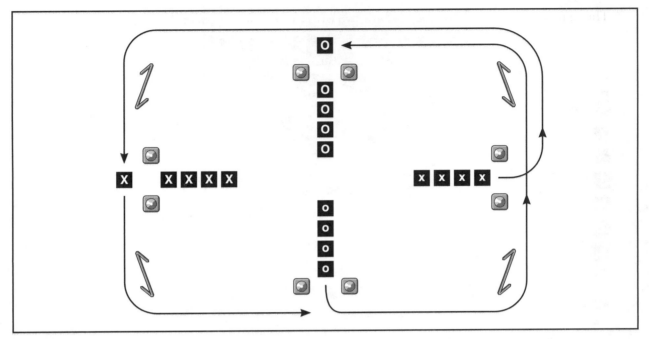

Diagram 5.13

light variations in a warm-up can be both fun and challenging to selected groups of students. As an example, to vary and develop problem-solving skills in the Inside-Outside Relay, use two *"Physio"-type* balls that are three to four feet in diameter. Instruct your students to move the ball around the course to their teammates anyway they want, as long as the ball remains on the floor; students can use their hands only, feet only, no hands or feet, and so on.

ORBITER

Purpose:

- To warm up using the interval training principle of work/relief, spatial awareness, and foot speed:
  - This is a perfect opportunity to discuss such scientific concepts as centripetal and centrifugal forces, gravitational pull, and orbit.

Materials:

- 4 folded mats
- 4 plastic bowling pins (or wooden clubs)

Procedure:

- Divide the class into four random groups.
- Assign a number to each member of each group (there will be four number 1s, four number 2s, etc.).

- The teacher calls out a number in random order (see diagram 5.14):
  - When a student hears her number called, she must run around the four folded mats and knock down her team's pin upon returning to her starting position.
- Points are assigned as follows: 4 for 1st place, 3 for 2nd, 2 for 3rd, and 1 for 4th (Dauer and Pangrazi 1986).

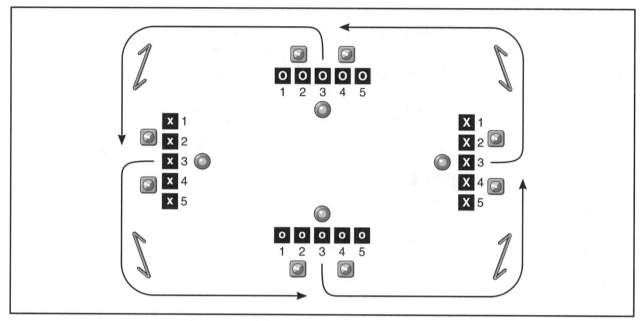

Diagram 5.14

PREDATOR AND PREY

Purpose:

- To warm up using the interval training principle of work/relief, spatial awareness, foot speed, and change of direction

Materials:

- Large area
- 1 large cone
- 4 small cones
- 1 sponge ball (a 6- to 8-inch diameter works well)

Procedure:

- Divide the class into two random groups (see diagram 5.15).
- One team is up (the prey), and the other team is in the field (predators).
- The students on the "prey" team partner up with a teammate so there are groups of pairs.
- Students get up, one pair at a time:
  - One teammate throws or kicks the ball anywhere in the large area he feels is appropriate.
  - The pair then races around a big cone and tries to get back between another set of smaller cones without getting hit by the sponge ball.
  - Partners may (and should) separate to help each other avoid getting hit by the ball.

- 1 point is awarded to each partner who safely gets back.
- 3 points are awarded to any pair that is successful.
- The team in the field (predators) gets control of the thrown or kicked ball and tries to hit or tag the "prey" with the ball:
  - Students should be encouraged to pass the ball to teammates, hit cutoffs, and cooperate to eliminate as many "prey" as possible.
  - To hit a "prey" player, the ball must be thrown as a "chest pass" to encourage control and stay within the objectives of the game (Dauer and Pangrazi 1986).

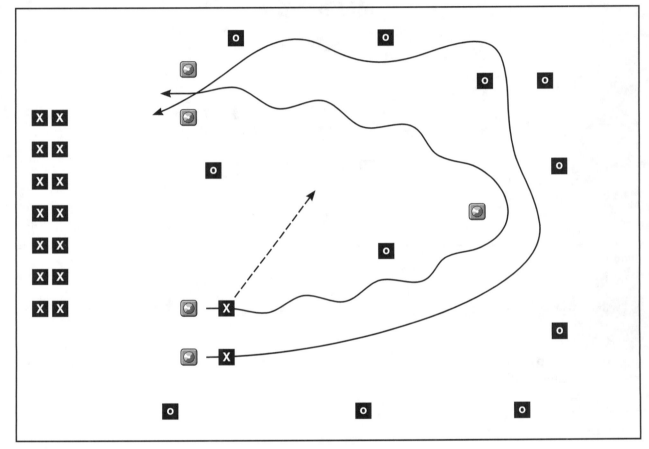

Diagram 5.15

VERTICAL JUMP AND PULL CIRCUIT

Purpose:
- To warm up while developing total body strength, endurance, and coordination

Materials:
- A volleyball net or wall with an 8-foot-high horizontal line drawn on it
- 6 hula hoops
- 12 cones on their sides with 6 hockey sticks placed across them, forming 6 hurdles
- 6 tall cones
- 6-8 jump ropes

- 6-8 scooters
- Floor space

Procedure:

- Divide the class into four random, equal-sized groups.
- Place the students at each of the four stations (see diagram 5.16):
  - Students work at their own capacity within a given station (30 to 60 seconds per station).
- Station 1—"V" jumps over the volleyball net or lined wall (jumps that would be used to block shots)
- Station 2— bounding circuit (up through hoops, down over hurdles, up over tall cones, down over hurdles, up through hoops, etc.)
- Station 3—students prone on scooters, propelling themselves using either butterfly-like or crawl-like swimming motions
- Station 4—rope skipping (any style but have students try adding double jumps)

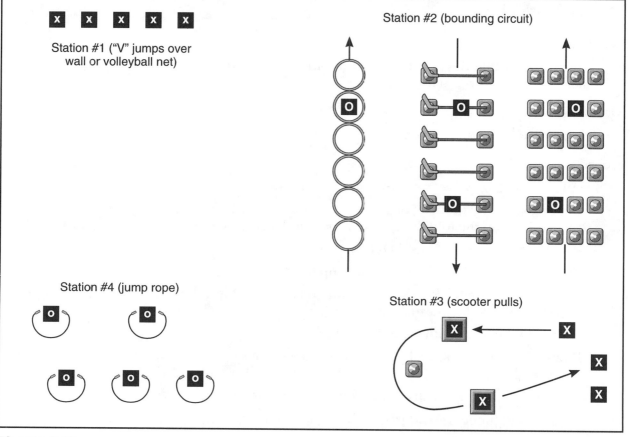

Diagram 5.16

SPEED DYNAMICS 1

Purpose:

- To warm up while developing speed techniques, helping students to be more responsive in rebounding off the floor

Materials:

- A large indoor or outdoor space

Procedure:

- Divide the class into two random, equal-sized groups.
- Call students by group (*1* or *2*, *A* or *B*, etc.), and have them run across the large designated space working on the following verbal cues (add a cue each time the students run):
  - Take a quick breath before running.
  - Hold your breath when running a short sprint (e.g., from first to second base).
  - Hold your stomach in when running (this will flatten the back).
  - Stand tall when running.
  - Keep your eyes focused on a conversational plane.
  - Keep your arms at a 90-degree angle, elbows in, thumbs up.

SPEED DYNAMICS 2

Purpose:

- To warm up while developing speed techniques, helping students to execute quicker foot placement on the floor with propulsion

Materials:

- A large indoor or outdoor space

Procedure:

- Divide the class into two random, equal-sized groups.
- Call the students by group (*1* or *2*, *A* or *B*, etc.), and have them run across the large designated space working on the following verbal cues (add a cue each time the students run):
  - Review the cues from Speed Dynamics 1 lesson.
  - Take quick skips with the toes pulled up (*toe up*).
  - Run upright with the knees straight down under the hips, the knee bending as if trying to strike the heel to the buttocks (*heel up*).
  - Skip with the toe up, knee up (foot under knee).
  - Power skip with the knee, heel, and toes pulled up as if trying to kick the buttock (*toe up, heel up, knee up*).
  - Perform "wall-claw" drills (ground prep and recovery):

    Have the students stand perpendicular to the wall, weight on the inside leg.

    With the outside foot, bring the toe, heel, and knee up in slow motion.

    Extend the lower leg, keeping the toe and heel up (as if clawing out in front of body).

    Straighten the leg with the foot (toes up) striking the ground, pulling backward (feel the weight/resistance of the foot pulling).

    As soon as the toe leaves the ground, recover as quickly as possible into toe up, heel up, knee up position.

    Repeat this process five times, then switch legs.
- Stress visualization and technical concepts with students throughout these tasks.

POWER AGILITY CIRCUIT 1

Purpose:

- To warm up while developing quick feet when changing directions

Materials:

- A large indoor or outdoor space

Procedure:

- Have the students spread out down one side of the gym or the teaching area:
  - Caution students to be conscious of spatial awareness to avoid collisions.
- Verbally cue students through the following circuit, stressing "quick feet" on nonjogging tasks:
  - Jog (30 seconds)
  - Side shuffle 15 to 20 feet to the left, then return to the right
  - Jog (30 seconds)
  - Side shuffle using power jumps 15 to 20 feet to the left, then return to the right
  - Jog (30 seconds)
  - Grapevine with the knees high (carioca) 15 to 20 feet to the left, then return to the right
  - Jog (30 seconds)

POWER AGILITY CIRCUIT 2

Purpose:

- To warm up while developing power in the thigh and hip flexor muscle groups

Materials:

- A large indoor or outdoor space

Procedure:

- Have the students spread out down one side of the gym or the teaching area:
  - Caution students to be conscious of spatial awareness to avoid collisions.
- Verbally cue students through the following circuit, stressing height on the skips and a good stretch on the lunges (30 seconds per cue):
  - Jog
  - Power skip for height
  - Jog
  - Lunge walk with a long stride (front knee over the front ankle)
  - Jog
  - Lunge walk with short stride (back knee next to the ankle of front foot)
  - Jog

POWER AGILITY CIRCUIT 3

Purpose:

- To warm up while developing vertical jump height off lateral movements

Materials:

- A large indoor or outdoor space

Procedure:

- Have the students spread out down one side of the gym or the teaching area:
  - Caution students to be conscious of spatial awareness to avoid collisions.
- Verbally cue students through the following circuit, stressing "quick feet" in nonjogging tasks (30 seconds per cue):
  - Jog
  - Side bound over a line (short jumps)
  - Jog
  - Side bound over a line (long jumps)
  - Jog
  - Side shuffle (2 steps right, 2 steps left)
  - Jog

BOUNDING CIRCUIT 1

Purpose:

- To warm up while developing the quadriceps, hamstrings, and calf muscles with implications for increasing vertical jump height

Materials:

- 6-8 jump ropes
- Volleyball net or 8-foot-high horizontal line drawn on wall
- 6-8 hockey sticks
- 6-8 cones

Procedure:

- Divide the class into four equal groups.
- Place each group at one of the four stations (see diagram 5.17):
  - Students work at their own capacity within a given station (30 seconds per station).
- Station 1—jump rope any style, as rapidly as possible
- Station 2—"V" jumps against the wall
- Station 3—lateral bounds over the hockey stick (stress speed)
- Station 4—forward bounding over cones placed on their sides; jog back to the start and repeat (stress height)

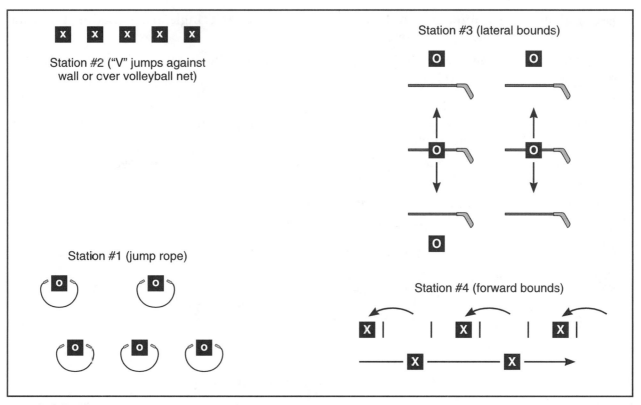

Diagram 5.17

BOUNDING CIRCUIT 2

Purpose:

- To warm up while developing the quadriceps, hamstrings, and calf muscles with implications for increasing vertical jump height

Materials:

- 6-8 jump ropes
- 6 folded mats

Procedure:

- Divide the class into four equal groups.
- Place each group at one of the four stations (see diagram 5.18):
  - Students work at their own capacity within a given station (30 seconds per station).
- Station 1—jump rope for height (two passes of the rope for each jump)
- Station 2—progressive squat-depth jumps:
  - Students start by standing in front of a folded 6-by-8-foot-mat (six such mats are placed in a row, 3 feet apart).
  - The student drops into a squat position with the thighs parallel to the floor and repeatedly jumps over each of the next mats in succession, landing on and jumping off the floor.
  - Emphasize arm swing and torso position during each jump (Smith 1996).
- Station 3—diagonal gathering jumps:

– Students jump approximately 4 feet forward at a 45-degree angle in a gathering jump, and then explode upward in a vertical jump.

– The student repeats this process, jumping 45 degrees to the opposite side (tracing a zigzag pattern) for the 30 seconds (Smith 1996).

• Station 4—pike jumps in place:

– Students jump vertically off the ground with the upper torso kept straight and the legs straight, flexing at the hips.

– When the legs are parallel with the ground, the student touches her toes and returns to a standing position before repeating jumps.

– Emphasize body control and getting off the ground quickly (Smith 1996).

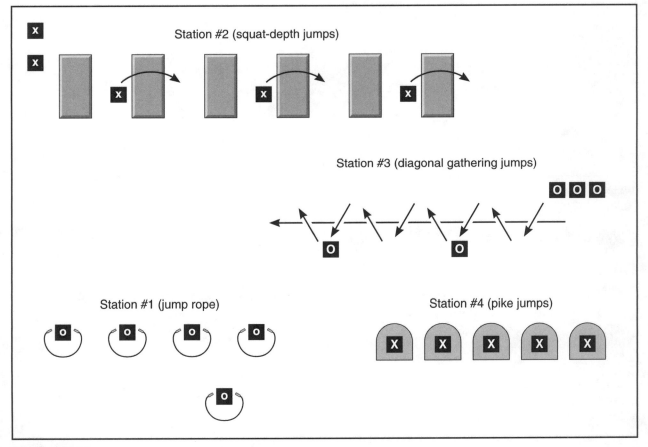

Diagram 5.18

MULTIDIRECTIONAL SPEED CIRCUIT

Purpose:

• To warm up while developing foot speed and multidirectional agility

Materials:

• 4 erasers

• 16 cones

• 3 parallel lines spaced 4 feet apart, 2 parallel lines spaced 15 feet apart, and 2 6-inch lines

Procedure:

- Divide the class into four equal groups.
- Place each group at one of the four stations (see diagram 5.19):
  - Students should give an all-out effort at each station and then rotate to the next station.
- Station 1—shuttle run:
  - Students run 15 feet and pick up an eraser; they then return to the starting line and drop the eraser, run back to the 15-foot line to retrieve a second eraser, and then run back past the starting line.
- Station 2—"N":
  - Students start at point *(A)* and run forward around cone *(B)*, then forward around cone *(C)*, up to a 6-inch line of tape denoted as point *(D)*; students touch the tape with their hands and then backpedal to point *(E)*.
  - Cones and tape points are spaced at distances of 5 yards apart by 1 yard over, except for point *(E)*, which lies directly in line with point *(D)*.
- Station 3—"O":
  - Students trace an "O"-shaped pattern by running forward around the first cone *(A)*, shuffle right to the second cone *(B)*, backpedal to the third cone *(C)*, shuffle left back to the starting position *(D)*, and then run forward up around the first cone again, looping it and returning to the starting position.
  - Cones are spaced 5 yards apart.

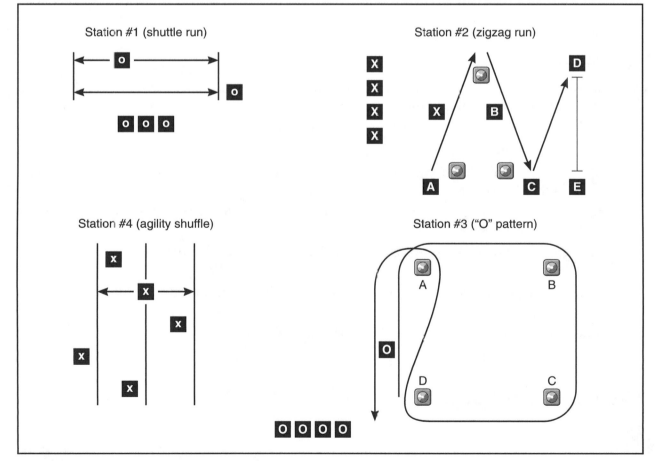

Diagram 5.19. Reprinted from Smith 1996.

- Station 4—three-line agility:
  - Students straddle the center of three parallel lines; on the "Go" signal, they repeatedly shuffle right and left across the outside lines, trying to cross as many lines as possible in a given time frame (30 seconds).
  - Lines are spaced 4 feet apart.

CARDIOVASCULAR AND COOPERATIVE TASKS

The warm-ups presented in this section require problem solving from a team perspective, fostering a sense of cooperation among team members. Equipment, body size, personal strengths and weaknesses of team members, and often an overall strategy need to be considered before attempting many of these tasks if a team is to be successful. Time should be given to students after explaining each warm-up to let them discuss and plot a strategy for their team.

CLEANUP

Purpose:

- To warm up using a cooperative effort among teammates while bending, reaching, and stretching during aerobic activity

Materials:

- 2 garbage bags (each stuffed with assorted "soft" objects such as shirts, baseball hats, sponge balls, etc.)
- 1 volleyball net or 4-6 mats balanced on their sides

Procedure:

- Section a volleyball court (or portion of the gym) off with a volleyball net or by forming a wall using four to six mats placed on their sides.
- Divide the students into two teams of equal number:
  - Place each team on opposite sides of the volleyball net or mats.
  - Provide both teams with a garbage bag and have them dump the contents onto the floor on their half of the court.
- On the command "Go," each team throws its "garbage" items over the net (mats) into its opponent's court.
- After a given period of time (approximately 2 minutes), stop the game and see whose yard looks cleaner:
  - Focus more on the fun and fitness benefits of the activity as opposed to counting articles and scoring.
  - Encourage teamwork among players and play two to three rounds.
    For variation, give students a countdown to maximize teamwork and strategies.

SHIP TO SHORE

Purpose:

- To warm up using a cooperative effort among teammates and group problem-solving skills while developing upper-body strength

Materials:

- 2 mats approximately 6 by 8 feet in size placed 10 feet apart
- 2-3 mats of a different color placed between the larger 6-by-8-foot mats
- 1 climbing rope

Procedure:

- Divide the class into two teams of mixed body types; select teams using birthdays, shirt colors, first initials, and so on.
- Explain the problem and give each team time to discuss how it will solve that problem (see diagram 5.20):
  - All teammates start on one mat (A), which is designated the ship.
  - They must all be safely transported to the other mat (B), the shore, without touching the different-colored floor (mats) between the ship and shore.
  - If they touch the floor, they must climb back on the ship and start again.
  - Students may want to tie their shoes together to form a whip and initially grab the rope.
  - Students must take care to swing the rope back to teammates on the ship.
  - Stronger students should go both first, to serve as catchers, and last, so other students are afforded help in getting from "ship to shore."

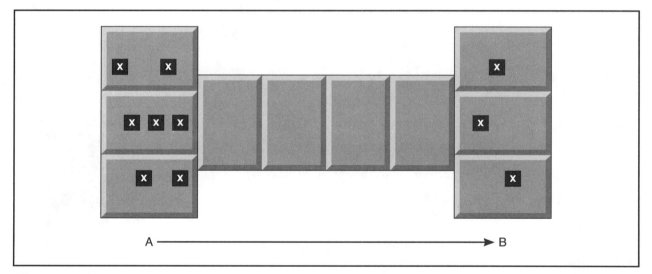

Diagram 5.20

RESCUE

Purpose:

- To warm up using a cooperative effort among teammates and group problem-solving skills while developing upper-body strength

Materials:

- 1 plastic sled
- 1 jump rope
- 4 small mats
- 1 larger mat

Procedure:

- Divide the class into two teams of mixed body types; select teams using birthdays, shirt colors, first initials, and so on.
- Explain the problem and give each team time to discuss how it will solve that problem (see diagram 5.21):
  - Teammates start on the smaller mats.
  - One student is designated as the "rescuer," and she uses the sled and rope to pull one or two others from the smaller mats to the large mat (safe island).
  - A "rescuer" may only serve in that role once and then must remain on the safe island.
- Time each team to make the experience more competitive.

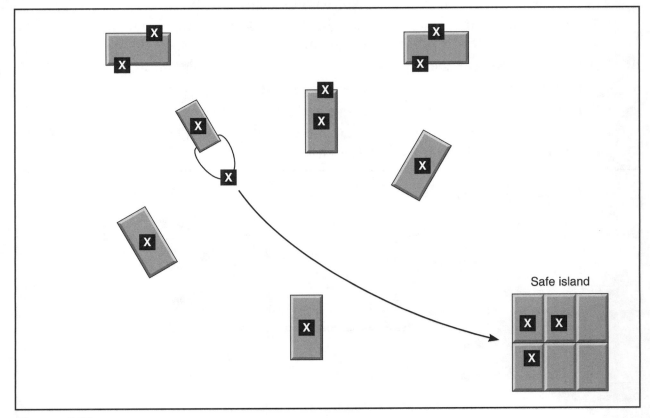

Diagram 5.21

AMOEBA

Purpose:

- To warm up while focusing on the social skills of cooperation and trust

Materials:

- 1 very large rope or a series of ropes tied together (a tug-of-war rope is ideal)
- A large space or field
- Cones
- Benches
- Mats
- Chairs

Procedure:

- Design an obstacle course (maze) using the cones, benches, mats, and chairs (see diagram 5.22).
- Either work with the class as a whole or divide the class in half based on numbers and space.
- Tie the students into the rope (forming an amoeba) with just enough space to move slightly:
  - The group members then attempt to move as a unit through the obstacle course by communicating with one another and changing shape as needed to be successful.
  - Try it walking or running, or time each group to provide variation (AS&S 1994).

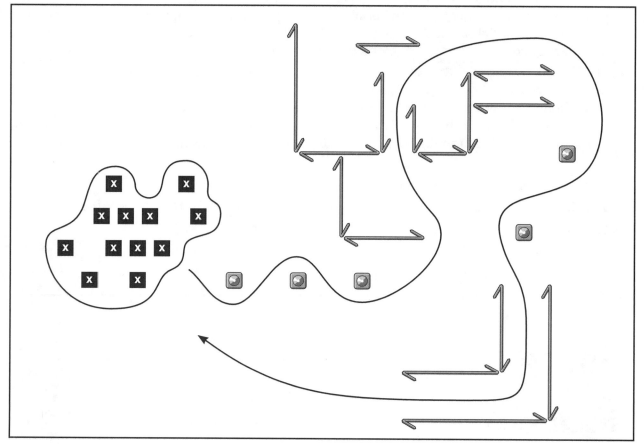

Diagram 5.22

JUNKYARD RELAY

Purpose:

- To warm up using a cooperative effort among teammates and group problem-solving skills while developing foot speed

Materials:

- 4 carpet samples
- 4 jump ropes
- 4 hula hoops
- 4 baseball gloves
- 4 cones
- 4 footballs

- 4 softballs
- 4 basketballs
- 4 Whiffle balls
- 4 sponge balls

Procedure:

- Place the students into four relay teams with equal numbers of players (see diagram 5.23).
- At the opposite end of the gym, in front of each team, place a hula hoop on the floor. In each hoop place one of the aforementioned materials. Each hoop should have one carpet sample, one jump rope, one baseball glove, and so on. Add more equipment if necessary; there should be at least one piece of equipment for each member of the team.
- On the signal "Go," the first student runs down to the hoop, picks up an item, and returns to the team, handing it to the second student in line; the second student carries the first item down to the hoop and returns with the first item plus another item, handing the two of them to the third student; the third student carries these two items down to the hoop, gets a third item, and returns to the fourth student, until all the equipment, including the hoop, is returned to the relay line:
    - For variety, have the students work in pairs.
- The first team to retrieve all the items from its hoop and sit in a straight line wins.
- Give students 1 minute before the race to discuss strategy:
    - What should be picked up first?
    - Who should go first or last?

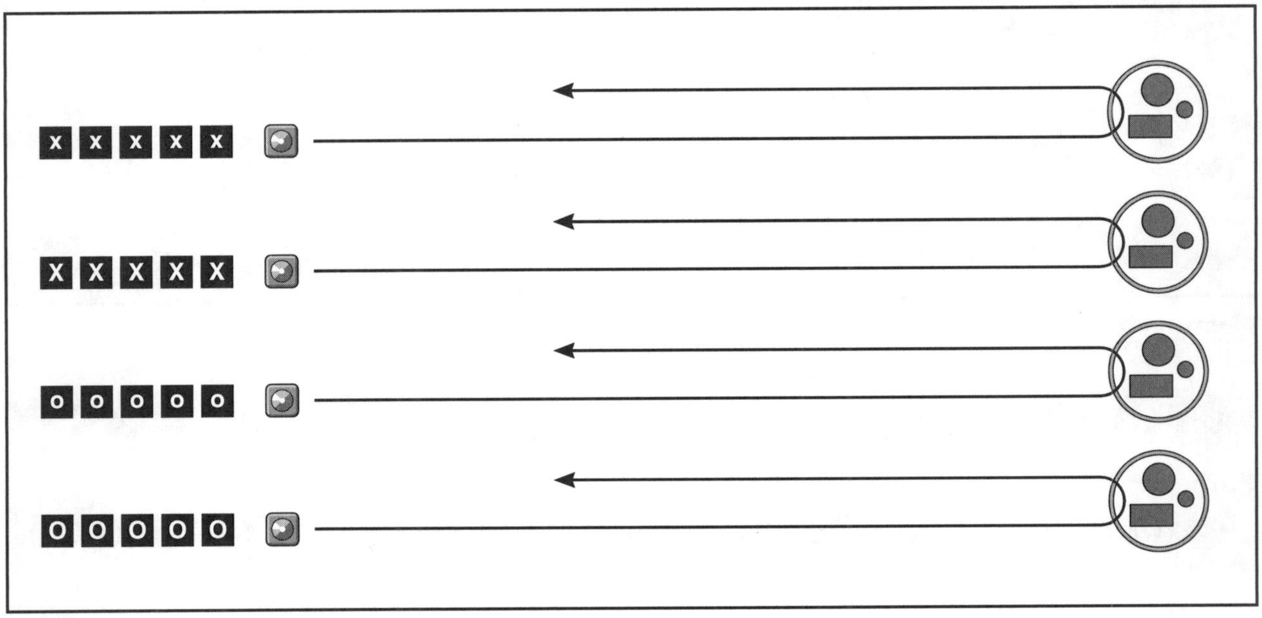

Diagram 5.23

BASKETBOWL

Purpose:

- To warm up using basketball, bowling, and fitness skills in a game of spatial awareness and cooperative effort both within and among teams

Materials:

- 4 basketballs (each of a different color)
- 1 bowling pin
- 3 mats
- 3 jump ropes
- 8 cones
- 1 basketball hoop

Procedure:

- Divide the class into four relay teams of equal number.
- Position the teams at the four corners of the gym as illustrated in diagram 5.24, phase 1:
  - The first person in each line has a basketball.
- On the command "Go," the first student in each line "bowls" the basketball at the bowling pin located in the center of the gym:
  - If the ball misses the pin, the student chases after his ball, picks it up, and returns it to the next player in line by handing it off.
  - Stress safety and spatial awareness in chasing after balls and moving throughout the gym.
  - Play continues in a relay format until someone's ball hits the pin, knocking it over.
- When the pin is knocked over, the teacher yells out the color of the ball that struck the pin.
- Upon hearing a color called, students move into phase 2 of the game:
  - The team whose color is called lines up at the basketball hoop and starts to shoot shots in a relay fashion (1 point per basket).

    For variety, award 2 points for a foul shot, 1 for a layup.
  - The other three teams must each run and line up at one of the three mats set at the opposite end of the gym from the basketball hoop.
  - The first person in line picks up the jump rope placed on the mat and jumps three times before handing it to the second student in line.
  - Each team member jumps three times in this manner, handing off to the person behind her in a relay fashion until each team member has had a turn.
  - When a team is done, it should sit down.
  - When all three teams are sitting, play is stopped, and the shooting team's score is recorded.
  - Stress cooperation, both within and among teams.
- Rotate each team clockwise to the next corner of the gym and play another round until each team has been to every corner of the gym.

Phase 1

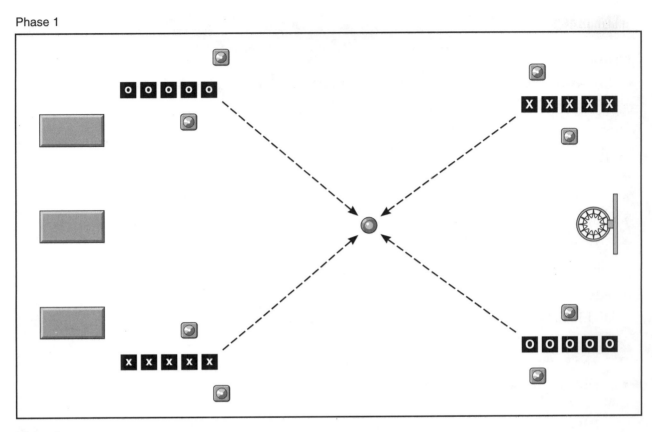

Phase 2

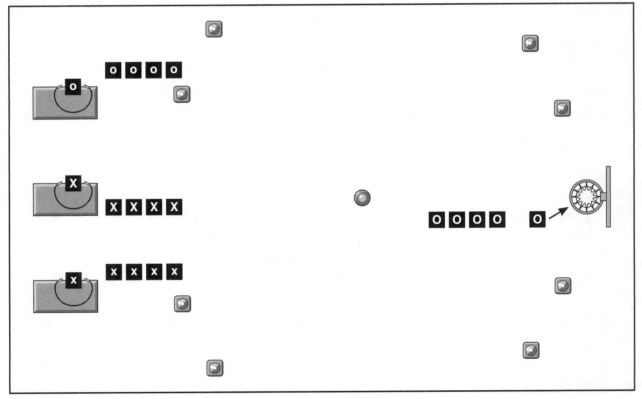

Diagram 5.24

FARMER

Purpose:

- To warm up by bending, reaching, and running, using a cooperative team effort

Materials:

- 16 cones
- 12 tape balls or rolled up socks
- 4 hula hoops

Procedure:

- Divide the class into four relay teams of even numbers.
- Place three cones and one hula hoop in front of each team as shown in diagram 5.25:
  - Place a tape ball next to each cone.
- On the signal "Go," the first team member runs through the "field," *harvesting* the tape balls, and places all three of his balls into his team's hula hoop at the end of the gym before running back to the relay line and tagging the next team member:
  - For variation, have students run a "reverse-suicide" drill whereby they pick up the first ball and run it to the hoop, come back to the second ball and run it to the hoop, and then come back for the third ball and run it to the hoop before returning to their line of teammates, as opposed to harvesting all three balls at once.
- The next team member runs down to his team's hoop, picks up the three tape balls and *plants* them next to the cones (returns them to their original position) before tagging off his teammate.
- This cycle of harvesting and replanting continues until every team member has gone two times.
- The team that finishes first and sits in a straight line wins.

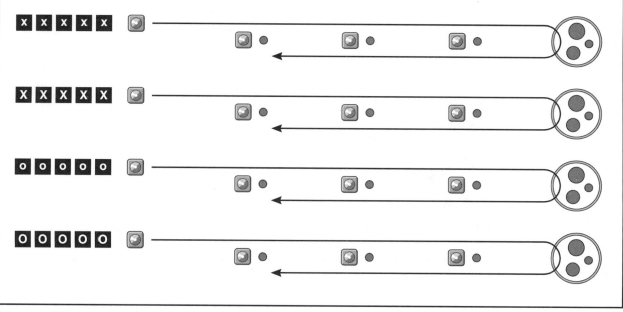

Diagram 5.25

BALL THIEF

Purpose:

- To warm up playing a game of cooperative effort that requires spatial awareness, running, bending, and problem solving

Materials:

- 4 hula hoops
- 32-40 balls of varied shapes and textures, split evenly among the 4 hoops

Procedure:

- Divide the class into four groups of equal numbers.
- Each team starts by sitting behind a hoop filled with 8 to 10 balls (see diagram 5.26).
- On the command "Go," students from one team run to the hoop(s) of another team and "steal" a ball, bringing it back and placing it in their hoop:
  - Students are only allowed to carry one ball at a time.
  - Stress safety with respect to moving throughout the gym, and stress spatial awareness.
  - All four teams are doing this simultaneously.
- After 2 to 3 minutes, the teacher yells "Stop," and all the students immediately "freeze":
  - The team with the most balls in its hoop wins.
  - Play two to three rounds.

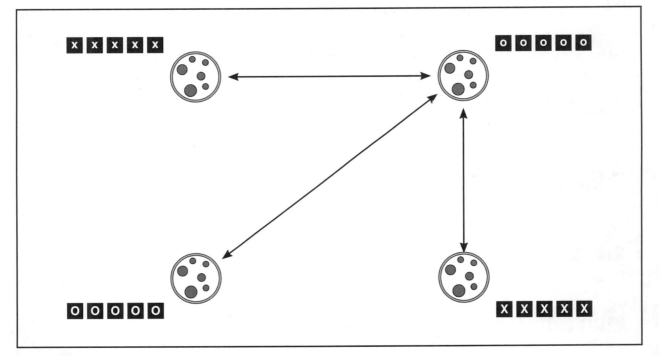

Diagram 5.26

TEAM CARRY

Purpose:

- To warm up using a game of cooperative effort and problem solving

Materials:

- 10-12 exercise mats
- 2 metal poles approximately 6 feet long and 2 to 3 inches in diameter

Procedure:

- Divide the class into two teams of equal numbers or work with the class as a whole:
  - Time the team(s) to create a more competitive atmosphere.
- Students must figure out how to most efficiently transport team members from point *(A)* to point *(B)*, staying within the following guidelines:
  - Only two team members may walk from point *(A)* to point *(B)* in any one given transport.
  - Two team members must return to point *(A)* with the metal pole after each transport, but no student may be a *carrier* more than twice (refer back to diagram 5.20).
- Give students time to plot a strategy before starting the contest:
  - Who should be carriers?
  - Who should ride?
  - How should they ride?
  - Can more than one student ride at a time?
  - What order should the team go in?

JUMPING/LANDING ACTIVITIES

Jumping and landing play a large part in almost all physical activities that involve games, gymnastic moves, or track and field events. The warm-ups contained in this section will help your students jump higher, land more safely, and do both with more control, thus enhancing their performances. Care should be taken to follow the progressions we outline and to stress sound biomechanical principles when teaching the jumping activities.

SAFETY FALLS

Purpose:

- To warm up while introducing safe landing techniques that have application to gymnastics, obstacle courses, track and field, and life-threatening emergencies such as evacuating a second-floor room during a fire; these techniques apply even to *stopping, dropping,* and *rolling* from a variety of heights

Materials:

- 6-8 folded exercise mats to create jumping platforms
- A well-matted area for landing (wrestling/floor exercise mat or extra exercise mats)

Procedures:

- Have the students practice jumping and landing safely in place on the floor:
  - As soon as they land, have the students lower their center of gravity and hips by bending their knees.
  - At the same time as they land, have the students bring the dominant arm across their bodies with their heads turning to follow the hand.
  - The chin should be tucked.

- This combined motion of bending their knees, throwing their arms across their bodies, and tucking their chins should initiate a roll.
- The student's head and neck are protected as the weight of the student becomes distributed along the back of the arm, shoulder, and upper back.

- After the students have mastered this basic technique, progressively increase the height from which they jump, using two, three, four, and even up to six stacked, folded mats:
  - Caution students to keep their "heads up" when jumping to prevent their bodies from leaning forward out of the jump.
  - Upon feeling their feet hit the ground, they should immediately initiate the fall technique of lowering the body, throwing the arm, and turning the head while tucking the chin.

JUMP-ROPE ACTIVITIES

Purpose:

- To warm up by developing agility, coordination, and body awareness, all while deriving cardiovascular benefits

Materials:

- 1 jump rope per student

Procedure:

- Stationary rope jumping—ropes are held in a stationary position:
  - Lateral jumps—side to side, or forward and backward over a rope placed on the floor

    Lateral jumps over an elevated rope—side to side, or forward and backward over a rope held at a variety of heights (6 inches, 12 inches, etc.) by two other students

    Parallel jumping—two ropes are held off the ground at the same height and parallel to each other:

    Students jump into and out of the ropes.
  - Perpendicular rope jumping—two ropes are held at 90-degree angles to each other and students jump them in any pattern they wish:

    Students should be encouraged to experiment with different patterns.
  - Incline jumps—back and forth over a rope that progressively gets higher (e.g., from floor to about 3 feet high)
- Traditional rope jumping—each student has a rope and jumps at her own pace:
  - Double-foot landings
  - Single-foot landings
  - Alternating feet (with or without traveling)
  - Crisscrossing jumps with the hands
  - Two rotations of the rope for each jump
- Partner rope jumping—a moving rope involving two or more participants:
  - Doubles—one person turns the rope as she and her partner jump.
  - Partners swing—two partners turn the rope while a third student jumps.
  - "Double Dutch"—two partners turn two ropes while a third student jumps both ropes.

GRID DRILLS

Purpose:

- To warm up while developing agility, foot speed, balance, jumping ability, and coordination

Materials:

- A series of "grid" stations placed on the floor using a "high stepper," 8 old tires, 8 hula hoops, or tape to create the grids (diagram 5.27)

Procedure:

- Students should strive to complete each of the five drills both correctly and in as little time as possible:
  - Double bound up and back:

    The students bound forward off both feet up the right side of the grid and then come back down the left side.

    Be sure the students keep their knees and ankles together.

    Encourage students to use their arms to help in jumping.
  - Double bound zigzag pattern (laterally):

    The students start by bounding into the right box, then bound diagonally into the second left box, back to the third right box, on to the fourth left box, and out of the grid.
  - Four-corner reverses (two students can go at the same time from opposite ends of the grid):

    The students jump into the first right box, forward into the second right box, laterally to their left, back on the left side, and laterally to their right before repeating the sequence in a clockwise direction.

Diagram 5.27. Reprinted from Smith, Powell, and Belodoff 1992.

– 180-degree straddles:

The students jump into the first two boxes, landing with a foot in each box; they then jump into the air, turn 180 degrees, and land with their feet reversed, jumping again and turning 180 degrees; the process is repeated with the students continuing down the grid in this manner until they complete all four rows of boxes.

Be sure the students alternate the direction in which they spin when turning 180 degrees.

– 360-degree straddles (two students can go at the same time from opposite ends of the grid):

The students start with a foot in the first left and the first right boxes; they then jump into the air, turn 360 degrees, and land facing in the same direction.

Repeat five times.

Be sure the students alternate the direction in which they spin when turning 360 degrees (Smith, Powell, and Belodoff 1992).

BASIC PLYOMETRIC JUMPS

Purpose:

- To warm up while developing vertical jump ability

Materials:

- A large, flat area (surface)
- 6 raised platforms of between 4 and 12 inches in height (folded exercise mats work well if they are firm)

Procedure:

- The following exercises are ordered in sequence from lowest to highest intensity and should be performed in the order presented:
  - Stress proper jumping mechanics of bent knees and arm swing for each activity.
  - Note that previous plyometric experience, age, body weight, strength-to-mass ratio, and training surfaces will vary widely among middle school students. Some activities may need to be modified to safely meet the goals of your students (Smith 1996).
- Side-to-side line hops:
  - The student jumps side to side over a line with the knees and ankles held together.
  - The student's hips and center of gravity should remain over the line (30 seconds).
- Forward-and-backward line hops:
  - The student jumps forward and backward over a line with knees and ankles held together.
  - The student's hips and center of gravity remain over the line (30 seconds).
- Gathering jump / explosive jump:
  - The student jumps forward 3 to 4 feet, gathers himself into a ready position (knees bent, arms back), and explodes upward in a vertical jump (30 seconds).
- Diagonal gathering jump / explosive jump:
  - The student jumps forward 3 to 4 feet at a 45-degree diagonal angle into a "gathering posture" before exploding upward in a vertical jump (30 seconds).
  - Students should alternate the direction of the angle at which they jump—left, right, left, and so on.

- Jumps in place:
  - These three exercises are repetitive, explosive movements focusing on body control and neuromuscular reactivity to the floor.
  - Have the students perform each exercise 10 times.
  - Have the students try to minimize contact time with the floor between repetitions (Chu and Panariello 1988).
  - Pike jumps:

    The student jumps vertically with the upper torso remaining erect, the lower legs straight and raised to hip level, becoming parallel with the floor.

    The student strives to touch her toes before returning to the standing position.
  - Spread pike jumps:

    These jumps are performed the same as "pike jumps," except that the legs are spread at the top of the jump.
  - Single leg jumps:

    The student stands on one foot and flexes the other leg at the knee, grasping it with the hand as if stretching the quadriceps, then jumps off one foot and repeatedly circles, jumping as quickly as possible.
- Depth jumps:
  - Each of these exercises requires six raised platforms (boxes) or folded exercise mats placed in a row spaced 3 to 4 feet apart.
  - Squat depth jumps:

    The student stands on top of the first platform and steps off, dropping into a squat position with the thighs parallel to the floor before jumping up onto the next platform.

    The student continues in this manner until she finishes the series of five jumps (Chu and Panariello 1989a; Chu and Panariello 1989b).
  - Bounce depth jumps:

    The student steps forward and drops into a toe-touch landing with the heels raised, then immediately attempts to reverse the movement, jumping onto the next box until the series of five jumps is concluded.

HEALTH-RELATED FITNESS CONCEPTS

What better place to discuss *health-related fitness concepts* with students than in the gymnasium, especially when they feel their hearts pumping, muscles bulging, and lungs rapidly moving air in and out of their bodies? The *health-related fitness concept modules* are designed for use in the time slot between warm-up and skill-development activities. They offer a logical educational opportunity for delivering information on fitness and a lifetime of wellness.

Divided into 10 modular units of study, one for each month of the school year, these concepts target cardiovascular, pulmonary, and muscular systems along with nutrition and fitness. Table 6.1 gives an overview of the topics by month. These 10 units are then further divided into weekly topics. Table 6.2 clarifies a sample topic, contrasting each of the weekly focuses by presentation level (I, II, and III). You can use table 6.2 to guide you in shaping weekly

Table 6.1	Monthly Health-Related Fitness Concepts
September	The Heart (page 87)
October	The Lungs (page 89)
November	Muscles of the Chest (page 91)
December	Muscles of the Back (page 93)
January	Muscles of the Abdominal Wall (page 95)
February	Muscles of the Hip and Thigh (page 98)
March	Muscles of the Lower Leg (page 100)
April	Muscles of the Arm and Shoulder (page 102)
May	Eating for Health: A Nutritional Plan (page 104)
June	Physical Fitness: A Lifestyle (page 107)

Table 6.2 A Multilevel Approach to Teaching About the Muscles of the Back

Level I

Name	Function	Applied Activities	Strength Exercises	Flexibility Exercises
Upper-back muscles	Elevate collarbone	Pull-ups	Pull-ups	Lie in a supine position with the knees held over the hips and the hands behind the knees. Round the spine, moving the head and knees closer together. Maximize the stretch by extending the elbows out to the side, fully rounding the back.
	Move shoulder blades upward, downward, and back	Rope climbing Rowing a boat Raking leaves		

Level II

Name	Function	Applied Activities	Strength Exercises	Flexibility Exercises
Lats	Draw arms and shoulders down and backward; lengthen, draw in, and roll the arm posteriorly toward the middle of the body	Swimming (crawl)	Lat pull-downs	Self-hug with a slight forward bend
Traps	Raise the collarbone, raise and lower the shoulder blades, draw the shoulder blades toward the middle of the body	Lifting an object from the floor to the waist or higher	Shoulder shrugs	Clasp hands behind back and lift arms upward, pulling shoulders downward and back with the head slightly forward.
Rhomboids	Move the shoulder blades backward and up, and roll them slightly downward	Wrestling (pulling movements)	Seated rows using a cable attachment on a multi-purpose gym (e.g., Universal Gym)	Interlock fingers of both hands and press them out in front of the body while rounding the spine.

(continued)

Table 6.2 *(continued)*

| | | Level III | | |
Name	Function	Applied Activities	Strength Exercises	Flexibility Exercises
Latissimus dorsi	Extend, adduct, and rotate arm medially; draw shoulder downward and backward	Rock climbing Surfing	Pull-ups with resistance	"Cat-and-camel stretch" (rounding up and dipping down of the spine with opposite head and hip movement)
Trapezius	Elevate clavicle, adduct scapula, and elevate or depress scapula	Blocking in football	Upright rowing Power cleans	"Cat-and-camel stretch"
Rhomboideus major and minor	Move scapula backward and upward, slightly rotate it downward; adduct scapula	Apparatus stunts in gymnastics	Bent-over rowing with resistance	"Cat-and-camel stretch"

This table is reprinted with permission from the *Journal of Physical Education, Recreation & Dance,* April, 1995, page 71. The *Journal* is a publication of the American Alliance for Health, Physical Education, Recreation and Dance, 1900 Association Drive, Reson, VA 20191.

lessons throughout the month and to contrast the information you present from one year to the next during a student's middle school experience by changing *levels* each year.

As an example, during the first week of December we would discuss the *function* of the back muscles with our students (Level I for sixth-graders, Level II for seventh-graders, and Level III for eighth-graders). During week two, we would review function but also discuss *applied activities,* again by grade-appropriate level. During week three, we would present *strength exercises,* and we would present *flexibility exercises* during week four.

TEACHING TECHNIQUES

When teaching these concepts, remember to apply the teaching strategies discussed in chapter 3. Keep the presentation short (less than 2-1/2 minutes) and clear, using concise state-

ments to make key points to students. Do not expect all your students to grasp the information the first time they hear it, but, by repeating applied concepts throughout class, reviewing concepts during closure, and reviewing concepts in subsequent classes, the majority of your students will develop a better understanding and appreciation of their bodies.

Use the morning announcements in your school as a time to bring the entire school population a *public service announcement* from the Department of Physical Education targeting a wide range of fitness and nutrition issues. Keep the announcements brief and informative, and include suggestions that are easy to take and use. Diagrams, posters, and other graphically displayed information placed in such "high-traffic" areas as the cafeteria can also have a positive impact on students and teachers to promote better health!

VISUAL AIDS

We have found that visual aids also help students grasp these concepts more thoroughly. These are just a few examples of well-accepted delivery techniques, and there are certainly others. Be creative and dramatic in helping your students remember key concepts. Often, that magic moment you provide through teaching will last them a lifetime, which is, after all, our goal as teachers!

Here are five, easy-to-implement visual aids:

1. Design posters, similar to photo 3.1 previously presented on page 24, that contain not only the monthly module focus (Muscles of the Back), but also each of the weekly focuses as well (Function, Applied Activities, Strength Exercises, and Flexibility Exercises). Keep it simple, and use the posters as a starting point for class presentations. Notice that the muscle poster has an illustration of the "muscle" centered on it, showing both the shape of the muscle and its position in the body relative to other muscles. Weekly focuses are then presented around the centralized muscle (monthly focus) using brief statements to start class discussions, letting you go into more depth as you feel necessary. Later in this chapter, each focus for the monthly modules is detailed to guide you.

2. Use a bulletin-board display to create a "point of focus" in the gym by leaving posters prominently displayed for the entire month. This allows students to view the health-related fitness information not only under your direction but also at their leisure.

3. Use photographs and draw attention to television commercials, popular home equipment (steppers and stationary cycles, for example), and equipment in the school (free weights and Universal Gyms, for example) to help make the more-advanced fitness concepts clear and relevant.

4. As was suggested in chapter 3, wear T-shirts of muscles or body systems to help students more clearly visualize your chosen topic. These shirts can be purchased at college bookstores or through allied health supply catalogs. Wearing them helps your students in the immediate

sense, and they will look forward to seeing the shirts and wondering, "What will our teacher wear next?" This technique helps motivate, teach, and create interest.

5. Paint your body with watercolors for antagonistic groups or to isolate muscles, which is another way of eliciting positive student reaction. It works well for those muscles that may not conveniently fit on a shirt, as is the case with the triceps and biceps or quadriceps and hamstrings.

LEVELS OF KNOWLEDGE

Naturally, you would expect a ninth-grader to be more knowledgeable than a seventh-grader about health-fitness concepts. To help you present material that is appropriate for each grade level, the subsequent monthly modules suggest three levels of knowledge depth referred to as *Levels I, II,* and *III.* This teaching progression will work well for grades six through eight or seven through nine, depending on your situation, if *Level I* information is presented during the first year of middle school, *Level II* the second year, and *Level III* the third, or final year (refer to table 6.2). Monthly modules are categorized by the heart; the lungs; muscle systems (e.g., the chest, the back, etc.); eating for health: a nutritional plan; and physical fitness: a lifestyle. Using the teaching strategies mentioned earlier, you can develop posters for

One of the best learning experiences students can have is to experience a concept firsthand, which can leave a lasting impression. When discussing the effects of excess body weight, we like to give our students a rope and five-pound barbell plate. They strap it tightly to their abdomens and go through a portion of the class with this excess weight. They readily notice that they move more awkwardly, move more slowly, breathe heavier, fatigue sooner, and work at a higher heart rate. This experience adds more relevance to follow-up discussions regarding the stress excessive weight places on such body systems as the heart, lungs, and muscles.

each module and present information by appropriate levels as outlined.

You can assess your students' comprehension of the subsequent concepts through the discussions and question/answer sessions you have in presenting information. By keeping your presentations at grade-appropriate levels and drawing upon personal experiences from your classes, the majority of students will connect with and retain general concepts.

HEALTH AND FITNESS CONCEPTS

The 10 *health and fitness concepts* are presented by level and weekly focuses for your ease and convenience in using them. We have also included two to three important points to cover, with specific teaching tips and learning activities to help you present information to your students.

THE HEART

LEVEL I

Function (Week 1):

- The function of the heart is to circulate blood through the lungs and throughout the body.

Mechanics (Week 2):

- The heart pumps blood by contracting, or squeezing, blood out of its chambers. *You may wish to make a fist simulating a heart and pump it to demonstrate how the heart mechanically acts as a pump. Also, position the fist at the sternum to show placement of the heart in the body; this will have application for cardiopulmonary resuscitation (CPR) as well.*

- The heart has an internal "pacemaker" that regulates heart rate based on need. *When someone has an electrocardiogram (EKG) taken, it is a graphic representation of the electrical activity in the heart.*

Oxygen Transport (Week 3):

- Oxygen is carried in the blood.

- Blood is carried away from the heart in arteries and returns to the heart in veins. *Have students feel the vein on the inside of their elbow where the doctor usually draws blood. Tell them that blood "flows" from a vein but "spurts" from an artery because of the pumping action of the heart. Have them take their pulses on the carotid (neck) artery to feel the pulsing sensation.*

Volumes (Week 4):

- Blood-flow volume is determined by the amount of blood pumped out of the heart, the strength with which the heart contracts, the rate at which the heart beats, and the body's ability to take oxygen from the blood to create energy.

- A stronger, better-conditioned heart works more efficiently and beats at a lower rate. *Have students count their resting heart rates and compare the rate of a well-conditioned student with that of a poorly conditioned one.*

LEVEL II

Function (Week 1):

- The function of the heart is to deliver blood to the various systems and organs in the body, providing nourishment and energy. *Remind students that blood carries oxygen and nutrients.*

- Through circulation, the blood also removes the "waste products" of energy production.

Mechanics (Week 2):

- At rest, a normal heart rate is in the range of 60 to 80 beats per minute (lower for a well-conditioned individual). *Have students take their resting pulse rates at either the wrist (radial) or the neck (carotid) artery for one minute.*

The maximal heart rate someone can achieve is approximately 220 minus his age. *Have students calculate their maximal heart rates (220 – 15 = 205). Point out that as people get older, they do not have the same heart rate capacity.*

Oxygen Transport (Week 3):

- When someone exercises, blood is redistributed from organs and nonworking muscles to those muscles that need energy.
- This causes blood pressure to increase because blood becomes concentrated in certain body parts and the heart pumps faster and more strongly.

Make students aware that these changes are normal and that blood pressure and flow return to normal upon cooling down after exercise.

Volumes (Week 4):

- During exercise the amount of blood pumped out of the heart *increases*, the strength with which the heart contracts *increases*, the rate at which the heart beats *increases*, and the body's ability to take oxygen from the blood to create energy *increases*.
- A stronger, better-conditioned heart beats at a lower rate during easy exercise and has a greater capacity during all-out exercise.

Make students aware that a heart, like any other muscle, gets stronger with exercise and can therefore handle greater demands with less effort (greater efficiency).

Help your students determine their *target heart rate zone* (ideal training zone) by taking the concept of maximal heart rate (220 – age) one step further. Training between 70 percent and 85 percent of the age-predicted maximal heart rate will both allow students to train safely and stimulate positive cardiovascular changes. Students can calculate their own "target heart rate zone (THRZ)" as follows (we'll use a 13-year-old as an example):

220 – age = maximal heart rate
220 – 13 = 207 beats per minute
207 × .70 = 145   207 × .85 = 176

The THRZ is therefore 145 to 176 beats per minute.

LEVEL III

Function (Week 1):

- The function of the heart is to:
  - supply oxygen and nutrients to tissues as per demand by controlling blood flow and
  - pump deoxygenated blood from the body tissues to the lungs, removing lactic acid from the blood stream.

Mechanics (Week 2):

- The resting heart rate of a trained individual (40 to 60 beats/minute) is lower than that of an untrained individual (60 to 80 beats/minute) because she pumps more blood per beat and can better extract oxygen from her blood. *Have students count their resting heart rates for one minute and make comparisons between endurance athletes and nonendurance-type students.*

- Maximal heart rate is not affected by training; rather, it is a function of age (220 – age). *Have students calculate their maximal heart rates and point out that it does not matter if they are male, female, in great shape, or out of shape; it is age related.*

Oxygen Transport (Week 3):

- During exercise, blood is redistributed to the muscles that most need it, up to 10 times the normal amount in some cases.

- This redistribution rate causes other tissues and organs to receive less blood, increasing blood pressure throughout the body.

- Blood flow to the muscles is helped by an increased heart rate, contraction of muscles, the force of blood returning to the heart, increased blood pressure, and a more forceful movement of air in the lungs.

Discuss this redistribution of blood flow with students. Does more blood go to their skin to help cool them through sweating? (Yes.) Do they feel their heart and lungs more during exercise than at rest? (Yes.) Do their muscles tighten and contract harder during exercise? (Yes.) If they eat right before strenuous exercise, how do they feel? Do they find it difficult to both digest and exercise hard? (Yes, because their blood cannot adequately satisfy each system—digestive and muscular—at once.)

Volumes (Week 4):

- The heart of a trained individual is more efficient because he pumps more blood per beat at the same heart rate and can use oxygen more efficiently. *Discuss the effect of exercise on muscles with respect to hypertrophy and efficiency. A well-trained heart is a larger, stronger pump; the trained body is a better delivery system, and trained muscles are better receptors of oxygen.*

THE LUNGS

LEVEL I

Function (Week 1):

- The function of the lungs is to:
  - allow oxygen to enter the body and
  - rid the body of carbon dioxide.

Mechanics (Week 2):

- Oxygen enters the lungs through *inspiration*, or the *breathing in* of air.
- Carbon dioxide is removed from the lungs through *expiration*, or the *breathing out* of air.

Gas Exchange (Week 3):

- Oxygen and carbon dioxide transfer across lung tissue through diffusion. *Talk with students about pressure gradients (water always seeks lower ground). The pressure of carbon dioxide in the body is greater than outside the body so we breathe to get rid of CO_2. It is the buildup of CO_2 that stimulates breathing.*

Volumes (Week 4):

- The maximal amount of air the lungs can move in one breath is referred to as vital capacity.
- The amount of air moved in a normal resting breath is referred to as tidal volume. During exercise, the tidal volume increases and approaches the vital capacity. *Make students aware that during exercise, a larger volume of air is moved by lungs because they breathe deeper and more rapidly.*

LEVEL II

Function (Week 1):

- The function of the lungs is to:
  - move oxygen (O_2) into the bloodstream and
  - remove carbon dioxide (CO_2) from the bloodstream.

Mechanics (Week 2):

- The lungs move about six liters of air per minute at rest.
- During exercise, the lungs can move 20 to 30 times the amount of air they normally move at rest. *Make students aware that they breathe both deeper and faster during exercise and, thus, move more air.*

Gas Exchange (Week 3):

- The exchange of air is more efficient in a trained individual because of her ability to better extract and use oxygen than an untrained person can. *The cells of a trained person use oxygen better than those of an untrained person; the cells take oxygen from the blood and process it more effectively.*

Volumes (Week 4):

- During exercise, the tidal volume increases because this is a function of breathing depth.
- Vital capacity remains the same because this is a maximal capacity.

Help students to see this relationship as being similar to maximal heart rate (absolute) and resting heart rate, that increases during exercise based on cardiac demand.

LEVEL III

Function (Week 1):

- The function of the lungs is to:
  - enrich the bloodstream with O_2 and
  - remove CO_2 from the bloodstream and body.

Mechanics (Week 2):

- The amount of air breathed each minute is a function of breathing rate and depth.
- During exercise, individuals breathe both faster and deeper. *Make students aware that a normal resting breathing rate is 10 to 12 breaths per minute. During exercise, this may increase to 25 breaths per minute. Forty or more breaths per minute is referred to as hyperventilation.*

Gas Exchange (Week 3):

- Trained individuals have a higher VO_2max than do untrained individuals. *This means that they are capable of taking in and using more oxygen per minute and can therefore perform longer and better at higher levels of endurance exercise.*

Volumes (Week 4):

- The respiratory volumes of trained individuals are not much different from those of untrained individuals. *The trained person is just better able to use the oxygen he does get into the bloodstream.*

MUSCLES OF THE CHEST

LEVEL I

Function (Week 1):

- The function of the chest muscles is to:
  - flex the arms toward the front of the body,
  - adduct the arms, and
  - rotate the arms toward the front midline of the body.

Discuss the terminology of flexion (lessening a joint angle), adduction (adding to the body), and rotation with respect to a ball-and-socket joint by demonstrating these three movements as illustrated in photo 6.1.

Activities (Week 2):

- The muscles of the chest are used in activities such as:
  - throwing,
  - pushing, and
  - striking.

Demonstrate these three movements, and through discussion have students come up with examples of each skill (throwing a baseball, lacrosse ball, or football; pushing a shopping cart; blocking in football; doing a push-up; striking a tennis ball, etc.).

Photo 6.1   Demonstrating muscle function.

Strength Exercise (Week 3):

- An exercise that strengthens the chest muscles is push-ups.

Flexibility Exercise (Week 4):

- To stretch the muscles of the chest, place your fingertips behind your neck and pull your elbows to the rear.

LEVEL II

Function (Week 1):

- The chest muscles are made up of two muscles—the *pectorals* and the *intercostals*:
  - The pectorals flex, adduct, and rotate the arms toward the front midline of the body. *Briefly review these movements and terms with your students.*
  - The intercostals pull the ribs together when breathing out and raise the ribs when breathing in. *Have students take a deep breath and feel the movement of the rib cage and chest cavity. This is an ideal time to remind them of the concept of changing pressure gradients in the lungs, linking the lungs and chest muscles together for the students.*

Activities (Week 2):

- Activities that use the chest muscles include:
  - pitching (pectorals),
  - blocking (pectorals),
  - tennis forehand stroke (pectorals), and
  - breathing (intercostals).

Strength Exercises (Week 3):

- The chest muscles can be strengthened by such exercises as the:
  - bench press (pectorals),
  - parallel bar dips (pectorals), and
  - pull-over motion from a supine position (pectorals and intercostals).

Demonstrate these three exercises to your students because the strength training exercises of bench press and pull-overs may be new to them.

Flexibility Exercise (Week 4):

- An example of a flexibility exercise for the chest muscles would be lat pull-downs to the rear. *This is an ideal time to introduce the concept of antagonistic muscle groups; when a muscle contracts or shortens, its antagonist stretches or lengthens.*

LEVEL III

Function (Week 1):

- The pectoral and intercostal muscles of the chest can further be divided into two distinct muscles:
  - Pectoralis major and minor that flex, adduct, and rotate the arm medially (toward the center of the body).
  - Internal and external intercostals that draw adjacent ribs together during exhalation and elevate the ribs when inhaling.

Review the fundamental movements of the chest muscle group with students through demonstration, question-and-answer sessions, and discussion.

Activities (Week 2):

- Activities that use chest muscles include:
  - an iron cross in gymnastics (pectoralis major and minor),
  - an overhand serve with spin in tennis (pectoralis major and minor), and
  - cross-country skiing at near maximal capacity (internal and external intercostals).

Discuss how the chest muscles function in these exercises with your students.

Strength Exercises (Week 3):

- Exercises to strengthen the chest muscles include:
  - incline bench presses with an accentuated rotation of the arms toward the front at the end of the movement (pectoralis major and minor),
  - "pec deck" flys (pectoralis major), and
  - supine pull-overs with a dumbbell.

Use this time to teach about strength training equipment using equipment at your school or pictures of the previously mentioned exercises. What are some exercises students could do at home without weights?

Flexibility Exercise (Week 4):

- A good flexibility exercise for the chest muscles is the "extension" portion of the "pec deck" fly movement. *This is again an ideal time to address the concept of antagonistic groups and the importance of working both sides of the body—front to back, left to right, and top to bottom. Use this discussion as a lead-in to the "muscles of the back," which is the next module.*

MUSCLES OF THE BACK

LEVEL I

Function (Week 1):

- The function of the back muscles is to:
  - elevate the collarbone and
  - move the shoulder blades up, down, and/or back.

Demonstrate these movements with your class. This is an ideal time to wear a shirt that has the muscles printed on it, offering students a graphic display of the movements and muscles.

Activities (Week 2):

- The muscles of the back are used in activities such as:
  - pull-ups,
  - rope climbing,
  - rowing a boat, and
  - raking leaves.

Ask your students to be creative and come up with other examples of activities that use the back muscles. Be sure to contrast the function of the back muscles with that of the chest muscles, reviewing the muscle function of the chest group and the concept of antagonistic muscles.

Strength Exercise (Week 3):

- An exercise that strengthens the muscles of the back is pull-ups.

Flexibility Exercise (Week 4):

- To stretch the muscles of the back, lie in a supine position with the knees held over the hips and hands behind the knees. Round the spine, moving the head and knees closer together. Maximize the stretch by extending the elbows out to the side, fully rounding the back.

LEVEL II

Function (Week 1):

- The back muscles are made up of three muscles—the *lats*, *traps*, and *rhomboids*:
  - The lats draw the arms and shoulders down and back, drawing the arms in and rolling the arm toward the midline of the body in the rear.
  - The traps raise the collarbone, raise and lower the shoulder blades, and draw the shoulder blades toward the midline of the body in the rear.
  - The rhomboids draw the shoulder blades back and up and roll them slightly downward.

Briefly review these movements with your students, and contrast them to the movements of the chest group.

Activities (Week 2):

- Activities that use the back muscles include:
  - swimming the crawl stroke (lats),
  - lifting an object from the floor to a height higher than the waist (traps), and
  - pulling an opponent into your body while wrestling (rhomboids).

Have students think of other activities that use the back muscles.

Strength Exercises (Week 3):

- The back muscles can be strengthened by such exercises as:
  - lat pull-downs (lats),
  - shoulder shrugs (traps), and
  - seated cable rows (rhomboids).

Demonstrate these three exercises with your students using dumbbells, cable attachments on a high-low pulley, a "Universal"-type gym, or stretch bands to introduce resistance training principles and options.

Flexibility Exercises (Week 4):

- Examples of stretching the back muscles would be:
  - to give yourself a "self-hug" while adding a slight forward bend, pushing the elbows up and out to the front (lats),
  - to clasp your hands behind your back and lift your arms upward, pulling your shoulders downward and back while holding your head slightly forward (traps), and
  - to interlock the fingers of both hands and press them out in front of the body while rounding the spine (rhomboids).

LEVEL III

Function (Week 1):

- There are three main muscles of the back:
  - The latissimus dorsi, that extend, adduct, and rotate the arm toward the body, as well as draw the shoulder down and back
  - The trapezius, that elevate the clavicle, adduct the scapula, and elevate or depress the scapula
  - The rhomboideus major and minor, that move the scapula backward and upward, slightly rotate the scapula downward, and adduct the scapula

Review the fundamental movements of the back muscles with students through demonstration, question-and-answer sessions, and discussion. This is an ideal time to also review such anatomical terms as extension, adduction, and rotation.

Activities (Week 2):

- Activities that use back muscles include:
  - rock climbing (latissimus dorsi),
  - surfing (latissimus dorsi),
  - blocking in football (trapezius), and
  - apparatus stunts in gymnastics (rhomboideus major and minor).

Talk with your students about how the back muscles function and interact in these activities.

Strength Exercises (Week 3):

- Exercises to strengthen the back muscles include:
  - pull-ups with resistance (latissimus dorsi),
  - upright rowing (trapezius),
  - power cleans (trapezius), and
  - bent-over rowing with resistance (rhomboideus major and minor).

Use this time to teach about strength training equipment using equipment at your school or pictures of the previously mentioned exercises. What are some exercises students could do at home without weights?

Flexibility Exercise (Week 4):

- A good flexibility exercise that involves all the muscles of the back is the "cat-and-camel stretch" (a rounding up and dipping down of the spine with opposite head and hip movement). *This is a good time to point out to your students how animals (such as a cat) often stretch when they wake up or have spent time in a prolonged position, yet we as humans rarely do. What are the implications and ramifications of reduced or greater flexibility in the lower back?*

MUSCLES OF THE ABDOMINAL WALL

LEVEL I

Function (Week 1):

- The function of the abdominal muscles is to:
  - flex the spine,
  - compress the abdomen, and
  - bend the spine to the side.

Demonstrate flexion and bending of the spine with your students, and discuss the importance of "compressing the abdomen" with respect to maintaining correct posture, avoiding low back syndromes, and keeping internal organs in their proper place.

Activities (Week 2):

- The muscles of the abdominal wall are used in activities such as:
  - bending,
  - lifting, and
  - raising the legs.

Demonstrate these three movements, and through discussion, have students come up with examples of activities in which the abdominal muscles play a role.

Strength Exercise (Week 3):

- All types of crunches strengthen the abdominal muscles. *Demonstrate, and have your students try several types of crunches: feet up, feet on the floor, and rotation, for example.*

Flexibility Exercise (Week 4):

- All movements that hyperextend the spine stretch the abdominal muscles. *Have your students lie in a prone position, then have them "push up" their upper bodies while the hips and legs remain in contact with the floor. Caution them not to hyperextend the lower spine and neck at the same time.*

LEVEL II

Function (Week 1):

- The muscles of the abdominal wall are made of three distinct muscles—the *rectus*, the *transverse*, and the *obliques:*
  - The rectus abdominis muscles flex the spinal column.
  - The transverse abdominis muscles compress the abdomen.
  - The internal and external obliques compress the abdomen when both sides contract at the same time, but, when only one side contracts at a time, the spine bends laterally.

Have students perform these movements while feeling their various abdominal muscles contracting. This is also an ideal time to wear a T-shirt depicting the abdominal muscles because students will clearly see the striations of each muscle and you can remind them that muscles contract along these "lines of pull."

Activities (Week 2):

- Activities that use abdominal muscles include:
  - bending to the front (rectus abdominis),
  - posture (transverse abdominis), and
  - bending to the side (internal and external obliques).

Strength Exercises (Week 3):

- The abdominal muscles can be strengthened by:
  - pulling the knees to the chest while hanging from a pull-up bar (rectus and transverse abdominis) and
  - doing side-to-side bends (transverse abdominis and obliques).

Demonstrate these exercises with your students and/or include them in your warm-up circuit for the lessons this week.

Flexibility Exercises (Week 4):

- Examples of flexibility exercises for the abdominal muscles would include:
  - arching to the rear while hanging from a pull-up bar (rectus and transverse abdominis) and
  - twisting to the rear while sitting in an upright, seated position (transverse abdominis and obliques).

Review the concept of antagonistic muscle groups to contrast stretching and strengthening exercises.

LEVEL III

Function (Week 1):

- The abdominal wall is comprised of three distinct muscles:
  - The rectus abdominis flexes the vertebral column.
  - The transverse abdominis compresses the abdomen.
  - The internal and external obliques either bend the vertebral column sideways when one side of the body contracts or, when both sides of the body contract, compress the abdomen.

Review the fundamental movements of the abdominal muscle group with students through demonstration, question-and-answer sessions, and discussion.

Activities (Week 2):

- Activities that use the abdominal muscles include:
  - diving in pike and tuck positions (rectus abdominis),
  - doing an iron cross in a layout position (transverse abdominis), and
  - starting a round-off or a cartwheel (external and internal obliques).

Review muscle function by discussing how the abdominal muscles play a role in these movements.

Strength Exercises (Week 3):

- Exercises to strengthen the abdominal muscles include:
  - crunches on an abdominal machine (rectus and transverse abdominis) and
  - twisting movements on a rotary torso machine (transverse abdominis and obliques).

Use this time to teach about strength training equipment using equipment at your school or pictures of the previously mentioned exercises. Help students come up with abdominal exercises they can perform at home using no equipment.

Flexibility Exercises (Week 4):

- Flexibility exercises for the abdominal muscles might include:
  - raising one arm and the opposite leg while in a prone position (rectus and transverse abdominis) and
  - sitting in a twisting yoga position with one leg flexed and crossed over the other straight leg while turning the upper torso back into the bent leg (transverse abdominis and obliques).

This is again an ideal time to discuss antagonistic muscle function.

MUSCLES OF THE HIP AND THIGH

LEVEL I

Function (Week 1):

- The function of the hip muscles is to:
  - move the leg to the rear.
- The function of the thigh muscles is to:
  - straighten or bend the leg at the knee joint and
  - bring the knee toward the chest.

Activities (Week 2):

- The muscles of the hip and thigh are used in activities such as:
  - kicking,
  - running,
  - jumping, and
  - skiing.

Demonstrate these movements, and, through discussion, have students come up with other examples.

Strength Exercise (Week 3):

- An exercise that strengthens the hip and thigh muscles is squat jumps.

Flexibility Exercises (Week 4):

- To stretch the muscles of the hip and thigh:
  - Stand on one leg, bend the other knee, and pull the foot up to the rear.
  - Sit on the ground in a modified hurdler stretch to stretch the back of the straightened leg.

LEVEL II

Function (Week 1):

- The muscles of the hip and thigh are made up of three muscles—the *glutes*, the *quads*, and the *hamstrings*:
  - The glutes extend the thigh to the rear and outwardly rotate the thigh.
  - The quads extend the knee and flex the thigh.
  - The hamstrings flex the knee and extend the thigh.

Activities (Week 2):

- Activities that use the hip and thigh muscles include:
  - starts in sprinting (glutes and hamstrings)
  - maintaining a pike position (quads)
  - the start of a kicking movement (glutes and hamstrings)

Demonstrate each of these skills with your students and help them to understand the muscular activity relative to muscle function.

Strength Exercises (Week 3):

- Exercises that strengthen the muscles of the hip and thigh include:
    - lunges (glutes, hamstrings, and quads),
    - squats (glutes and quads), and
    - single leg curls with ankle weights (hamstrings).

Demonstrate these exercises with your students, and use this as an opportunity to teach strength training principles, familiarize students with equipment, and help students think of exercises they can perform at home to accomplish the same goals with respect to increasing strength.

Flexibility Exercises (Week 4):

- Exercises to stretch the hips and thighs might include:
    - While lying supine, pull one knee across the body and up toward the opposite shoulder (glutes).
    - Lie on one side, bend the top leg at the knee, and pull the foot back to the buttock (quads).
    - Place one leg up on a bench, bend forward from the waist, and touch the toes of the raised leg (hamstrings).

Use this opportunity to discuss "safe" stretches as opposed to contraindicated stretches. For example, when you are stretching the hamstrings from a standing position, your foot of the leg being stretched should be lower than the hip.

LEVEL III

Function (Week 1):

- The muscles of the hip and thigh can be divided into three distinct muscle groups—the *gluteals*, the *quadriceps*, and the *hamstrings*:
    - The gluteals extend and rotate the femur (upper leg).
    - The quadriceps extend the knee and flex the thigh.
    - The hamstrings flex the knee and extend the thigh.

Review the fundamental movements of the hip and thigh with students through demonstration, question-and-answer sessions, and discussion.

Activities (Week 2):

- Activities that use the hip and thigh muscles include:
    - the extension of the leg in jumping (gluteals),
    - the follow-through in punting (quadriceps), and
    - the recovery phase in pedaling a bicycle (hamstrings).

Discuss these activities with your students, and see if they can think of other activities that use the hip and thigh muscles.

Strength Exercises (Week 3):

- Strengthening exercises for the hips and thighs include:
    - straight leg extensions to the rear (gluteals),
    - leg presses (quadriceps), and
    - leg curls (hamstrings).

Use this time to teach about strength training equipment, using equipment at your school or pictures of the previously mentioned exercises. Help students create options for exercising at home without weights to achieve the same goals.

Flexibility Exercises (Week 4):

- Stretching exercises for the hips and thighs might include:
  - While lying on your back, grab one leg behind the knee and calf, and pull it up toward your head (gluteals).
  - Sit back on heels from a kneeling position (quadriceps).
  - With the knees bent, bend over from the waist from a standing position, and press the knees back until the legs are straight (hamstrings).

Discuss with your students the difference between stretching for fitness and stretching before a contest. Before a contest, it is more advantageous to do some large-muscle-group rhythmic activity (jogging) and then stretch with slight, controlled bouncing. Conversely, for fitness or postactivity stretching, static stretching is the way to go.

MUSCLES OF THE LOWER LEG

LEVEL I

Function (Week 1):

- The function of the lower leg muscles is to:
  - point the foot and
  - pull the toes back toward the knee.

Activities (Week 2):

- The muscles of the lower leg are used in activities such as:
  - kicking,
  - jumping,
  - running, and
  - skiing.

Demonstrate each of these activities with your students, and differentiate between the muscles on the back of the leg that point the foot and the muscles on the front of the shin that pull the foot up.

Strength Exercises (Week 3):

- Exercises that strengthen the muscles of the lower leg include:
  - heel raises and
  - walking with the toes pulled up.

Have your students try each of these exercises to better feel these muscles contract, relating them to function.

Flexibility Exercises (Week 4):

- Exercises to stretch the lower leg include:
  - Achilles tendon stretch, with the heels hanging off a stair or bench and
  - Modified lunge position, with the top of the back foot resting on the ground (the sole up)

Demonstrate each of these exercises with your students.

LEVEL II

Function (Week 1):

- The lower leg muscles are made up of two muscle groups—the *calves* (gastrocs and soleus) and the *tibialis*:
  - The calves increase the angle from shin to toes.
  - The tibialis lessens the angle from shin to toes.

Briefly review these movements with your students. Remember that pointing the toes is not extension as is usual for increasing an angle; it is plantarflexion. Point this "oddity" of anatomical phrasing out to students!

Activities (Week 2):

- Activities that use the lower leg muscles include:
  - raising the heels in jumping (calves) and
  - the recovery phase of the bicycle pedal (tibialis).

Can your students think of any other activities that use this muscle group?

Strength Exercises (Week 3):

- The lower leg muscles can be strengthened by:
  - plyometric jumping (*Point out to students that they have done these types of activities in some of the warm-up circuits.*) and
  - cycling with toe clips on. (*Explain to students that competitive cyclists are pulling up with one leg while pushing down with the other.*)

Flexibility Exercises (Week 4):

- To stretch the lower leg muscles:
  - Stand with your toes on a 2-by-4-inch board, letting the heels hang off in contact with the floor. Lean forward slightly to increase the stretch.
  - From a kneeling position, sit back on the heels with the toes pointed away from the body.

Once again review antagonistic muscle groups with your students, making application to the function of the ankle joint.

LEVEL III

Function (Week 1):

- The muscles of the lower leg:
  - plantarflex the foot by pointing the toes (gastrocnemius and soleus) and
  - dorsiflex the foot by pulling the toes up (tibialis anterior).

Review the fundamental movements of the lower leg muscles with students through demonstration, question-and-answer sessions, and discussion.

Activities (Week 2):

- Activities that use lower leg muscles include:
  - pointing the feet during gymnastic movements (gastrocnemius and soleus) and
  - the recovery phase of a running stride—knee, heel, toe up (tibialis anterior).

When discussing these activities with your students, relate activity to function.

Strength Exercises (Week 3):

- Exercises to strengthen the calf muscles include:
  - power cleans (gastrocnemius and soleus) and
  - rowing on a rowing machine with the feet strapped in (tibialis anterior).

Use this time to teach about strength training equipment and cardiovascular equipment (cycle and rower) that strengthen the lower leg muscles. Either relate to equipment at school or use pictures to make students aware of available exercise equipment. Help them develop exercises they can do at home to achieve their goals.

Flexibility Exercises (Week 4):

- To stretch the muscles of the lower leg:
  - Lean forward in a modified lunge, keeping the heel of the back foot pressed flat to the floor (calf).
  - Perform a standing thigh stretch with the ankle pulled into plantarflexion (tibialis anterior).

When doing these stretches with your students, help them to interrelate the muscles of the hips, thighs, and lower legs with respect to these movements and other activities; they all work together.

MUSCLES OF THE ARM AND SHOULDER

LEVEL I

Function (Week 1):

- The function of the arm and shoulder muscles is to:
  - bend the arm at the elbow joint,
  - straighten the arm at the elbow joint *(Discuss the concepts of flexion and extension as they relate to a hinge joint such as the elbow.)*, and
  - raise the arm at the shoulder joint.

Activities (Week 2):

- The muscles of the arm and shoulder are used in activities such as:
  - pulling,
  - pushing, and
  - raising the arms in lifting movements.

Demonstrate these three movements, and relate these actions to the muscles of the chest and back because the arm and shoulder muscles serve as secondary movers for many of the same activities involving chest and back function.

Strength Exercises (Week 3):

- Exercises that strengthen the arm and shoulder muscles include:
  - chin-ups,
  - push-ups, and
  - straight-arm dumbbell lifts.

Flexibility Exercises (Week 4):

- To stretch the muscles of the arm and shoulder:
  - Hang off a pull-up bar with the arms straight.
  - Bend one arm at the elbow and raise it so that the hand rests on the back of the neck; with the other hand pull the bent elbow across the back.

LEVEL II

Function (Week 1):

- The arm and shoulder muscles are made up of three muscles:—the *biceps*, the *triceps*, and the *deltoids*:
  - The biceps flex the forearm and turn the palm upward.
  - The triceps extend the forearm.
  - The deltoids abduct the arm.

Review these three terms and movements with the students through demonstration, and relate them to the function of the back and chest muscles in activity.

Activities (Week 2):

- Activities that use the arm and shoulder muscles include:
  - rowing (biceps),
  - throwing (triceps), and
  - overhead lifting (deltoids).

Strength Exercises (Week 3):

- Muscles of the arm and shoulder can be strengthened by such exercises as:
  - dumbbell curls (biceps),
  - press-downs on a high cable pulley (triceps), and
  - shoulder presses (deltoids).

Demonstrate these three exercises to your students using varied apparatuses that are available in your school.

Flexibility Exercises (Week 4):

- Examples of flexibility exercises for the arm and shoulder muscles are:
  - To stretch the biceps, hang the arms down at the sides, palms facing forward; then press the arms back while extending the wrists.
  - To stretch the triceps, place the arms in a "curl" position, with the finger tips touching the shoulders; pull the elbows together and elevate them as high as possible.
  - To stretch the deltoids, grab one wrist and pull the arm across the front of the body, parallel with the ground.

LEVEL III

Function (Week 1):

- The muscles of the arm and shoulder can be divided into three distinct muscles:
  - The *biceps brachii,* that flex the forearm and supinate the forearm and hand
  - The *triceps brachii,* that extend the forearm
  - The *deltoids,* that abduct the arm

Activities (Week 2):

- Activities that use the arm and shoulder muscles include:
  - wrestling (biceps brachii),
  - pushing down or away from the body (triceps brachii), and
  - pressing movements over the head (deltoids).

Review with your students how the arm and shoulder muscles coordinate during functions. Also review the concept of antagonistic muscle function.

Strength Exercises (Week 3):

- Exercises to strengthen the arm and shoulder muscles include:
  - barbell curls (biceps brachii),
  - dips (triceps brachii), and
  - straight-arm lateral, forward, or posterior raises with dumbbells (deltoids).

Take this time to teach about strength training equipment using the equipment you have available at your school and pictures of these exercises. Discuss exercises students can perform at home without weights to achieve the same exercise effect.

Flexibility Exercises (Week 4):

- Flexibility exercises for the arm and shoulder muscles include:
  - The fully extended position of any triceps exercise to stretch the biceps.
  - The fully flexed position of any biceps exercise to stretch the triceps.
  - Adducting the arm past the midline of the body to stretch the deltoid.

EATING FOR HEALTH: A NUTRITIONAL PLAN

LEVEL I

Foods and Nutrients (Week 1):

- Nutrients are divided into six categories; nutrients in three of these categories serve as energy sources based on body demands:
  - Fats
  - Carbohydrates
  - Proteins

Foods and Nutrients (Week 2):

- Nutrients are divided into six categories; nutrients in three of these categories serve as regulators during daily activities and normal body functions:
  - Water
  - Minerals
  - Vitamins

Nutrition and Athletic Performance (Week 3):

- Elite athletes may be put on special performance diets, but generally:
  - the needs of an athlete are comparable to those of the nonathlete with respect to foods eaten, and
  - the required amount of food consumed (calories) may vary based on expenditure and body-weight demands.

Students need to be made aware that at their level and age, a good, well-balanced diet should be adequate to meet their athletic needs. They should be discouraged from following "fad-type" diets that they have been exposed to through television or in the print media.

Energy Balance (Week 4):

- A balance in calories consumed and calories expended maintains body weight. An imbalance can result in:
  - weight loss or
  - weight gain.

This is an ideal time to discuss basic weight-control principles of eating behaviors relative to exercise patterns because they have an impact on weight loss or gain. These concepts are discussed in greater detail in Levels II and III.

LEVEL II

Foods and Nutrients (Week 1):

- Nutrients that serve as a source of energy come from a variety of foodstuffs:
  - Fat sources include oils, butter, red and other meats, mayonnaise and creamy salad dressing, nuts, and chocolate.
  - Carbohydrate sources include cereal and grain products, pastas, starchy vegetables, sugar and honey, and dried fruits.
  - Protein sources include meat, fish, nuts, cereal, and dairy products, including eggs.

Foods and Nutrients (Week 2):

- Each nutrient that serves as a regulator has distinct functions:
  - Water serves to transport nutrients, remove cellular waste, and regulate temperature.
  - Minerals aid in the buildup and breakdown of other nutrients.
  - Vitamins function as chemical regulators and promote growth and life maintenance.

Nutrition and Athletic Performance (Week 3):

- If an athlete generally eats well-balanced meals, then *water regulation* and the *pregame meal* may have a favorable impact on performance:
  - Water should be ingested when thirsty and as part of the regular diet during warm weather and periods of strenuous activity.
  - Pregame meals
    - should be eaten more than two hours before contest,
    - should contain familiar foods,
    - should contain a high percentage of carbohydrates, and
    - should avoid gas-producing foods, whole milk, and caffeine.

Energy Balance (Week 4):

- Energy balance can be divided into three areas:
  - To promote weight loss, you need to

    create a 3,500 calorie differential to lose one pound of fat,

    reduce food intake, and

    increase caloric expenditure through aerobic exercise.
  - To gain weight, you need to

    create a 2,500 calorie differential to gain one pound of muscle,

    increase food intake, and

    reduce aerobic exercise and increase muscle mass through strength training.
  - To maintain weight, you need to

    maintain a balance between caloric intake and caloric expenditure.

Discuss these concepts at greater length with your students through a question-and-answer format. Have you ever gained or lost weight? Have any of your students? Share and relate these experiences with the class as a whole.

LEVEL III

Foods and Nutrients (Week 1):

- Each nutrient that serves as a source of energy has distinct characteristics:
  - Fat functions

    as a concentrated source of energy that is easily stored,

    as a primary energy source during aerobic activity, and

    as a means to transport fat-soluble vitamins.
  - Carbohydrate functions

    as an efficient short-term energy source and metabolic primer for aerobic activity.
  - Protein functions

    to repair and maintain tissue,

    to break down antibodies, enzymes, and hormones, and

    to serve as a minor contributor of energy during exhaustive work.

Foods and Nutrients (Week 2):

- Each nutrient that serves as a regulator has distinct functions:
  - Water serves to

    transport nutrients,

    remove cellular waste, and

    regulate temperature.
  - Minerals can be further classified as either *"trace"* or *"large"*.

    There are 14 trace minerals. Some of the more common ones are iron, zinc, iodine, and fluorides.

    Large-quantity minerals include sodium, calcium, potassium, phosphorus, magnesium, sulfur, and chlorine.

– Vitamins can also be broken down into two categories—*fat soluble* and *water soluble*.

Fat-soluble vitamins include A, D, E, and K.

Water-soluble vitamins include B_1, B_2, niacin, B_6, B_{12}, and C.

Nutrition and Athletic Performance (Week 3):

- For the most part, an athlete need only vary the number of calories consumed based on activity, not his percentages of calorie source. Performance should be optimal with a standard dietary recommendation of:
  - Carbohydrates—55 percent, with less than 10 percent simple sugars and more than 45 percent complex
  - Fats—30 percent, with less than 10 percent from saturated sources
  - Protein—15 percent

Discuss the eating habits of your students with them. You might have them list the foods they eat one day and then categorize the foods with respect to fats, carbohydrates, and protein. This is a perfect time to help them learn to read labels on food sources!

Energy Balance (Week 4):

- The key to weight control is a balanced caloric intake and expenditure. The basic four food group plan will help to maintain a healthy balance of food in the diet:
  - Milk and dairy products (2 servings)
  - Meat and high-protein foods (2 servings)
  - Vegetables and fruits (4 servings)
  - Cereals and grains (4 servings)

Reinforce the importance of a well-balanced diet with your students, bringing together all the concepts taught in this month's focus.

PHYSICAL FITNESS: A LIFESTYLE

LEVEL I

Cardiovascular Benefits (Week 1):

- A lifestyle of physical fitness has several cardiovascular benefits:
  - Improved cardiovascular fitness
  - Improved oxygen flow throughout the body
  - Quicker recovery after exercise

Relate these three benefits back to the earlier discussions you had with students when presenting the heart and lung modules. The "physical fitness: a lifestyle" concept is a logical way to end the year because it ties together so many of the other concepts presented monthly.

Body Composition Benefits (Week 2):

- A physically fit lifestyle also promotes body composition changes:
  - Greater lean body mass
  - Reduced body fat

These two changes relate directly to the "nutrition" module presented last month.

Muscular Strength and Endurance Benefits (Week 3):

- Regular physical activity helps to develop:
  - stronger muscles and
  - greater muscular endurance.

Relate these changes to any of the many muscle groups discussed throughout the year.

Flexibility Benefits (Week 4):

- A program of regular stretching, that should be included as part of an overall physical fitness program, will help promote flexibility in those muscles that are stretched.

LEVEL II

Cardiovascular Benefits (Week 1):

- A lifestyle of physical fitness promotes many cardiovascular changes, including:
  - a stronger heart muscle,
  - a lower resting heart rate,
  - a more controlled blood pressure,
  - an improved circulation to muscles,
  - an improved coronary circulation, and
  - a reduction in mental tension.

Be sure to relate these changes back to other topics you discussed with your students throughout the year, particularly with respect to the heart and lungs.

Body Composition Benefits (Week 2):

- Regular physical activity promotes a leaner, more fat-free body, that serves to:
  - improve your appearance and
  - improve your self-image.

Both of these factors are of concern to the middle school student (whether or not they care to discuss it). Reinforce the positive effect regular exercise can have on their mental outlook as well as physical appearance.

Muscular Strength and Endurance Benefits (Week 3):

- A lifestyle that regularly uses muscles can help an individual to improve her:
  - performance in sports,
  - physical ability to meet emergencies, and
  - posture.

Flexibility Benefits (Week 4):

- A well-rounded physical fitness program that includes stretching can help an individual to:
  - improve her sports performance and
  - reduce muscle tension.

LEVEL III

Cardiovascular Benefits (Week 1):

- A regular lifestyle of physical fitness can favorably affect a number of risk factors associated with coronary heart disease; it can:
    - reduce blood fats, including low-density lipids (LDL),
    - increase protective high-density lipids (HDL),
    - possibly offer resistance to atherosclerosis, and
    - lower the risk of a heart attack.

Review these risk modifications with your students relative to aerobic exercise and the effects such exercise has on the heart and lungs as discussed earlier in the year.

Body Composition Benefits (Week 2):

- Not only will a physically fit individual have a lower percent body fat, but he will also have:
    - a greater work efficiency and
    - a lower susceptibility to disease.

Help raise student awareness that fat is like a metabolic wasteland where you get no return for your blood flow in terms of productivity. Leaner people perform better at physical tasks and tend to be more disease free.

Muscular Strength and Endurance Benefits (Week 3):

- Like body composition, the physically fit, stronger individual has:
    - a greater work efficiency and
    - less potential for back problems and injury.

Being overweight and lacking abdominal strength are two of the leading causes for back syndromes, both of which are preventable through a balanced program of regular physical activity.

Flexibility Benefits (Week 4):

- A program of regular stretching enhances both an ideal body composition and the increased muscular strength and endurance associated with a physically active lifestyle by:
    - allowing for a greater work efficiency and
    - decreasing the potential for back, joint, or muscle injury.

Be sure to reinforce the concept of a "balanced" program when discussing physical fitness with your students (aerobic, strength, and flexibility components). The means through which they achieve a high level of fitness is a choice of lifestyle, and, as teachers, we can provide a number of options and the motivation for doing so!

chapter 7

SKILL-DEVELOPMENT ACTIVITIES

Chapters 7, 8, and 9 provide numerous activities through which to teach your students the concepts discussed in this book. These three chapters are truly the *"heart"* of the book and offer easy-to-use, fun activities for a variety of team and individual-movement experiences. In this chapter, teaching cues and activities are presented for skill development. Most of the skills center on catching/throwing, kicking, and/or striking and form the basis for the team activities in the following chapter. Some of the skills presented here, however, lend themselves to the individual and partner activities found in chapter 9.

For your ease in using this chapter, skills are presented under the headings of catching/throwing, kicking, and striking. Under each heading, skills are further subdivided by sport (e.g., striking—softball, racket-related, volleyball, etc.). Finally, for each specific skill (e.g., forearm pass), teaching cues are provided under the heading *Technique,* that tells you what students should concentrate on, and *Skills Practice,* that gives you suggestions for specific drill activities. Drills are listed for each skill, from easiest to most difficult. These drills are de-

signed to be used in the 13-minute *skill-development module* presented in table 3.1 (page 18). We find that two to three drills per day, progressing from individual to partner drills or from part-

We use the *skill-development drill module* to evaluate students relative to the *benchmarks* discussed in chapter 4. We tend to notice those students who are struggling—those we have to give extra cues or attention to. When class is over, we jot their names down on a piece of paper (it's usually only two to three names per class). When we have their class again, and we are working on the same skill area (e.g., catching/throwing), we pay a little more attention to the students on the list, either removing their name from the list if they show progress or leaving it there if they continue to struggle. At report card time, we simply check off all the students not on our lists (which is the majority of them) and make appropriate comments relative to those students not yet at level. This method proves to be both effective and efficient.

ner to small group, work best in keeping the students active. Diagrams 7.1 through 7.16 are provided to clarify drill formations, while photos 7.1 through 7.17 will help to illustrate key body positions.

The following suggestions will help you create skill-development drills that coincide with the many game activities presented in the next two chapters. As you read through chapters 8 and 9, refer back to this chapter to reinforce teaching cues from lesson to lesson while selecting drills that are appropriate for the chosen activity of the day.

The individual and partner drills will also allow you to quickly evaluate the progress of students through observation. This will help you in filling out the *portfolio assessment card* discussed in chapter 4 (page 32).

Table 7.1 lists all the skill activities presented in this chapter by their major headings (catching/throwing, kicking, and striking) with page numbers for your ease of reference.

Table 7.1   Skill Activities by Groupings

Catching/Throwing		Kicking		Striking	
Basketball-Related Skills		**Football-Related Skills**		**Floor Hockey-Related Skills**	
Bounce Pass	(page 116)	Placekicking	(page 131)	Stickhandling	(page 136)
Chest Pass	(page 117)	Punting	(page 131)		
Defensive Stance/				**Racket-Related Skills**	
Positioning	(page 117)	**Soccer-Related Skills**		Strokes	(page 137)
Dribbling	(page 118)	Dribbling	(page 132)		
Overhead Pass	(page 119)	Heading	(page 132)	**Softball-Related Skills**	
Rebounding	(page 119)	Passing Long	(page 134)	Hitting	(page 138)
Shooting a Layup	(page 120)	Passing Short	(page 134)		
Shooting an Outside		Throw-Ins	(page 134)	**Volleyball-Related Skills**	
Shot	(page 120)	Trapping	(page 135)	Forearm Pass	(page 139)
				Overhead Pass	(page 140)
Football-Related Skills				Overhead Serve	(page 142)
Cadence	(page 121)			Underhand Serve	(page 143)
Catching	(page 121)				
Handoff	(page 122)				
Passing	(page 123)				
Pass Patterns	(page 123)				
Quarterback/Center					
Exchange	(page 124)				
Stance	(page 125)				
Lacrosse-Related Skills					
Catching	(page 126)				
Scooping	(page 127)				
Throwing	(page 127)				
Softball-Related Skills					
Catching	(page 128)				
Throwing	(page 130)				

GENERAL PASSING DRILLS

Several of the *drills* presented in this section can be used to practice a wide variety of skills. As an example, Partner Drills (diagram 7.1) work well for practicing catching/throwing skills (bounce passes), kicking skills (short soccer passes), or striking skills (forearm volleyball passes). Although the drills are described in detail, use the diagrams to help you fully understand them.

PARTNER DRILLS

As shown in diagram 7.1, Partner Drills have students working in pairs and merely passing a ball back and forth between them. This drill could easily be expanded to include a third child as well.

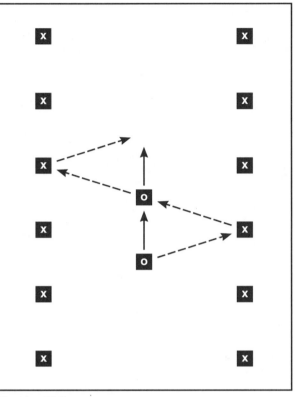

Diagram 7.2

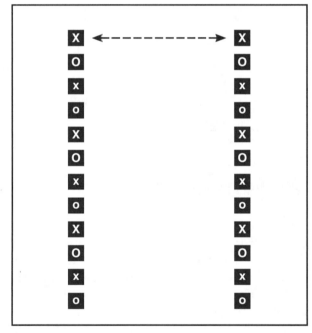

Diagram 7.1

GAUNTLET DRILL

In the Gauntlet Drill (diagram 7.2), a student *(O)* runs through a gauntlet formed by his classmates *(Xs)*. The *O* student passes to every other *X* student while alternating sides

of the gauntlet, and the *Xs* pass back to the *O* student as he progresses through the gauntlet.

After passing through the gauntlet, the *O* student can reverse direction and pass to those students he missed on the way down, or the next student who goes can simply start on the opposite side of the gauntlet so that all the *Xs* do in fact get a turn.

When done, the *O* student should go to the end of the *X* line. The first *X* student then steps out to become an *O*, continuing the drill.

SPOKE DRILL

The Spoke Drill (diagram 7.3) can be used to give one student *(X)* repetitious practice at a particular skill. Placed in the middle of a circle, she passes to each *O* student, who passes right back to her, working her way around the circle. When she *(X)* has passed to everyone in the circle, she joins the circle, and one of the *Os* becomes an *X*.

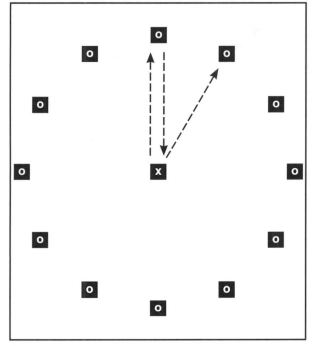

Diagram 7.3

Many of the drills we present lend themselves to being more challenging by simply adding another ball to the drill. By having several balls in motion at one time, students need to anticipate, react, and make judgments more rapidly. In the Gauntlet Drill, several students can be passing through the gauntlet at one time, creating a greater challenge for the students forming the gauntlet. Two balls could be used in the Spoke Drill, with the center student passing to *every other student* in the circle (a skip pass), thus increasing the intensity level of every student in the drill. In a Partner Drill, use two balls, with one student throwing a bounce pass while the other student throws a chest pass. It will not only prove challenging; it will be fun as well!

THREE-PERSON PASSING DRILL

The Three-Person Passing Drill (diagram 7.4) has three teammates *(Xs)* running side by side in a line down a court or field. The center X passes to his right. Still moving as a group, the X on the right now passes back to the center X. Upon receiving the ball back, the center X

passes to the X on his left, who returns the ball, continuing the drill.

To be successful, students must move forward as a group and anticipate the pass coming to them. It is also a good idea to repeat this drill several times so that every student gets a chance to be in the middle position.

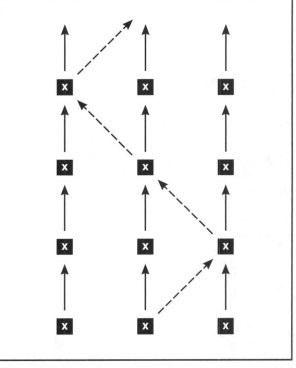

Diagram 7.4

THREE-PERSON WEAVE DRILL

The Three-Person Weave Drill (diagram 7.5) is similar to the Three-Person Passing Drill in that students start out three abreast and move down the floor as a unit. The big difference is that after passing the ball, the student follows her pass by sprinting up to and around the person she passed to, continuing down the court.

WALL DRILLS

Wall Drills (diagram 7.6) are good to use when every student has a ball and you want a high-repetition practice drill. Simply have students line up around the gym facing the walls, pass-

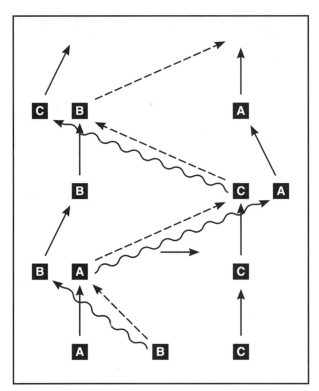

Diagram 7.5

ing and catching a ball rebounded off the wall (or kicking and trapping a ball or wall volleying a ball).

CATCHING/THROWING

Keep in mind that many of the *skills* presented under this heading overlap with game and sport activities. For example, a bounce pass is used in both basketball- and team handball-related games. Many of the *techniques* overlap as well. When catching a bounce pass, football, or lacrosse ball, students should "keep their eyes on the ball." Use these similarities among skills to help reinforce key concepts with students as you present a variety of catching/throwing experiences.

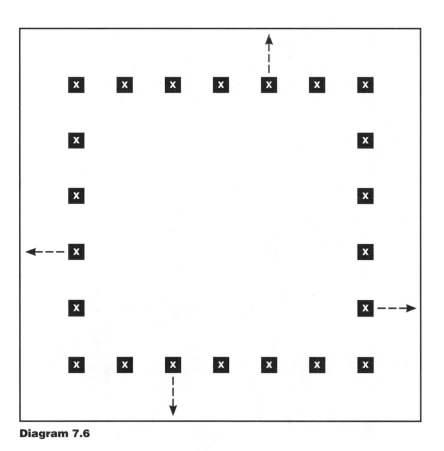

Diagram 7.6

BASKETBALL-RELATED SKILLS

BOUNCE PASS

Technique

To execute the bounce pass effectively, students should

- aim to pass at a spot on the floor two-thirds the distance from their partners;
- step into each pass and catch; and
- receive a pass by (see photo 7.1)
    1. keeping their eyes on the ball;
    2. making a target with their hands, fingers spread;
    3. placing one hand up as if "stopping traffic" to stop the ball; and
    4. placing the other hand on the side to control the pass.

Skills Practice

Have the students pass and catch with a partner(s) using the

- Partner Drills (see page 113),
- Gauntlet Drill (see page 113),
- Spoke Drill (see page 113),
- Three-Person Passing Drill (see page 114), and
- Three-Person Weave Drill (see page 114).

Photo 7.1 Catching a bounce pass.

CHEST PASS

Technique

To execute the chest pass correctly, students should

- aim at their target when passing;
- step into each pass and catch; and
- receive a pass by
  1. keeping their eyes on the ball and
  2. making a target with their hands, fingers spread.

Skills Practice

Have the students pass and catch alone using the

- Wall Drills (see page 114).

Have the students pass and catch with a partner(s) using the

- Partner Drills (see page 113),
- Gauntlet Drill (see page 113),
- Spoke Drill (see page 113),
- Three-Person Passing Drill (see page 114), and
- Three-Person Weave Drill (see page 114).

DEFENSIVE STANCE AND POSITIONING

Technique

To execute an effective defensive stance and properly position themselves defensively, students should (see photo 7.2)

- assume an athletic stance—feet spread slightly wider than shoulder-width, knees flexed, weight on the front part of the feet in a position of *"comfort"*;
- square their bodies to the person they are guarding;
- mirror the ball—hand down on the ball side, up on the nonball side in the passing lane;
- run (cut off) their players sideline to sideline or end line to midcourt, preventing them from penetrating toward the basket; and
- use a drop step to recover if they start to get beat.

Skills Practice

Have students practice their stance

- mirroring the teacher and
- working with a partner(s)
  1. One partner dribbles and the other plays defense.

Photo 7.2   The defensive stance.

DRIBBLING

Technique

To execute the dribble effectively, students should

- keep fingers spread;
- push the ball firmly to the floor; and
- dribble every time they move with the ball.

Skills Practice

Have students practice dribbling

- in place—right hand only, left hand only, alternating hands on each dribble;
- while tracing various lines on the floor;
- while moving throughout the gym, changing the direction of their dribble, avoiding contact with other students;
- in place—weaving the ball in and out between their legs in a figure-eight pattern;
- back and forth through their legs while walking around the gym; and
- in different directions using only visual directions given by a leader.

OVERHEAD PASS

Technique

To execute the overhead pass effectively, students should

- aim at their target when passing;
- keep their arms extended with the ball held high; and
- step into each pass.

Skills Practice

Have the students pass and catch alone using the

- Wall Drills (see page 114).

Have the students pass and catch with a partner(s) using the

- Gauntlet Drill (see page 113),
- Spoke Drill (see page 113), and
- a full-court rebounding and outlet drill:
  1. One student shoots, then cuts to the corner.
  2. Her partner rebounds the shot and passes an overhead outlet pass to the corner, then cuts up court.
  3. The student in the corner passes back to the student cutting up court who will dribble and repeat the process at the other end as they now switch roles as the *shooter* and *rebounder*.

REBOUNDING

Technique

To execute a rebound effectively, students should

- jump vertically, reaching with both hands;
- hold the ball high upon landing with the arms extended (on the offensive end), taking the ball right up again without a dribble; and
- hold the ball high upon landing with the arms extended (on the defensive end), throwing a two-handed *"overhead"* pass to an outlet.

Skills Practice

Have the students form a relay line and rebound off the backboard:

- One student shoots a soft *"jump shot"* off the backboard so that the next student can rebound.
- The next student rebounds, then goes right up to shoot a soft *"jump shot"* repeating the drill (see diagram 7.7).

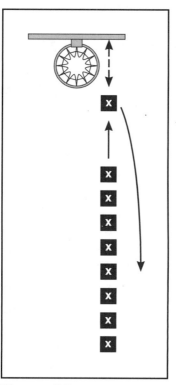

Diagram 7.7

SHOOTING A BASKETBALL (LAYUP)

Technique

To execute the layup effectively, students should

- keep their eyes on the *"box"*;
- jump off the foot opposite their shooting hand; and
- push the ball up into the box off their fingertips.

Skills Practice

Have students practice layups from

- one line, with each student rebounding his own shot and
- two lines—one line shoots while the other rebounds (see diagram 7.8).

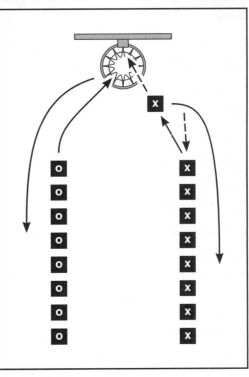

Diagram 7.8

SHOOTING A BASKETBALL (OUTSIDE SHOT)

Technique

To execute the outside shot effectively, students should

- Form a comfortable base of support
  1. with the feet spread slightly wider than shoulder-width;
  2. with the foot of the shooting hand slightly forward; and
  3. with the body squared to the rim.
- Position their arms
  4. to form a *"window,"* holding the ball above their heads;
  5. to form a straight line with the shoulder, elbow, and shooting hand (in line with the flight of the ball at the rim);
  6. to distribute the weight of the ball more toward the thumb, index, and middle finger; and
  7. to *"wave good-bye"* as if reaching over the rim.

Skills Practice

Have students practice shooting

- from around the perimeter of the *"bucket"* and
- from one line:
  1. Student shoots outside the *"key."*
  2. Student follows her shot.
  3. Student rebounds.
  4. Student shoots a layup.

FOOTBALL-RELATED SKILLS

CADENCE

Technique

To execute a cadence effectively, students should

- realize that the purpose of a cadence is to set a team into motion as a unit;
- realize that different teams use different cadences; and
- use the cadence that your school district uses, for example:
  1. "set"—students set feet, bend legs, and place hands on thighs;
  2. "down"—students assume the three-point stance; and
  3. "hut"—students move into motion out of the three-point stance.

Skills Practice

Have students practice using a cadence

- by lining up and talking them through the proper checkpoints for each part of the *"cadence"*;
- by lining up in conjunction with your calling out a *"cadence"*; and
- by working in groups of three, rotating through each position:
  1. One as a *"back"*
  2. One as a *"center"*
  3. One as a *"quarterback,"* calling out the cadence for his group

We also use the concept of *cadence* (and have fun doing so) to teach about offsides from a defensive perspective. Have half your students line up in a defensive stand 5 yards from the ball. Have the other students act as offensive linemen following the lead of two students who play center and quarterback. By having a quick huddle with the offense, the cadence can be varied (e.g., "set, down, hut," or "set, down, hut 1, hut 2, red, 95, hike") to set the "offensive line" into motion. The defensive line should be taught to react to movement of the ball or movement of the offensive line. Have fun watching all the sutdents who twitch, jump, fall, stutter step, and just plain react with confusion. After several tries, the students improve, and then you can switch offensive and defensive responsibilities.

CATCHING

Technique

To execute catching a football effectively, students should

- keep their eyes on the ball;
- move toward the ball;
- provide a target by spreading their fingers and forming a "frame";
- position their bodies behind or under the ball; and

• use their hands to guide the ball into their bodies.

Skills Practice

Have students pass and catch with a partner(s) using the

- Partner Drills (see page 113) and
- Three-Person Passing Drill (see page 114).

HANDOFF

Technique

To execute the handoff effectively, students should

- run straight with their arms properly positioned (it is the quarterback's responsibility to get them the ball):
    1. Hold the *outside* arm at a right angle, palm up, forearm just above the belt line.
    2. Hold the *inside* arm parallel to the bottom arm, elbow high, framing the abdominal area (see photo 7.3).

Skills Practice

Have students practice handoffs

- using a line drill as in teaching the "cadence"
    1. with the students running out of a three-point stance with the proper hand position.
- by working in groups of three, rotating through each position:
    2. One as a *"back"*
    3. One as a *"center"*
    4. One as a *"quarterback,"* handing off to the back

Photo 7.3 Receiving the handoff.

PASSING

Technique

To execute the pass effectively, students should

- step into each pass;
- throw overhand with the elbow held high; and
- position their hands so that
  1. their fingers are spread on the back half of the ball's laces;
  2. they release the ball one finger at a time: pinkie, ring, middle, and index;
  3. they release the ball with the front tip angled up slightly; and
  4. they aim for their target with their hands on the follow-through.

Skills Practice

Have the students pass and catch with a partner(s) using the

- Partner Drills (see page 113).

PASS PATTERNS

Pass patterns are illustrated in diagram 7.9. Demonstrate and briefly discuss their use with respect to long- and short-yardage situations. There are of course variations for these basic patterns, but these six patterns will give your students a good basis from which to start.

Technique

To have an effective understanding of basic pass patterns, students should

- run each of the following patterns:
  1. curl in,
  2. square out,

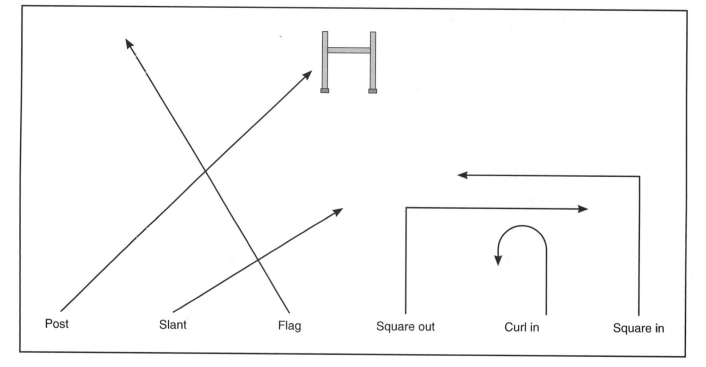

| Post | Slant | Flag | Square out | Curl in | Square in |

Diagram 7.9

3. square in,

4. slant,

5. post, and

6. flag.

Skills Practice

Have the students practice pass patterns by

- observing you run them and
- having the students work in groups of three, rotating through each position:

  1. One as the *"quarterback"* who calls the cadence and pattern
  2. One as the *"receiver"* who runs the patterns
  3. One as the *"center"* who hikes the ball

Sometimes we will use students to demonstrate proper positioning for a skill or to demonstrate a drill. As an example, we might use three modified football players to demonstrate a proper stance, the quarterback/center exchange, or a handoff. I often use girls from my seventh- and eighth-grade volleyball team to demonstrate proper forearm (bump) and overhead (set) passes. By using these students to demonstrate, or teach:

- talented students get a chance to showcase their knowledge and skills. Other students see that someone their own age can in fact do what they may perceive as difficult; and we then use these students as mentors in partner or group drills, benefiting everyone!

QUARTERBACK/CENTER EXCHANGE

Technique

To execute the quarterback/center exchange effectively,

- centers should

  1. assume a modified three-point stance;
  2. spread the fingers of the dominant hand on the laces of the football; and
  3. hike the ball up to the buttocks with a quarter turn (ball pointing leg to leg).

- quarterbacks should

  4. stand square to the center with the knees bent;
  5. hold hands under the buttocks of the center, fingers spread, heels of the hand touching, wrists pulled back as far as possible, and the hands angled so the throwing hand is on top;
  6. receive the hiked ball firmly between their hands; and
  7. drop back three steps, starting with the dominant foot to throw, or turn and step to the side for a handoff.

Skills Practice

Have students practice the quarterback/center exchange

- working in pairs, playing each position.

STANCE

Technique

To assume a proper stance, students should

- stand on a line:
  1. Spread their feet slightly wider than shoulder-width
  2. Place their left heels on the line with the right toes on the line so that the feet are offset
  3. Bend the legs
  4. Place their right hands on the ground to form a triangle with their feet
  5. Tilt their heads up so the eyes can look straight ahead (see photo 7.4)

Skills Practice

Have students practice the stance by

- talking them through the proper checkpoints while they stand on a line;
- calling out a cadence and having them go through the proper checkpoints; and
- working in groups of three, rotating through each position:
  1. One as a *"quarterback,"* calling out the cadence
  2. One as a *"center,"* assuming a modified stance
  3. One as a *"back,"* assuming the three-point stance

Photo 7.4 The three-point stance.

LACROSSE-RELATED SKILLS

CATCHING

Technique

To execute the catch effectively, students should

- step into each catch and
- receive a pass by
  1. providing a target by holding their sticks up, away from their bodies (see photo 7.5);
  2. keeping their eyes on the ball; and
  3. letting the stick "give" with the ball.

Skills Practice

Have students pass and catch

- alone using Wall Drills (page 114) and
- with a partner(s) using the
  1. Partner Drills (page 113),
  2. Three-Person Passing Drill (page 114), and
  3. Three-Person Weave Drill (page 114).

Photo 7.5 Giving a good target.

SCOOPING

Technique

To execute scooping effectively, students should

- keep their eyes on the ball;
- hold the stick with the hands spread shoulder-width apart;
- hold the bottom hand on the side of the hip;
- get the body (hips) low as if shoveling (see photo 7.6); and
- move to the ball, sliding the stick in under it.

Skills Practice

Have students practice scooping

- on their own and
- using the Traditional Relay Lines Drill (see diagram 7.10).

Photo 7.6   Scooping a ground ball.

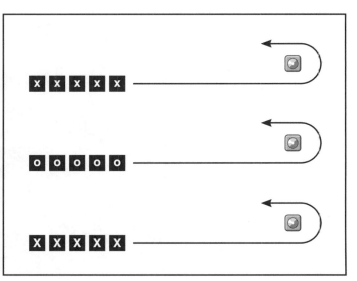

Diagram 7.10

THROWING

Technique

To execute the throw effectively, students should

- step at their targets and
- hold their sticks
  1. with their hands high;
  2. away from their bodies; and
  3. with a backward tilt of 45 degrees.

- use a throwing motion similar to softball/baseball, with (see photo 7.7)
    4. the top hand traveling in a throwing motion;
    5. the head of the stick following through at the target; and
    6. the bottom hand just holding the stick, relaxed.

Skills Practice

Have students pass and catch

- alone using Wall Drills (page 114) and
- with a partner(s) using the
    1. Partner Drills (page 113),
    2. Three-Person Passing Drill (page 114), and
    3. Three-Person Weave Drill (page 114).

Photo 7.7 Using the lacrosse stick to throw the ball.

SOFTBALL-RELATED SKILLS

CATCHING

Technique

To execute a catch effectively, students should

- expect every ball to come to them;
- preplan what to do with the ball, based on the game situation; and

- be in a relaxed, athletic stance (see photo 7.8):
  1. knees bent, feet slightly wider than shoulder-width;
  2. weight forward on the feet;
  3. hands down, separated and loose; and
  4. step in as the pitch is delivered.
- play *ground balls* by charging them:
  5. staying low, squared to the ball;
  6. hands in front of the body, coming together on the ground; and
  7. gathering the ball into the body.
- play *fly balls* by
  8. getting the body into position under the ball;
  9. moving into the ball if a throw is necessary; and
  10. holding the hands up, with a "soft" give upon catching, pulling the ball into the body.

Skills Practice

Have students practice catching with a partner(s) and no glove:

- Roll the ball back and forth.
- From a roll, gather the ball in and throw it halfway to their partners.
- Toss fly balls to each other underhand.

Photo 7.8 The ready position.

THROWING

Technique

To execute a throw effectively, students should

- step at the target;
- throw overhand; and
- keep the throwing elbow high.

Skills Practice

Have students throw and catch

- alone using Wall Drills (page 114) and
- with a partner(s) using the
  1. Partner Drills (page 113),
  2. Zigzag Gauntlet Formation (see diagram 7.11), and
  3. Line Relay (see diagram 7.12).

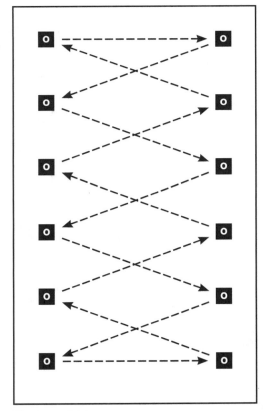

Diagram 7.11

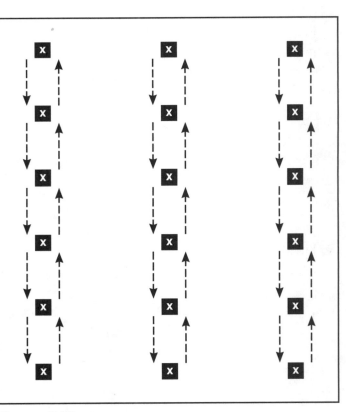

Diagram 7.12

KICKING

As with the "catching/throwing" skills, many of the *skills* presented under this heading overlap between game and sport activities. For example, placekicking and punting are used in both soccer- and football-type games. Many of the *techniques* overlap, too. Use these similarities to help students "revisit" key concepts as you present kicking drills.

FOOTBALL-RELATED SKILLS

PLACEKICKING

Technique

To execute a placekick effectively, students should

- tee the ball up at a 45-degree angle;
- turn the ball so the laces face away;
- use a soccer-style approach:
  1. Three steps back (starting with the kicking foot)
  2. Two steps over (toward the nonkicking foot)
- keep their eyes on the ball when approaching and contacting it;
- use a sweeping, "soccer-style" kick with the leg fully extended; and
- have the foot follow through at the target.

Skills Practice

Have students practice placekicking by

- kicking off tees for distance;
- kicking at targets; and
- kicking over targets: hurdles, fences, mats, soccer goals, football uprights, and so on.

PUNTING

Technique

To execute a punt effectively, students should

- extend their arms, holding the ball level at waist height;
- *drop* the ball as they step and kick (they should not *toss* the ball);
- keep their eyes focused on the ball;
- follow through with their leg fully extended; and
- change their body angle to affect the ball trajectory:
  1. forward for distance and
  2. upright for shorter, higher kicks.

Skills Practice

Have students practice punting, starting with round balls and progressing to footballs, by

- dropping balls onto the foot, lightly making contact, and
- punting for
  1. distance,
  2. height,
  3. accuracy, and
  4. to a partner.

SOCCER-RELATED SKILLS

DRIBBLING

Technique

To execute the dribble effectively, students should

- keep the center of gravity over the ball and
- control the ball with the inside, outside, or bottom of the foot.

Skills Practice

Have students practice dribbling by

- dancing laterally back and forth across the ball, touching it lightly and alternating feet and
- lightly placing one foot on the ball and hopping on the other foot:
  1. forward on right foot;
  2. forward on left foot;
  3. backward on right foot; and
  4. backward on left foot.
- dribbling without hitting each other, stopping under control on a signal (whistle) and
- dribbling through a Slalom Course of cones (see diagram 7.13).

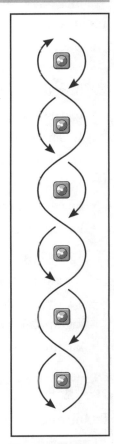

Diagram 7.13

HEADING

Technique

To execute a head ball effectively, students should

- keep their eyes on the ball;
- contact the ball with the center of the forehead; and
- step into the ball with the nondominant foot forward.

Skills Practice

Have students practice heading

- working with a partner(s) using a variety of *soft*-type balls (playground, sponge, soccer, etc.) and changing roles every five times:
  1. Jump off feet and head a stationary ball held by partner (see photo 7.9).
  2. Head a tossed ball from a sitting position, feet out straight.
  3. Head a tossed ball out of an *all-fours* position.
  4. Head a tossed ball advancing forward while their partners (the tossers) back up (retreat), catching and retossing the ball.

Photo 7.9   Heading a stationary ball.

We have a number of success stories to profess, as no doubt you do, too. Perhaps this is what motivates us to teach—seeing the joy on a student's face when she finally conquers a task. Much of our success comes from using a variety of progressions in teaching skills, modifying the balls used in performing the skills, and as we have mentioned throughout this book modifying game activities so students repetitively practice these skills. A student named Reginald comes to mind when we discuss the skill of *heading* a soccer ball.

Reginald moved to us about a year ago from another school district and had a real fear of heading a ball. Although he was intelligent and could grasp the concept involved with the skill and could analyze how to head, he had a real fear of doing so. In his old school, he had to use only soccer balls from a standing position to practice this skill, and he remembered getting headaches from doing so. By watching other students go through our drills, he noticed that no one was in pain. Using a soft, Nerf-type ball, he gave it a try and progressed, not only drill-wise but also in terms of the firmness of the balls he was heading, up to a volleyball. Just the other day in a game of *modified 6-on-6 soccer*, Reginald headed a real soccer ball out of his defensive end without even giving it a second thought. When we pointed this out to him after class, he beamed with pride, not only because he had overcome his fear but because we had noticed!

PASSING LONG

Technique

To execute a long pass effectively, students should

- plant the nonkicking foot next to the ball;
- approach the ball from a 45-degree angle;
- *"sweep"* the kicking foot through the ball, making contact with the instep; and
- lean back slightly to provide lift to the ball.

Skills Practice

Have students practice with a partner using two grids (see diagram 7.14) by

- passing from their grids, lifting the ball into their partners' grids and
- passing from their grids, going to an open corner of their grids, and receiving a pass back from their partners.

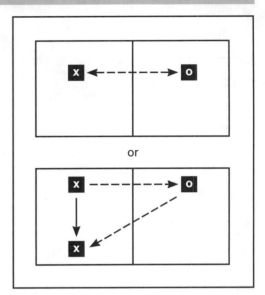

Diagram 7.14

PASSING SHORT

Technique

To execute a short pass effectively, students should

- plant the nonkicking foot next to the ball;
- center their weight over the ball to keep the pass down;
- turn the kicking foot out, contacting the ball with the inside of the foot; and
- follow through at the target with the kicking foot.

Skills Practice

Have students practice with a partner in one grid (see diagram 7.15) by

- passing back and forth with short instep passes within their grids and
- passing, going to an open area within their grids, and receiving a pass back from their partners.

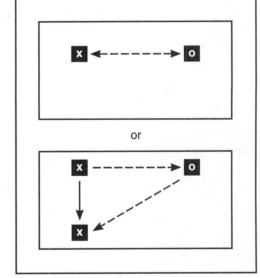

Diagram 7.15

THROW-INS

Technique

To execute a throw-in effectively, students should

- run into the pass, throwing with one foot forward while dragging the back foot;

- keep their arms extended, ball held high, equal pressure on both hands; and
- aim at an area to *lead* their teammates (see photo 7.10).

Skills Practice

Have students practice throw-ins by

- working with a partner:
  1. One throws while the other traps and passes back (switch after five times).
- working in threes out of the Triangle Formation (see diagram 7.16):
  2. One throws; the next traps, touches, and passes to the third, who picks it up as a goalie and throws, continuing the drill.

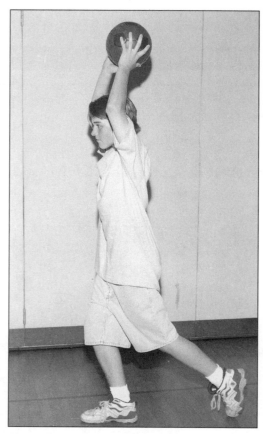

Photo 7.10 The soccer throw-in.

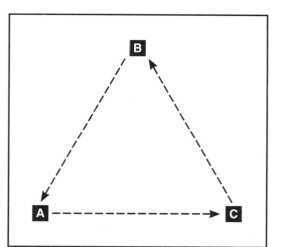

Diagram 7.16

TRAPPING

Technique

To execute a trap effectively, students should

- keep their eyes on the ball;
- use "*soft*" parts of their bodies to trap (stop and control) the ball (e.g., instep, inner thigh, chest);
- "*give*" with the ball to "*deaden*" it, pushing the ball to the ground; and
- "*one touch*" the ball for control before kicking.

Skills Practice

Have the students practice trapping with a partner(s) using the

- Partner Drills (see page 113),

- Triangle Formation (see page 135),

- Spoke Drill (see page 113),

- Gauntlet Drill (see page 113), and

- Zigzag Gauntlet Formation (see page 130).

STRIKING

The striking *skills* presented under this heading will provide your students with diverse *drills* using numerous lever lengths for striking; various sized balls to strike; and fly, bouncing, and rolling balls to deal with. The drills are fun, challenging, and effective for developing basic striking *techniques*.

FLOOR HOCKEY-RELATED SKILLS

STICKHANDLING

Technique

To stickhandle effectively, students should

- hold the stick with hands shoulder-width apart (bottom hand up, top hand down) and the *blade always on the ground*;

- *"push"* and *"draw"* the stick to control the ball; and

- execute the pass by

  1. keeping their eyes on the ball;

  2. stepping into each pass;

  3. pushing the ball with the blade, following through at the target;

  4. keeping their weight over the ball to keep it down;

  5. turning the wrists upward to lift the ball; and

  6. shooting as if *passing* to a spot in the net.

Skills Practice

Have the students practice stickhandling with a partner(s) using the

- Partner Drills (see page 113),

- Triangle Formation (see page 135),

- Gauntlet Drill (see page 113),

- Zigzag Gauntlet Formation (see page 130),

- Three-Person Passing Drill (see page 114),

- Three-Person Weave Drill (see page 114),

- Traditional Relay Lines with pass back to teammates (see page 127),

- Line Relay (see page 130), and

- Slalom Course (see page 132).

RACKET-RELATED SKILLS

STROKES

Technique

To execute a racket-type stroke effectively, students should

- turn their bodies perpendicular to the flight of the ball;
- change body shape based on the location of the ball: high, low, or waist high (see photos 7.11 through 7.13);
- differentiate between swinging for control (accuracy) and swinging for power (distance); and
- make contact as they
  1. keep their eyes on the ball;
  2. shift their weight forward through the ball; and
  3. recover for the next shot by assuming an *"athletic stance,"* with the striking lever centered in front of the body.

Photo 7.11   The overhand stroke (Pillo Polo).

Photo 7.12   The ground stroke (Paddleball).

Photo 7.13   The forehand stroke (hand hockey).

Skills Practice

Have the students practice racket-type strokes

- alone using Wall Drills (see page 114) and
- with a partner(s):
    1. alternately volleying off the wall;
    2. using Partner Drills (see page 113) and volleying over a line, bench steps, cones, a net; and
    3. increasing the length of the striking lever: hand, paddle racket, tennis racket.

SOFTBALL-RELATED SKILLS

HITTING

Technique

To execute a hit effectively, students should

- position themselves so that
    1. they are perpendicular to the object being struck;
    2. they spread the feet slightly wider than shoulder-width;
    3. they bend the knees assuming a *"comfortable"* stance;
    4. they extend the elbows from the body; and
    5. they start the bat from the same position each time.

- do the following when hitting:
  6. Step at the pitcher
  7. Try to see the ball make contact with the bat
  8. Drive off the back foot, stepping lightly on the big toe of the front foot

Skills Practice

Have students practice hitting

- a ball off a tee;
- rolled up socks tossed from the side;
- six-inch playground balls pitched with a bounce;
- a ball while playing *"pepper"* with a partner; and
- a regular softball thrown underhand.

VOLLEYBALL-RELATED SKILLS

FOREARM PASS (BUMP)

Technique

To execute the forearm pass effectively, students should

- assume a ready position with the
  1. body squared to the ball;
  2. outside foot forward;
  3. hands out in front of the body;
  4. eyes on the ball; and
  5. body rocking in motion.
- actively pass the ball by
  6. dropping into a semi-squat, partial sitting position;
  7. locking out the arms at a 45-degree angle to the floor;
  8. pushing the thumbs and heels of the hands together and downward to more fully supinate the forearms (see photo 7.14);
  9. move two steps into the ball, then three steps back to recover; and
  10. drive the ball with the legs, not the arms.

Skills Practice

Have students practice bumping

- alone:
  1. Repeatedly passing to themselves
  2. Using Wall Drills (see page 114)
- with a partner(s):
  1. Using Partner Drills (see page 113), as one tosses and one bumps
  2. Using Partner Drills (see page 113), bumping back and forth
- with a Spoke-Drill formation (see page 113), but with students volleying as a group.

Photo 7.14   The forearm pass (bump).

Volleyball is another one of those activities in which we find that a number of students fear a regulation ball, react too slowly to use it, or just don't have the skills to do so. We find that using a beach ball for low-functioning classes enhances our drills and student success immensely with respect to group volleying and even game activities. Next we progress to a number of optically colored "floater" balls on the market today, and, for those students at a high skill level, we do use regulation volleyballs while suggesting they wear long-sleeve shirts to reduce the "stinging" sensation they might experience on their forearms.

OVERHEAD PASS (SET)

Technique

To execute the overhead pass effectively, students should

- assume a ready position with
  1. the body angled 45 degrees between where the ball is and where the set will go and
  2. the eyes on the ball.

- actively set the ball by
  3. dropping into a semi-squat, partial sitting position;
  4. raising the arms overhead, with the index fingers and thumbs forming a diamond with the hands almost touching and the fingers firm;
  5. driving the ball with the legs, letting the arms extend to impart flight (see photo 7.15); and
  6. setting to an area, letting the striker move into the ball.

Skills Practice

Have the students practice setting

- alone:
  1. Repeatedly setting to themselves
  2. Using Wall Drills (see page 114)
- with a partner(s):
  3. Using Partner Drills (see page 113), as one tosses and one sets
  4. Using Partner Drills (see page 113), setting back and forth
- with a Spoke-Drill formation (see page 113), but with students volleying as a group.

Photo 7.15 Setting the ball.

OVERHEAD SERVE

Technique

To execute the overhead serve effectively, students should

- assume a ready position
  1. Turning the body out toward the sideline
  2. Placing the nondominant foot forward
  3. Holding the ball at head level with fingertips of the nonstriking hand
- actively serve by
  4. tossing the ball 2 feet into the air without a spin (if not struck, the ball should land on the end line in front of the nondominant foot) and
  5. bringing the body square to the net, rotating the hips as in a *"throwing motion."*
- make ball contact with
  6. the hand cupped, on the heel of the hand in line with the thumb;
  7. the arm at full extension; and
  8. the arm slightly in front of the body (see photo 7.16).

Photo 7.16 The overhead serve.

Skills Practice

Have the students practice serving

- tossing a ball, letting it land in a *hula hoop* placed in front of the nondominant foot;
- using Wall Drills (see page 114);
- using Partner Drills (see page 113); and
- over a net in groups of six to nine on each side of the net (start close and move back from the net as the serves become more successful).

UNDERHAND SERVE

Technique

To execute the underhand serve effectively, students should

- assume a ready position
  1. Placing the nondominant foot forward, bending slightly forward from the waist
  2. Holding the ball in the nonstriking hand, palm up, arm extended out in front of the body, slightly higher than the waist
  3. Making a fist with the striking hand, knuckles turned down, arm straight, held to the rear
  4. Keeping their eyes on the ball
- actively serve by
  5. swinging the arm forward like a pendulum;
  6. contacting the ball with the fist; and
  7. striking the ball out of the hand at a 45-degree angle to the floor (see photo 7.17).

Photo 7.17   The underhand serve.

Skills Practice

Have the students practice serving

- using Wall Drills (see page 114);

- using Partner Drills (see page 113);

- over a net in groups of six to nine on each side of the net (start close and move back from the net as the serves become more successful).

chapter 8

TEAM-ORIENTED ACTIVITIES

Watch television at almost any hour of the day or night, and you cannot help but get caught up in the fast-paced age of change. Computerized technology such as television and audio remotes and coast-to-coast telecommunication updates all facilitate change, creating excitement and desire for immediate gratification. As a people, we have come to demand change, even expect it, in almost all facets of daily living. Exercise is no exception. Just look at the diverse, high-tech exercise equipment available in the marketplace for individuals looking for fun and enjoyment through diversity as they develop fitness. Your students are no different.

The following *team-oriented activities* are designed for use as alternatives to the more traditional sport-activity units of basketball, football, and other sports. These activities are structured to involve more students in a particular game activity and provide more opportunity for skill development through repetition and reinforcement. In general, they are high-paced, ever-changing, fun activities that challenge students of all levels while maximizing the opportunity for success.

Each *team-oriented activity* is ready to be "inserted" into the modular lesson format (table 3.1), much as you did with the *warm-ups* and *health-related fitness concepts*. For ease of reference, activities are presented as in chapter 7 under the general headings of catching/throwing, kicking, and striking. Although activities are categorized by one of these predominant skills, there is, of course, overlap in many fitness/sport activities and skills areas. Within each level, games are listed alphabetically. Table 8.1 lists activities by predominant skill and classification level to help you quickly find a particular game or activity.

Activities are grouped as well in a progression from the easiest to the most advanced, as denoted by their classification of entry level (I), intermediate (II), or exit level (III). Although the comparative degree of difficulty among some of the activities or skills is minimal, we have attempted to establish a logical progression for each category, taking into account things such as lever length (short to long), eye-hand eye-foot coordination (large ball to small/stationary ball to moving ball), and team strategies (end-line games to smaller goal games), all while promoting fitness, problem solving, and social skills in a fun, action-packed environment.

Each activity follows a similar format to help you maximize its use:

- Section 1 states a *purpose* to help you identify the major skills that are targeted.

- Section 2, *assessment objectives*, provides two to three benchmarks that relate back to tables 4.4 (page 34) and 4.5 (page 35). Use the benchmark criteria to help in evaluating students for a given activity.

- Section 3 lists the *materials* you will need to effectively run your class.

- Section 4 refers you back to chapter 7 for appropriate *skill-development activities*.

- Section 5 describes the *activity* in detail, often with options for adding even more variety to your class.

At the end of each activity, in boldface type, a *teaching focus* is provided to help you "zero" in on the important teaching points of the lesson. This format will provide you with a blueprint for a "tried-and-tested" activity module.

We have a sign over our gym doors that reads, "Come and be surprised! . . ." It is a motto that students embrace as they develop greater skills and fitness levels over three years of modular programming.

Table 8.1 Team Activities Listed by Predominant Skill and Level

Catching/Throwing	Kicking	Striking
Basketball Shoot-Out (I) (page 147)	Amoeba Soccer (I) (page 170)	Beach Volleyball (I) (page 191)
Beat "Michael Jordan" (I) (page 147)	Elephant Ball (I) (page 171)	Big-Ball Tennis (I) (page 192)
Hooper (I) (page 148)	End-line Soccer (I) (page 173)	Boxball (I) (page 192)
Hot Shots (I) (page 150)	Partner Kickball (I) (page 174)	End-line Hockey (I) (page 194)
Pass-Over (I) (page 150)	Punt-Over (I) (page 175)	Hand Hockey (I) (page 195)
Platform Football (I) (page 151)	Two Base-Alley	Sock-Over (I) (page 196)
Team Handball (I) (page 153)	Kickball (I) (page 175)	Targetball (I) (page 197)
Basket-A-Rama (II) (page 154)	Captain and Crew (II) (page 177)	Four-Corner
Platform Basketball (II) (page 155)	Modified Six-Player	Hockey (II) (page 198)
Quadrant Football (II) (page 156)	Soccer (II) (page 179)	Modified Cricket (II) (page 199)
Reaction Ball (II) (page 158)	Multicone Soccer (II) (page 180)	One-Wall
Repeat Baseball (II) (page 159)	Obstacle Kickball (II) (page 182)	Handball (II) (page 201)
Three Base-Basketball/	Scotch Foursome (II) (page 184)	Pillo Polo (II) (page 202)
Football (II) (page 161)	Indoor Soccer (III) (page 185)	Punch Ball (II) (page 203)
Ultimate Football (II) (page 162)	Medal Play (III) (page 186)	Quadrant
Arena Football (III) (page 164)	Speedball (III) (page 187)	Volleyball (II) (page 204)
Full-Court Basketball (III) (page 165)	Ultimate Rugby (III) (page 189)	Sticks and Kicks (II) (page 205)
Goal Ball (III) (page 166)		Three-Court
3-on-3 Half-Court		Volleyball (II) (page 207)
Basketball (III) (page 167)		Floor Hockey (III) (page 208)
Transitional Lacrosse (III) (page 168)		Garbage-Can
		Baseball (III) (page 209)
		Paddle Tennis (III) (page 211)
		Softball (III) (page 211)
		Volleyball (III) (page 212)
		Walleyball (III) (page 213)

CATCHING/THROWING

The game activities presented here focus on *catching/throwing* skills. They involve shooting, rolling, passing, running, catching, teamwork, and cooperation and will develop a variety of fitness components, as well as the intended catching/throwing skills.

Remember that activities are listed alphabetically by level of difficulty. If you refer to table 8.1 on page 146, you can quickly locate a particular game activity by page number.

CATCHING/THROWING SKILLS

BASKETBALL SHOOT-OUT (I)

Purpose:

- To develop catching/throwing skills related to basketball

Assessment Objectives:

- To what extent can students dribble with either hand?
- When receiving a pass, do students move to the ball?
- Can the students use a variety of shots to make baskets?

Materials:

- 1 basketball for each student
- As many baskets as possible

Skill Development:

- See *basketball-related skills* (page 116): dribbling, chest pass, bounce pass, and shooting.

Activity:

- Divide the class into as many teams as there are baskets.
- Each team shoots, one player at a time, from a relay format starting at the foul line:
  - First shot is a foul shot (2 points).
  - Follow up shot by rebounding and taking a layup (1 point).
  - Return ball to next player with a chest or bounce pass.
- Play four quarters of 3 minutes each:
  - Add up scores after each quarter.
  - Rotate baskets each quarter.
- **Stress working at individual skill levels to learn and improve performance.**

BEAT "MICHAEL JORDAN" (I)

Purpose:

- To develop a wide variety of shots and shooting accuracy while also teaching students to follow their shots

Assessment Objectives:

- To what extent do students follow the release of their shots?
- Do students take the easiest shot available?
- Do students use correct form in shooting a one-handed jump shot?

Materials:

- 1 basketball per student
- As many baskets as possible

Skill Development:

- See *basketball-related skills* (page 116): dribbling, shooting, and rebounding.

Activity:

- Divide the class into equal groups at each basket.
- Have students at each basket count off sequentially.
- Each student plays in order—one student at a time against an imaginary "Michael Jordan."
- When playing, the student must shoot a shot from outside the "key" and follow it up with a layup. Students keep repeating this process:
  - 1 point is awarded for each basket made.
  - For each missed shot, "Michael Jordan" is awarded 2 points.
  - The first person (student or "Michael") to reach 10 points wins, and the next student plays.
- You may wish to have students rotate baskets after they play, having all the students who beat "Michael" playing at one basket, in a sort of tournament.
- **Stress proper shooting and rebounding techniques.**

HOOPER (I)

Purpose:

- To develop catching and throwing skills in a game of spatial awareness while building team and cooperative effort

Assessment Objectives:

- Do students move to the ball or wait for it to come to them?
- Do students use a variety of passing techniques to get the ball to the *"hoopers"*?
- To what extent do students cooperate to achieve their goals?

Materials:

- Large gym space or field
- 1 basketball for every 3 students
- 4 hula hoops
- Pinnies (2 colors)

Skill Development:

- See *basketball-related skills* (page 116): chest pass, bounce pass, and overhead pass.

Activity:

- Randomly divide the class into two equal teams (see diagram 8.1).
- Place two students from each team in the end zone:
  - These students are referred to as the *"hoopers."*
  - Each is given a hula hoop and must keep both his hands on the hoop at all times.
- Each team attacks its own end zone in order to score:
  - Players must use a variety of passes to move the ball toward their own end zone.
  - Students cannot run with the ball.
  - A team scores when its passes a ball into its end zone, through its hoop before the ball hits the ground.

    1 point is awarded for each score.
  - After a score, on an interception, or on a dropped pass, the other team is awarded the ball.
- **Stress movement without the ball, proper passing techniques, cooperation, and teamwork** (Rohnke 1989).

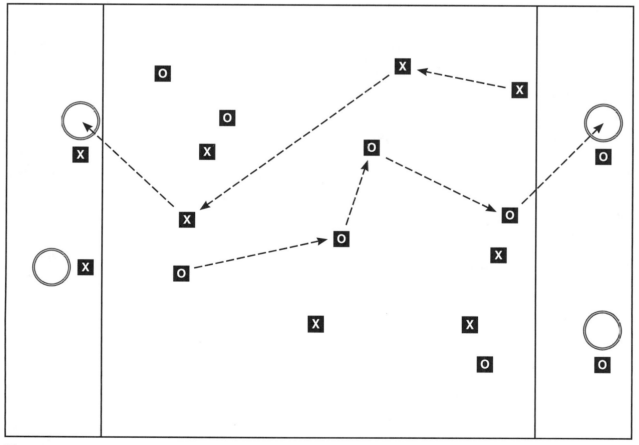

Diagram 8.1

HOT SHOTS (I)

Purpose:
- To develop catching/throwing skills related to basketball

Assessment Objectives:
- Do students shoot the basketball from a variety of areas?
- Can the student shoot both a jump shot and a layup?
- Can the student dribble without looking at the ball?

Materials:
- 1 basketball for each student
- As many baskets as possible

Skill Development:
- See *basketball-related skills* (page 116): dribbling, chest pass, bounce pass, and shooting.

Activity:
- Equally divide the students among the number of available baskets.
- Each student gets to shoot for 1 minute:
  - Other students count the number of successful shots.
  - Shots outside the "key" count as 2 points.
  - Shots taken inside the "key" count as 1 point.
- Each minute, another student shoots until there is a winner at each basket.
- Winners play off to determine a class *"hot shot"* champion.
- **Stress shooting technique and strategies for maximizing points.**

PASS-OVER (I)

Purpose:
- To develop catching/throwing skills using a football

Assessment Objectives:
- Can the students throw a football for accuracy?
- To what extent can students catch a football while standing still?
- Do students move to an open zone without the football?

Materials:
- 1 football for every 2 students

Skill Development:
- See *football-related skills* (page 121): passing and catching.

Activity:

- Divide the class into two teams and then into two groups per team.
- Set the teams into position as per diagram 8.2:
  - *x* plays in an offensive area and tries to intercept throws from *O* to *o*, throwing the footballs to *X* players.
  - Players score by successfully throwing a ball to their end zone and having a teammate catch a pass in that zone (only players designated *O* and *X* can score points).
- Receivers must stay within their designated zones, and those throwing must stay within theirs:
  - All catches are rethrown to the appropriate middle zones.
- Use 8 to 12 balls, and start play by tossing the balls to the middle zones.
- Play four quarters and record the score after each quarter:
  - Rotate zones after each quarter.
  - Switch sides at halftime.
- **Focus on throwing accurate spirals, catching technique, and moving without the ball to create a passing lane.**

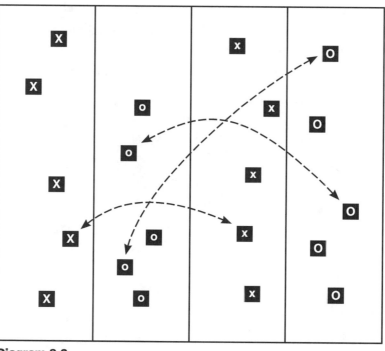

Diagram 8.2

PLATFORM FOOTBALL (I)

Purpose:

- To develop passing/catching skills with a football while analyzing, and solving problems about, defensive situations through movement without the ball

Materials:

- Large gym space

- 4-6 Nerf-type footballs for the game activity
- 1 real football for every 2 students
- Pinnies (2 colors)

Skill Development:

- See *football-related skills* (page 121): passing and catching.

Activity:

- Divide the class into two teams (see diagram 8.3).
- Within each team, members are positioned either on a mat or on the floor:
  - Floor players serve as the quarterbacks.
  - Mat people serve as the receivers.
- On the command "Go," players on a given team try to pass the ball to their receivers on the mats:
  - 1 point is awarded for each successful catch.
  - After a catch, the ball is then thrown back to any one of the "quarterbacks."
  - Opposing players try to intercept the ball and throw it to their receivers.
  - Use a multiple number of balls to maintain a high level of activity.
- Rotate receivers and quarterbacks every few minutes so students have an opportunity to play in both roles.
- **Stress passing accuracy and movement without the ball to form passing lanes.**

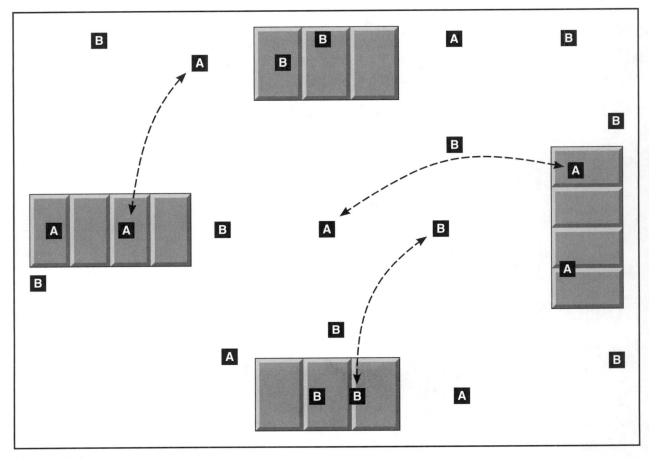

Diagram 8.3

TEAM HANDBALL (I)

Purpose:

- To develop catching/throwing skills at varied levels (ground, bounce, fly, and line drive) with round balls and to develop team concepts of movement without the ball—using triangles and filling lanes for maintenance of court balance

Assessment Objectives:

- Can students catch a ball while moving?
- To what extent do students move without the ball?
- Do students create passing lanes for themselves?

Materials:

- 1 softball for every 2 students
- 1 basketball for every 2 students
- 1 football for every 2 students
- 1 sponge-type ball that bounces
- 2 plastic bowling pins
- 8 cones
- Pinnies (preferably 2 or 3 colors)

Skill Development:

- See *basketball-related skills* (page 116): bounce pass, chest pass, and overhead pass.

Activity:

- Divide the class into three even teams:
  - Choose a system for rotation (round-robin, king of the court, etc.).
- Set the teams into position as shown in diagram 8.4 (two groups on the court, one on the sideline).
- The bowling pins serve as goals and are placed approximately 2 to 3 feet from the end walls of the gym:
  - A goal is scored if the bowling pin falls in any way.
  - 1 point is awarded for each goal.
  - Form a crease by placing four cones around each pin.
  - Only the defensive team is allowed in the crease.
  - Relate the "crease" to other sports (hockey, lacrosse, etc.).
  - Each team should have a goalie.
- Explain the team concept of positions for goalies, forwards, backs, and centers:
  - Review offensive balance using triangles.
  - Review court balance by filling lanes.
  - Encourage students to apply math concepts in passing off the walls, shooting off the walls at angles to the pin, and by using bounce passes and bounce shots.

- Play 3-minute games, then switch on-court groups with sideline groups.
- Explain the rules:
  - Each game starts with a jump ball. After a goal is scored, play resumes with another jump ball at center court.
  - Players may only take three steps with the ball or three dribbles or hold the ball for 3 seconds.
  - Players are encouraged to pass the ball.
  - Defense is played in a basketball-type fashion.
- **Focus on game sense through spatial awareness and passing the ball quickly from player to player.**

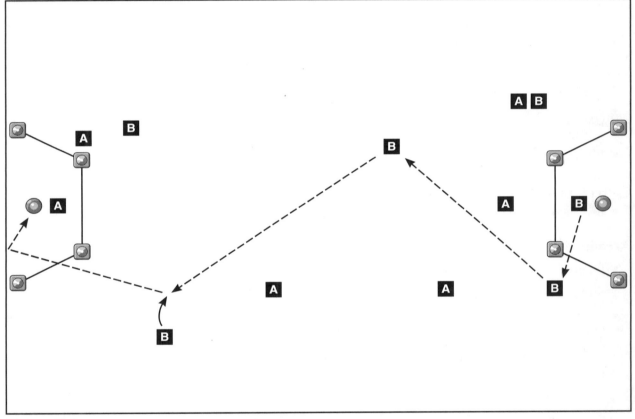

Diagram 8.4

BASKET-A-RAMA (II)

Purpose:

- To develop catching/throwing skills related to shooting a basketball

Assessment Objectives:

- Can the student shoot both a jump shot and a layup?
- Do students use their vertical jumping ability when rebounding?
- Can the student dribble without looking at the ball?

Materials:

- 1 basketball for each student
- As many baskets as possible

Skill Development:

- See *basketball-related skills* (page 116): dribbling, bounce pass, chest pass, and shooting.

Activity:

- Divide the students evenly at each available basket.
- Two balls are placed on the foul line at each basket.
- On the command "Go," two students go head-to-head and try to score three baskets at a given basket:
  - The first student to win keeps the court and the next student challenges him.
  - The losing student rotates to the next basket so students are competing against a large number of their classmates (Dauer and Pangrazi 1986).
- **Stress shot selection and rebounding skills.**

PLATFORM BASKETBALL (II)

Purpose:

- To develop throwing and catching skills along with shooting skills in a modified basketball-type game and to stress the use of triangles to create passing lanes and movement without the ball

Assessment Objectives:

- When receiving a basketball pass, do the students step toward the ball?
- When shooting a basketball, do students focus on an appropriate target?

Materials:

- 2 basketball baskets
- 1 basketball for every student
- 7 mats (4-by-8-foot)

Skill Development:

- See *basketball-related skills* (page 116): dribbling; bounce, chest, and overhead passes; shooting; and rebounding.

Activity:

- Divide the class into two or three even teams based on class size (two teams play at a time).
- One team (A) takes up positions on the mats (platforms) as depicted in diagram 8.5 (one or two players per mat works best).
- The other team (B) members serve as chasers and are not allowed on the mats. They are encouraged to move without the ball, being conscious of passing lanes.
- Each team is given a ball before starting the game, and a third ball is introduced later.

- Play is started, and the *"platform"* team tries to score at one end of the gym while the *"chasing"* team tries to score at the other.
- The *"platform"* team tries to move the ball from mat to mat using quick passes (chest, bounce, etc.) until it is able to take a good shot (2 points per basket).
- The *"chasing"* team is allowed to pass or dribble the ball until it can take a good shot (2 points per basket).
- Either team can steal the ball from the other team provided the *"platform"* team stays on the mats and the *"chasers"* stay off.
- After a basket, the ball is given to the nearest player on the other team.
- Play 2- or 3-minute games before rotating teams from platform to chaser. If using three teams, rotate one team in and one team out every 3 minutes (or let winners keep the court).
- **Encourage students to pass the ball while focusing on the naturally predetermined passing lanes.**

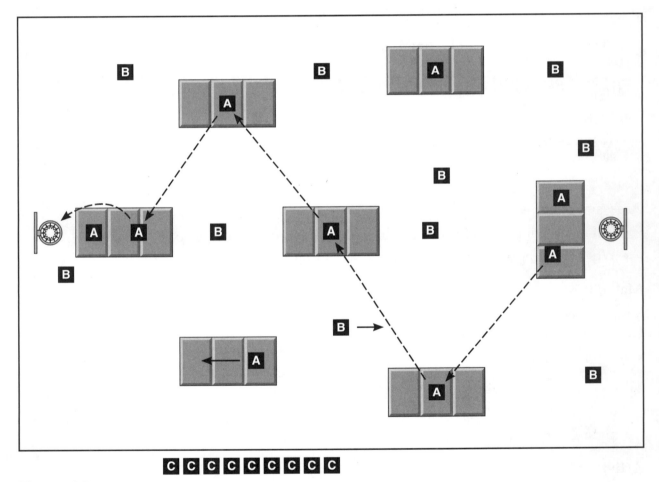

Diagram 8.5

QUADRANT FOOTBALL (II)

Purpose:

- To develop passing/catching skills with a football

Assessment Objectives:
- Can the students throw accurate forward passes?
- Can the students throw a football for distance?
- Can the students successfully catch forward passes?

Materials:
- Large gym space
- 4 large mats
- Pinnies (2 colors)
- 2-4 sponge-type footballs for the game activity
- 1 football for every 3 students

Skill Development:
- See *football-related skills* (page 121): stance, cadence, handoff, quarterback/center exchange, and pass patterns.

Activity:
- Divide the class into two equally numbered teams and set the students into position as denoted in diagram 8.6.

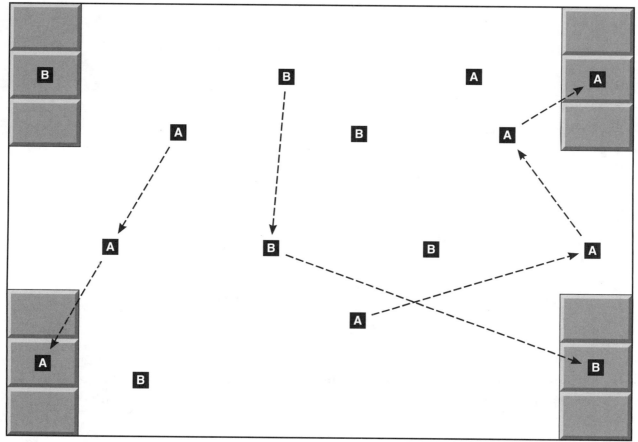

Diagram 8.6

- Players on the floor try to move the ball close to their respective mats at diagonally opposed ends of the gym by passing from teammate to teammate:
  - No one is allowed to run with the ball.
  - Passed balls may be intercepted.
  - A dropped pass is a turnover.
  - 1 point is scored for each ball successfully passed to and caught on a mat.
  - After a touchdown, the ball is given to the closest defensive player.
- Play four quarters, and rotate the mats each quarter, as well as the receivers:
  - Use two to four balls at one time to maintain a high level of activity and decision making.
- **Stress movement without the ball and strategies for scoring, taking into account the mats are at each end of the gym.**

REACTION BALL (II)

Purpose:
- To develop catching/throwing skills at varied levels (ground, bounce, fly, and line drive) with round balls and to develop team concepts of movement without the ball using triangles and filling lanes for maintenance of court balance

Assessment Objectives:
- Can students catch and release a ball while moving?
- To what extent do students move without the ball?
- Do students create passing lanes for themselves?

Materials:
- 1 softball for every 2 students
- 1 basketball for every 2 students
- 1 football for every 2 students
- 1 sponge type-ball that bounces
- 2 plastic bowling pins
- 8 cones
- Pinnies (preferably 2-3 colors)

Skill Development:
- See *basketball-related skills* (page 116): chest, bounce, and overhead passes.

Activity:
- Divide the class into three even teams:
  - Choose a system for rotation (round-robin, king of the court, etc.).
- Set the teams into position as shown in diagram 8.4, page 154 (two groups on court, one on sideline).

- The bowling pins serve as goals and are placed approximately 2 to 3 feet from the end walls of the gym:
  - A goal is scored if the bowling pin falls in any way.
  - 1 point is awarded for each goal.
  - Form a crease by placing four cones around each pin.
  - Only the defensive team is allowed in the crease.
  - Relate the "crease" to other sports (hockey, lacrosse, etc.).
  - Each team should have a goalie.
  - *A 10-second shot clock is in effect,* that forces students to focus more on *"fast breaking,"* taking the game to a higher level of play whereby problem solving becomes almost automatic (a reaction).
- Explain the team concepts of positions for goalies, forwards, backs, and centers:
  - Review offensive balance using triangles.
  - Review court balance by filling lanes.
  - Encourage students to apply math concepts by passing off walls, shooting off walls at angles to the pin, and using bounce-type passes and shots.
- Play 3-minute games, then switch on-court groups with sideline group.
- Explain the rules:
  - Each game starts with a jump ball. After a goal is scored, play resumes with another jump ball at center court.
  - Players may only take three steps with the ball, take three dribbles, or hold the ball for 3 seconds.
  - Players are encouraged to pass the ball.
  - Defense is played in a basketball-type fashion.
- **Focus on game sense through spatial awareness and passing the ball quickly from player to player.**

REPEAT BASEBALL (II)

Purpose:

- To develop catching/throwing skills relative to softball/baseball, as well as associated striking skills

Assessment Objectives:

- Can students catch both fly and ground balls?
- Can students throw a ball accurately?
- To what extent can students strike balls of varied sizes?

Materials:

- A large gym space
- 4 large mats
- 1 safety bat
- Various-sized indoor-type balls for the game activity

- 1 indoor-type softball for every 2 students

Skill Development:

- See *softball-related skills* (pages 128 and 138): catching, throwing, and hitting.

Activity:

- Divide the class into two equal teams.
- Set up teams as denoted in diagram 8.7, using unfolded mats as bases.
- Play starts with the teacher pitching to the first batter (underhand, softball-type pitch):
  - Use a variety of soft, indoor-type balls, and reduce the size of the ball each inning.
  - There are no "foul" balls. Any contact with the bat puts the ball in play.
  - The batter hits the ball and continues to run the bases in order until called out by the teacher.
  - 1 point is awarded for each base safely reached.
  - The team in the field must get control of the ball and throw the ball to two bases (double play) before throwing the ball home to the catcher, stopping play (the batter is out).
  - After everyone on the first team has been up, teams switch.
- **Stress proper hitting, fielding, and throwing techniques.**

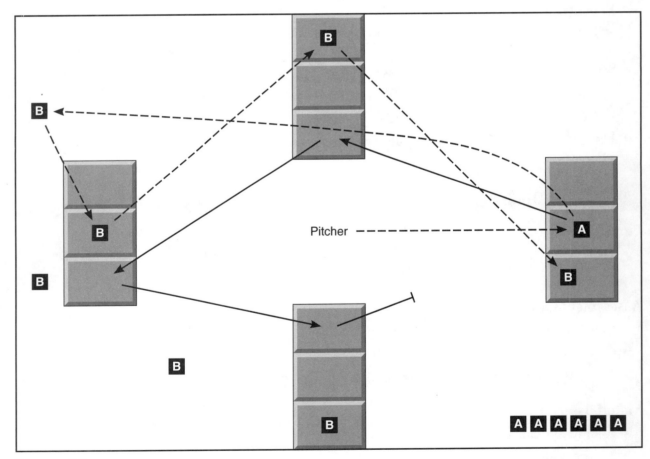

Diagram 8.7

THREE BASE-BASEBALL/FOOTBALL (II)

Purpose:

- To develop punting and placekicking skills, along with throwing/catching skills

Assessment Objectives:

- Can students kick a stationary football with proper technique?
- Can students master kicking a moving target?
- Do the students use proper mechanics when catching and throwing a football?

Materials:

- 1 football for every student
- 1 kicking tee
- 5 cones
- 3 large mats

Skill Development:

- See *football-related skills* (page 131): punting and placekicking.

Activity:

- Divide the class into two even teams.
- Set the teams into position as per diagram 8.8 (*A* players are up, *B* players in the field):
  - *A* players must stay in the "dugout" until they are up.
  - *B* players spread out in the field as in baseball.
- Everyone on one team gets up, then teams switch.
- The player who is *"up"* puts the ball into play by kicking it:
  - Kicking off a tee in the first inning
  - Punting it the second inning
- After kicking the ball, the player runs to first and third bases and home plate as many times as possible before the team in the field controls the ball, throws the ball to two bases, and then home, stopping play:
  - Players score 1 point for every base they touch.
  - Alternative scoring methods might include
    automatic points for hitting the far wall with a kick (5 points for a homer);
    home run plus earned points;
    an automatic out for catching a fly ball; and
    3 points for catching a fly ball but play continues.
- **Stress catching, throwing, and kicking skills (mechanics).**

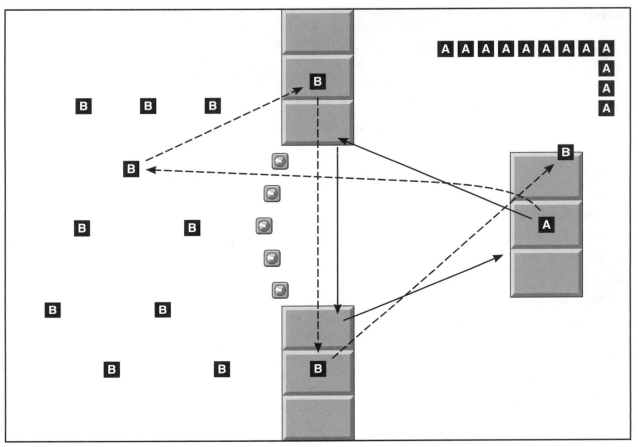

Diagram 8.8

ULTIMATE FOOTBALL (II)

Purpose:
- To develop the skills of catching/throwing, open-field running, dodging, and placekicking

Assessment Objectives:
- When throwing a football, do the students step with the proper foot?
- Can the students catch a football while moving toward the ball?
- Can the students catch a football while moving away from the ball?
- Do students transfer their weight to the outside foot when making a dodge?
- Can the students kick a stationary ball as in placekicking?

Materials:
- 1 football for every 2 students
- 1 kicking tee
- Pinnies (preferably 2 colors)

Skill Development:
- See *football-related skills* (page 121): catching and passing.

Activity:

- Divide the class into two teams.
- Set the teams into position as per diagram 8.9.
  - Play starts with one team kicking off to the other team.
- Receiving team gets control of the ball and moves ball toward its end zone using either lateral passes or forward passes among teammates:
  - The ball may not be held for more than 5 seconds.
  - Defense is played in basketball style.
  - No more than three steps can be taken with the ball.
- An interception or a dropped ball constitutes a turnover.
- A touchdown is scored when a ball is successfully passed and received in the offensive end zone:
  - 6 points is awarded for each touchdown.
- **Stress movement without the ball to get open and movement with the ball in the form of dodging and fleeing; also stress throwing on the run.**

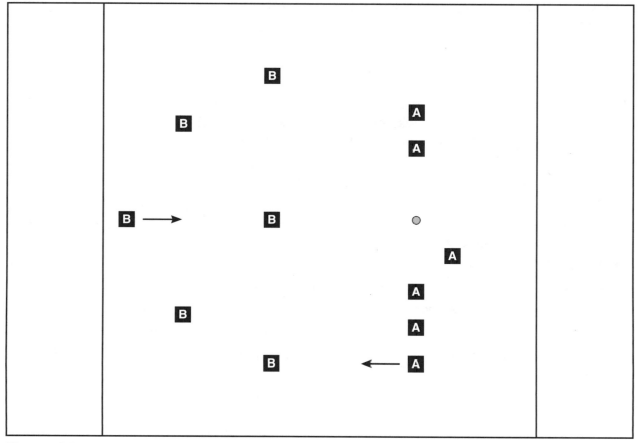

Diagram 8.9

ARENA FOOTBALL (III)

Purpose:

- To develop kicking, passing, and catching skills relative to football

Assessment Objectives:

- Can students run a proper pass pattern and catch the ball?
- Are students more successful at kicking a stationary or a moving ball?
- Do students realize the different roles (positions) necessary to make a team successful?

Materials:

- 12 cones for sideline markers
- 1 modified football for every 3 students
- 1 pinny for every 2 students
- 1 tear-away flag belt for each student

Skill Development:

- See *football-related skills* (page 121): stance, cadence, handoff, quarterback / center exchange, and pass patterns.

Activity:

- Divide the class into two teams.
- Within the two teams there will be an offensive team and a defensive team (students should be encouraged to rotate among positions: quarterback, center, line, etc.). Students stay, however, on offense or defense until halftime, at which time they switch.
- One team, determined by a coin toss, kicks off to start play.
- The other team's offensive unit gets control of the ball and tries to return it:
  - The team has four plays to reach either midcourt (midfield) for an automatic first down or the opponent's end zone for a score. Offensive and defensive alignments should be relative to football, similar to the alignment shown in diagram 8.10.
- All football rules apply:
  - Players are "tackled" by ripping one flag off their belts.
  - Rushing is held off to a count of "two-one thousand."
  - All extra points must be rushed (1 point) or passed into the end zone (2 points).
  - Offensive and defensive teams are rotated in and out according to downs and the game situation.
- **Focus on setting students up in proper positions and running logical football-type plays.**

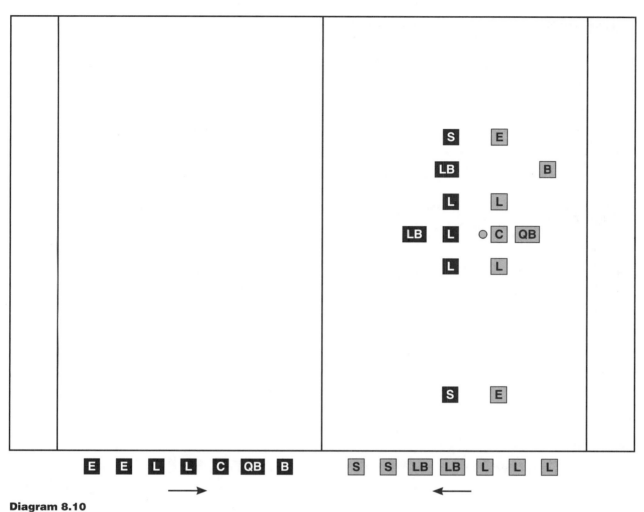

Diagram 8.10

FULL-COURT BASKETBALL (III)

Purpose:

- To develop catching/throwing skills related to basketball

Assessment Objectives:

- To what extent do students fill lanes to balance the court?
- Do students move without the ball?

Materials:

- 1 basketball for each student
- As many baskets as possible

Skill Development:

- See *basketball-related skills* (page 116): dribbling, chest and bounce passes, shooting, and defensive stance.

Activity:

- Divide the class into teams of five.

- Explain the rules for full-court basketball:
  - Establish boundary lines.
  - When a ball changes possession after a rebound or a basket, the defensive team must drop back to its half of the court (no pressing).
  - Defensive team plays a 2-1-2 zone.
  - Offensive team should be encouraged to move without the ball through the passing lanes.
- Play 4- or 5-minute games based on class size, and rotate teams accordingly.
- **Focus on team play, movement, and court balance.**

GOAL BALL (III)

Purpose:

- To develop catching/throwing skills at varied levels (ground, bounce, fly, and line drive) with round balls and footballs and to develop movement without the ball using triangles and filling lanes to maintain court balance

Assessment Objectives:

- Do students catch and throw with proper mechanics?
- How well do the students move to get open without the ball?
- Can students catch and throw while moving?

Materials:

- 1 softball for every 2 students
- 1 basketball for every 2 students
- 1 football for every 2 students
- 1 sponge-type ball that bounces
- 2 goals or mats
- 8 cones
- Pinnies (preferably 2 colors)

Skill Development:

- See *basketball-related skills* (page 116): bounce, chest, and overhead passes.

Activity:

- Divide the class into two even teams, and then subdivide each team into two groups.
- Set the teams into position as shown in diagram 8.11 (two groups on court, two on sideline).
- Goals are either used or formed by turning and standing two mats on their ends:
  - A goal is scored if the ball hits the net inside the goal or the two inner panels of the mat.
  - 1 point is scored for each goal.
  - Form a crease by placing four cones around each goal.
  - Only the defensive team is allowed in the crease.
  - Relate the "crease" to other sports (hockey, lacrosse, etc.).

- Explain the team concepts of positions for goalies, forwards, backs, and centers:
  - Review offensive balance using triangles.
  - Review court balance by filling lanes.
- Play 3-minute games, 6-on-6, then switch on-court groups with sideline groups.
- Explain the rules:
  - Each game starts with a jump ball.
  - Players may only take two steps with the ball.
  - Players are encouraged to pass the ball (sideline players may be used).
  - Defense is played in a basketball-type fashion.
- **Focus on game sense through spatial awareness and passing the ball quickly from player to player.**

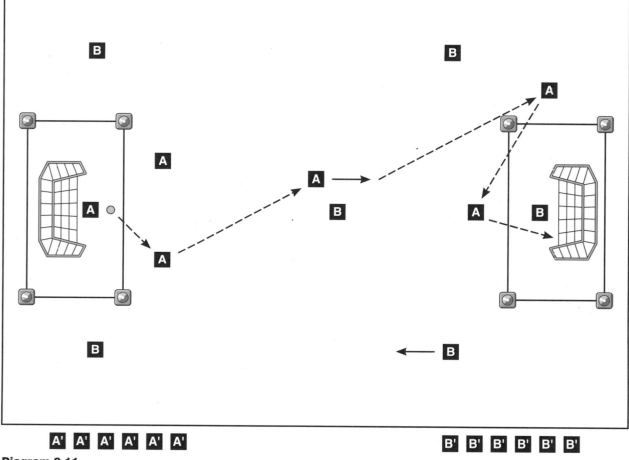

Diagram 8.11

3-ON-3 HALF-COURT BASKETBALL (III)

Purpose:

- To develop catching/throwing skills related to basketball while playing as a team

Assessment Objectives:
- Can students see other players while still controlling their dribbling?
- Do students realize and perform their roles in certain set plays (e.g., pass and pick away, etc.)?

Materials:
- 1 basketball for each student
- As many baskets as possible

Skill Development:
- See *basketball-related skills* (page 116): dribbling, chest and bounce passes, shooting; *teach*:
  - pass and pick away,
  - pass and pick to, and
  - pick-and-roll.

Activity:
- Divide the class into teams of three.
- Explain the rules for half-court basketball:
  - Establish boundary lines.
  - A ball hitting the rim by one team must be brought out past the foul line by the defensive team before it goes on offense.
  - When starting the game, starting play after a basket, or when a foul is called, the ball starts up top and must be "checked."
  - The defensive team must play a zone or man-to-man defense (structure the defense).
- Play 3- or 4-minute games based on class size, and rotate teams.
- **Focus on team concepts of passing, picking, and defense.**

TRANSITIONAL LACROSSE (III)

Purpose:
- To develop scooping, passing, and catching skills relative to lacrosse

Assessment Objectives:
- Can students throw at a still target while standing still using a lacrosse stick?
- Can students catch and throw with a lacrosse stick while moving?
- In transitional play, do the students pass to the open player?

Materials:
- 4 floor hockey (or spongy softball-size balls) balls
- 1 lacrosse stick for each student
- Cones
- 2 large mats
- 1 (4-by-6-foot) mat or an indoor hockey cage

Skill Development:

- See *lacrosse-related skills* (page 126): scooping, throwing, and catching.

Activity:

- Divide the class into two teams.
- The object of the game is for the at-bat team to throw the ball as far as possible using a lacrosse stick and then score points by running quickly between the two bases (see diagram 8.12):
  - 1 point is awarded per base.
- Bonus points can be added for long-distance accuracy:
  - 5 points is awarded for hitting the far wall.
  - 10 points is awarded for hitting the far basketball backboard.
- The "fielding" team tries to catch a fly ball (3 points) or scoops a ground ball, passing the ball at least once to a teammate who then shoots it into the goal:
  - Bounce shots should be encouraged but must be taken from behind the two cones designating the "target area."
- Missed shots are scooped up and brought back out past the "target area" before being shot again.
- When a goal is scored, play stops and the next member of the "throwing" team is up.
- Everyone gets up on one team, and then teams switch positions.
- **Focus on the fundamental skills of scooping, passing, and catching.**

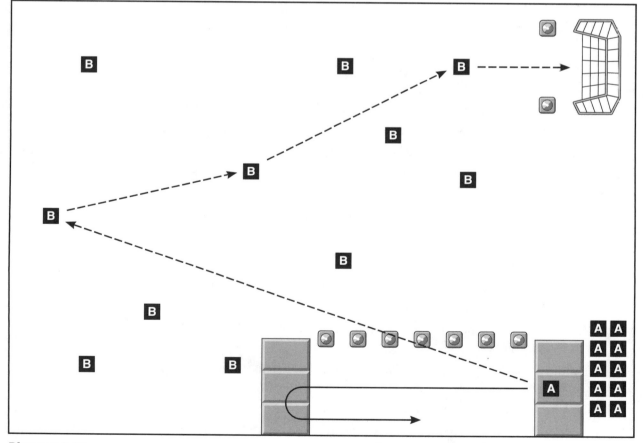

Diagram 8.12

KICKING

The predominant skill targeted under *kicking* is, of course, kicking, but many of these activities also involve catching/throwing skills, as well as cooperative teamwork, problem solving, and strategy development. Once again, activities are listed alphabetically by level.

KICKING SKILLS

AMOEBA SOCCER (I)

Purpose:

- To develop the following soccer skills: dribbling, short passes, long passes, trapping, head balls, and goalie skills (including punting); to develop movement without the ball using triangles and filling lanes for maintaining field balance

Assessment Objectives:

- Can students adjust their kicking styles to hit a small target?
- Can students control a moving ball without first trapping it?
- To what extent can students kick a rolling ball for accuracy?

Materials:

- 1 soccer ball for every 2 students
- 8 cones or 4 soccer goals

Skill Development:

- See *soccer-related skills* (page 134): passing, trapping, and throw-ins.

Activity:

- Divide the class into two even teams (or four if you have a large class).
- Set the teams into position as shown in diagram 8.13 (use two fields if you have four teams).
- Explain the team concept of balance, keeping in mind that there are no boundaries and positions:
  - Review offensive balance using triangles.
  - Review field balance by filling lanes.
- Explain the rules:
  - All players except the goalie must use their feet, in keeping with soccer rules.
  - There are two goalies per goal.
  - There is no out-of-bounds, and goals can be scored in either direction through the designated cones and/or soccer goals.
  - 1 point is awarded per goal (ball passing through cones at a height of no higher than the goalie's head).
  - Two to three balls are in play at one time.
- **Focus on game sense through spatial awareness and physical conditioning because of the magnitude of field and number of balls in play.**

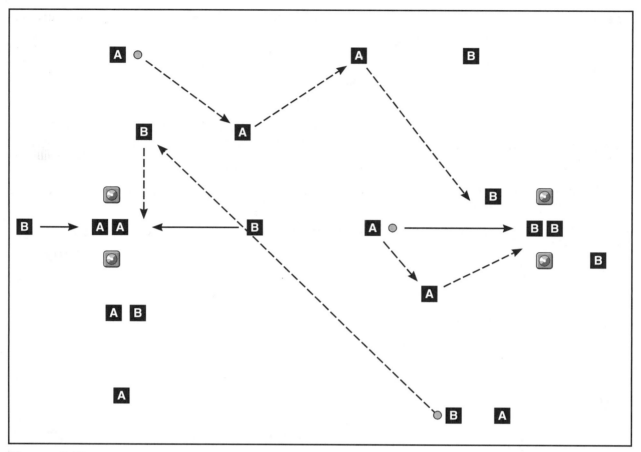

Diagram 8.13

ELEPHANT BALL (I)

Purpose:
- To develop the soccer skills of trapping, kicking, and goalkeeping

Assessment Objectives:
- Do students apply the proper trapping techniques to the situation?
- Do the students use the proper kicking technique on the oversized ball?
- Do goalkeepers move their bodies and their hands to make a save?

Materials:
- Large indoor or outdoor area
- Pinnies (2 colors)
- 1 ball, 3 or 4 feet in diameter
- 1 soccer ball for every 3 students

Skill Development:
- See *soccer-related skills* (page 134): passing and trapping.

Activity:

- Divide the class into two even teams.
- Set the teams into position as shown in diagram 8.14 (half the team is in goal in the end zone, and half the team is in between the two end zones trying to score).
- Goalies must stay within their designated end zones:
  - They may use any part of their bodies (including hands) to prevent balls from hitting the wall behind them.
  - All saves are returned to the offensive area by rolling the ball.
- The offensive players must abide by soccer rules and try to trap and shoot the balls (or pass to a teammate), scoring goals by hitting the wall behind the end zones:
  - Offensive players are not allowed in the end zones.
  - Offensive players should use an instep kick to move the ball because of its large size.
  - Chest traps become important for controlling the ball.
- Designate a certain height as acceptable for a goal, and count each goal as 1 point.
- Rotate goalies and offensive players every 3 minutes.
- **Focus on trapping and passing.**

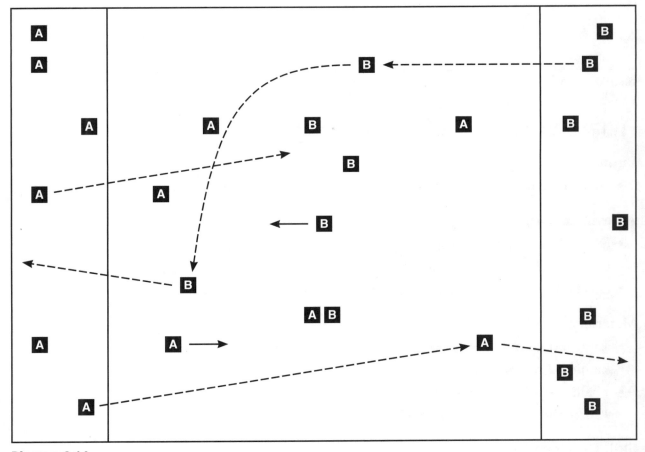

Diagram 8.14

END-LINE SOCCER (1)

Purpose:

- To develop trapping and kicking skills in a game-oriented environment and to develop catching skills with respect to the goalie portion of the game

Assessment Objectives:

- Do students use a variety of traps to meet a variety of situations?
- To what extent do the goalkeepers move their bodies behind their hands when making saves?
- Are students moving when making contact with a ball?

Materials:

- 1 soccer ball for each student
- 8 cones

Skill Development:

- See *soccer-related skills* (page 132): dribbling, passing, and trapping.

Activity:

- Divide the class into three even teams.
- Set the teams into position as shown in diagram 8.15 (*A* players in one end zone, *C* players in the other, and *B* players on offense in between the two end zones).

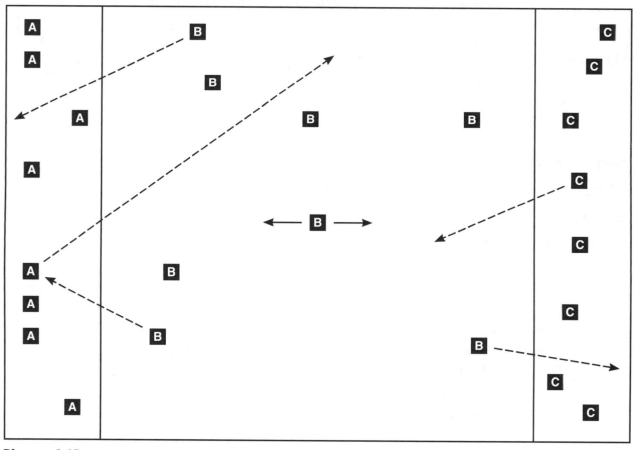

Diagram 8.15

- Goalies must stay within their designated end zones:
  - They may use any part of their bodies (including hands) to prevent balls from hitting the wall behind them.
  - All saves are returned to the offensive area.
- The *B* players must abide by soccer rules and try to trap and shoot the balls (or pass to a teammate), scoring goals by hitting the wall behind the end zones:
  - Offensive players are not allowed in the end zones.
  - Offensive players can score at either end of the gym.
- Designate a certain height as acceptable for a goal, and count each goal as 1 point:
  - Use balls and start play by tossing the balls to the offensive team.
- Rotate teams every 3 minutes.
- **Focus on trapping and passing and/or trap, turn, and pass.**

PARTNER KICKBALL (I)

Purpose:

- To develop kicking skills and apply them in a game setting that requires communication among teammates

Assessment Objectives:

- Do the students strategically place their kicks when up at bat?
- Do the students communicate and cooperate to limit the opposing team's score?
- To what extent do students use relay-type passes to achieve their goals?

Materials:

- 1 round, soft ball for every student
- 1 kicking tee .
- 4 large mats

Skill Development:

- See *football-related skills* (page 131): placekicking.

Activity:

- Divide the class into two teams.
- Pair each player from one team with a player on the other team (partners):
  - The partner on one team is the only player who can get her partner out, thus everyone must be involved in the game.
- One team gets up while the other team plays in the field as illustrated in diagram 8.7:
  - The player at bat kicks the ball off the tee and then runs continuously to as many bases as possible, up to four:
  - Dodging and fleeing tactics are to be encouraged.
  - 1 point is awarded for each base safely achieved.

- The fielding team must catch the ball and quickly relay it to the partner of the batter who in turn hits the runner with the ball using a chest pass and kickball rules (it cannot bounce or hit the runner in the head):
  - The focus is not on getting outs, but on limiting points.
  - Teamwork and communication skills are essential for success.
- After everyone on one team has been up, the teams switch.
- **Stress communication and the use of strategy for both the kicking and the fielding teams.**

PUNT-OVER (I)

Purpose:

- To develop punting kicking skills, along with catching skills

Assessment Objectives:

- Can students kick a moving ball using their legs as a lever arm?
- Do students move their feet as well as their hands when catching a punted ball?

Materials:

- 1 round ball and 1 football for every 2 students
- 16 cones

Skill Development:

- See *football-related skills* (page 131): punting.

Activity:

- Divide the class into two teams, then divide each team into two groups.
  - Set the teams into position as shown in diagram 8.2. *o* plays in an offensive area and tries to intercept punts from *x* to *X*, punting them to players in the *O* zone.
  - Players score by successfully punting a ball to their end zone and having a teammate catch a punt in that zone (only the *X* and *O* players can score points).
- Receivers must stay within their designated zones, those students punting must remain in theirs:
  - All catches are repunted to the appropriate middle zones.
- Use 8 to 12 balls, and start play by tossing the balls to the middle zones.
- Play four quarters, and record the score after each quarter:
  - Rotate zones after each quarter.
  - Switch sides at halftime.
- **Focus on contact when punting, catching technique, and moving without the ball to create a kicking lane.**

TWO BASE-ALLEY KICKBALL (I)

Purpose:

- To develop punting and placekicking skills, along with throwing skills

Assessment Objectives:

- Can students kick both a stationary and a moving ball?
- Can students throw with proper technique to hit stationary and moving targets?

Materials:

- 1 round, soft ball for every student
- 1 kicking tee
- As many cones as possible
- Large mats

Skill Development:

- See *football-related skills* (page 131): punting and placekicking.

Activity:

- Divide the class into three even teams.
- Set the teams into position as shown in diagram 8.16 (*A* players on one side of the alley, *B* players on the other, and *C* players up at bat):
  - *A* players must stay on their side of the alley.
  - *B* players must stay on their side.
  - *C* players are up first.

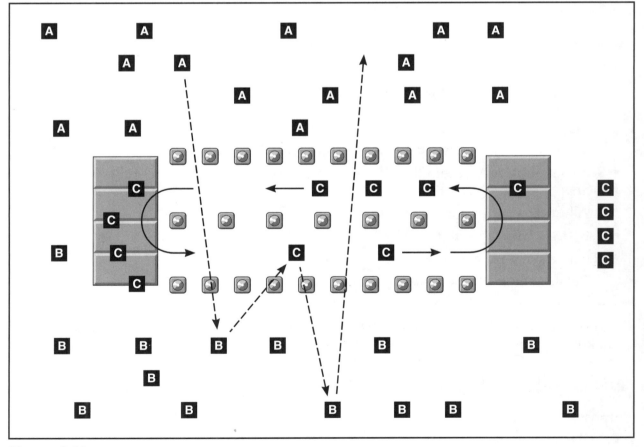

Diagram 8.16

- Everyone on one team gets up, then teams rotate (*A* to *B*, *B* to *C*, and *C* to *A*).
- The player who is "up" puts the ball into play by kicking it:
  - Punting it the first inning
  - Kicking off a tee the second inning
- After kicking the ball, the player runs to the far base and chooses to stay there, letting the next kicker get up, or run home:
  - Players score points (1) whenever they reach the base nearest to the dugout.
  - Players continue to run until they are hit by a thrown ball (chest pass) when they are off the base, at which time they return to the dugout to sit.
  - When all runners remain on a base for more than 3 seconds, play is discontinued and the next kicker is "up":

    There can be any number of runners on either of the two bases at any given time.
- **Runners must always stay to the right side of the alley when running (just like traffic) for safety reasons:**
  - **Stress safety, decision making, and cooperation.**

CAPTAIN AND CREW (II)

Purpose:

- To develop the skills of kicking (punting, long kicks, and short kicks) using the rules and strategies of golf

Assessment Objectives:

- Can students use a wide variety of kicking skills to meet a given situation?
- Can students use the strategies of teamwork to produce the best results?
- To what extent can students relate to the game of golf as a lifetime activity?

Materials:

- 1 soccer ball or volleyball per student
- 1 scorecard per 4 students
- 6 cones
- 6 folded mats
- 6 sticks with flags

Skill Development:

- See *football-related skills* (page 131): punting and placekicking.

Activity:

- Divide the class into groups of four players:
  - Fill out a scorecard for each group (diagram 8.17).
- Set the teams into position as shown in diagram 8.18 using a shotgun approach (a foursome starts at each hole).

- Explain the rules of golf using a *captain and crew* format:
  - Each player in the foursome tees off by punting his ball from behind the folded mat toward the appropriate cone and flag:

    This counts as one shot.
  - Players in that foursome decide which shot (punt) is in the best position for the next shot, and place their balls there.
  - Each player then takes another shot, kicking the ball off the ground (as if using a fairway wood or iron):

    This counts as the second shot.
  - Players continue to collectively select the best shot for all to kick from until one of the foursome's shots hits the cone.
  - The number of shots taken are counted and recorded for each hole.
  - The foursome moves to the next hole and tees off when the hole is clear, again using a punt as the drive.
  - After all six holes have been played, the scores for each hole are tallied and multiplied by three to obtain an 18-hole score.
  - The scorecard should be signed and verified by players in the foursome before being handed in to the teacher.
  - Scores are then posted on the master "leader board" for each foursome, much as it is in a real golf tournament.
- **Stress the rules and strategy of golf, along with appropriate kicking skills to accomplish selected strategies. Also, stress communication and cooperative skills in selecting the best shots to use.**

Names	Holes					
	1	2	3	4	5	6

Diagram 8.17

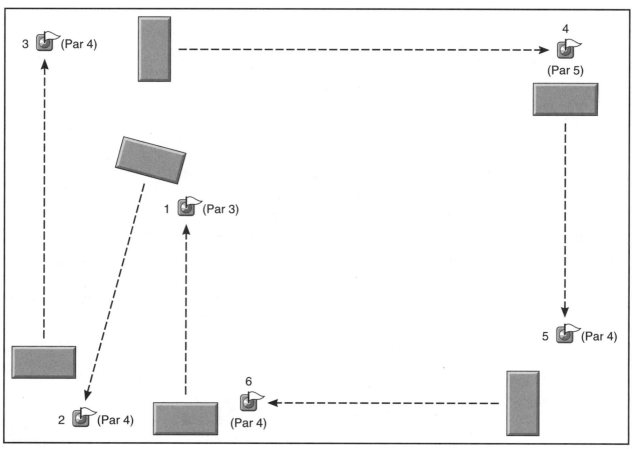

Diagram 8.18

MODIFIED SIX-PLAYER SOCCER (II)

Purpose:

- To develop the following soccer skills: dribbling, short passes, long passes, trapping, throw-ins, head balls, and goalie skills (including punting); to develop movement without the ball using triangles and filling lanes for maintaining field balance

Assessment Objectives:

- Can students trap and kick a ball in a controlled sequence?
- Can students kick a moving soccer ball without trapping it first?
- Do students demonstrate proper game sense by moving the ball out to the side to open up the middle of the field?

Materials:

- 1 soccer ball for each student
- 8 cones

Skill Development:

- See *soccer-related skills* (page 132): dribbling, heading, trapping, and passing.

Activity:

- Divide the class into four even teams.
- Set the teams into position as shown in 8.19.
- Explain the team concepts of positions for goalies, forwards, backs, and centers:
  - Review offensive balance using triangles.
  - Review field balance by filling lanes.
- Explain the rules:
  - All players, with the exception of the goalies, must use their feet in keeping with soccer rules.
  - Teams play 5- to 7-minute games, with 1 point awarded for each goal (ball passing through cones at a height no higher than the goalie's head).
  - Rotate teams after every game (round-robin, winners stay, etc.)
- **Focus on game sense through spatial awareness and positioning to maximize soccer skills.**

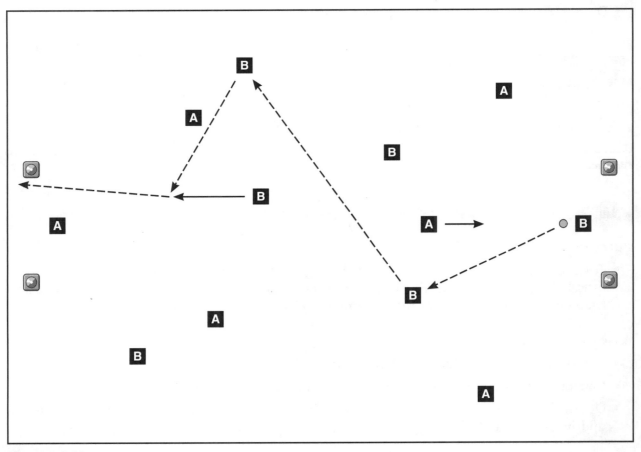

Diagram 8.19

MULTICONE SOCCER (II)

Purpose:

- To develop the following soccer skills: dribbling, short passes, long passes, trapping, throw-ins, and head ball skills; to develop movement without the ball using triangles and filling lanes for maintaining field balance

Assessment Objectives:

- To what extent do students keep the ball on the ground using the inside of their feet to kick the ball?
- Do students form triangles to form passing lanes and maintain possession?
- Do students move with and without the ball?

Materials:

- 1 soccer ball for each student
- 16 cones per field or court

Skill Development:

- See *soccer-related skills* (page 132): dribbling, trapping, and passing.

Activity:

- Divide the class into four even teams.
- Set the teams into position as shown in diagram 8.20, but do so on two fields (game is similar to real soccer except that the ball must hit the cones to score and therefore requires more ball control).

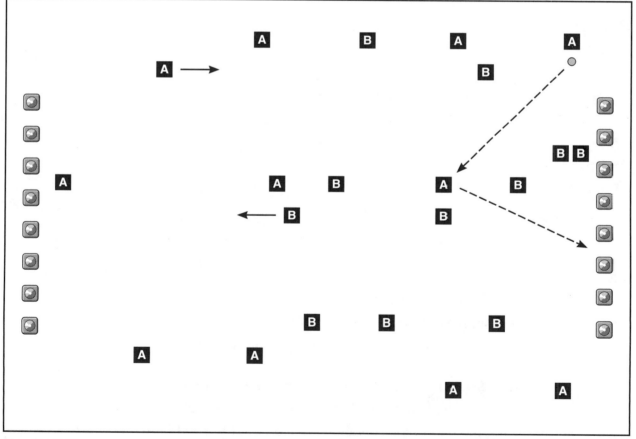

Diagram 8.20

- Explain the team concepts of positions for forwards, backs, and centers:
  - Review offensive balance using triangles.
  - Review field balance by filling lanes.
- Explain the rules:
  - All players must use their feet in keeping with soccer rules.
  - Teams play 5- to 7-minute games, with 1 point awarded for each goal (ball must hit cones to count as a goal).
  - Rotate teams after every game (round-robin, winners keep field, etc.).
- **Focus on game sense through spatial awareness, positioning to maximize soccer skills, and ball control to hit cones.**

OBSTACLE KICKBALL (II)

Purpose:

- To develop punting and placekicking skills, along with throwing/catching skills

Assessment Objectives:

- Can students progress from kicking a stationary ball to kicking a moving ball?
- Do students use proper hand position when catching and throwing a football?

Materials:

- 4 floor mats
- 2 jump ropes
- 2 junior basketballs and a container to hold them
- 1 basketball basket
- 2 bowling pins
- 1 placekicking tee
- 1 football for each student

Skill Development:

- See *football-related skills* (page 131): punting and placekicking.

Activity:

- Divide the class into two even teams.
- Set up the gymnasium as shown in diagram 8.21.
- The team that is up has each player kick off, one at a time, in turn (placekick first time up, punt second time up):
  - After kicking, players run to first base and jump rope five times.
  - Next, they run to second base and either shoot a basket or make three attempts.
  - After returning the ball to the container, they proceed to third base and must set up the bowling pin using only their feet.
  - Finally, they run home.

- The fielding team must first get control of the kicked ball, then throw to its first-base player, who catches the ball and jumps rope five times:

  - Fielding-team players then throw the ball to their second-base player, who either makes a basket or makes three attempts.

  - The ball is then thrown to the third-base player, who sets up the bowling pin using only her feet before throwing the ball home to the catcher.

- The first team to complete the circuit and get the ball home scores a point.

- After everyone on a team has been up, the teams switch positions.

- **Stress catching, throwing, and kicking skills, plus cooperative skills with players on the fielding team.**

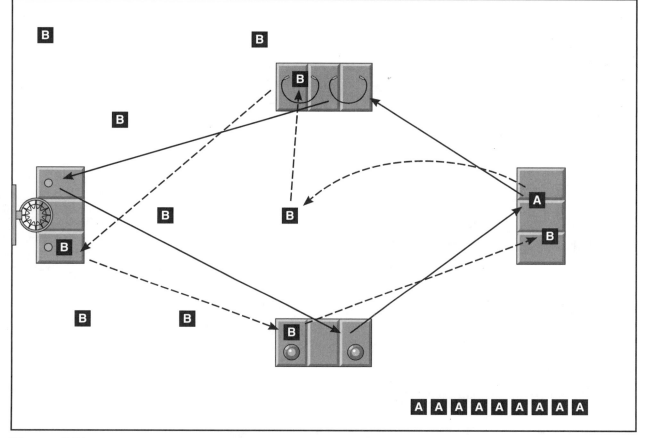

Diagram 8.21

So many of our game activities lend themselves to observable assessment. Obstacle kickball is one of the best because the teacher can observe each student individually with respect to timing and coordination, fine motor skills, and problem solving. Because a student must jump rope, shoot a basket, and set a pin upright without the use of his hands, a teacher may want to use this activity in the beginning of the year as a screening tool to look at overall class function. You may also want to change or create your own three "obstacles" to look at a particular skill(s).

SCOTCH FOURSOME (II)

Purpose:

- To develop the skills of kicking (punting, long kicks, and short kicks) using the rules and strategies of golf

Assessment Objectives:

- Can students use a wide variety of kicking skills to meet a given situation?
- To what extent can students relate to the game of golf as a lifetime activity?

Materials:

- 1 soccer ball or volleyball for every 2 students
- 1 scorecard per 4 students
- 6 cones
- 6 folded mats
- 6 sticks with flags

Skill Development:

- See *football-related skills* (page 131): punting and placekicking.

Activity:

- Divide the class into groups of four players:
  - Within each group, divide the players into teams of pairs.
  - Fill out a scorecard for each group (see diagram 8.17).
- Set the teams into position as shown in diagram 8.18 using a shotgun approach (a foursome starts at each hole).
- Explain the rules of golf using a *scotch-foursome format*:
  - Each team of pairs selects a player to tee off first by punting his ball from behind the folded mat toward the appropriate cone and flag.
  - This counts as one shot.
  - The second shot is taken by the pair's partner who did not tee off and is taken from the exact location where the tee shot lands.
  - The shot is taken from the ground as if using a fairway wood or iron.
  - Pairs keep alternating shots until they successfully hit the cone and flag, completing the hole.
  - The number of shots taken is counted and recorded for each hole by pair.
  - The foursome moves to the next hole and tees off when the hole is clear while continuing to alternate shots between partners.
  - After all six holes have been played, the scores for each hole are tallied and multiplied by three to obtain an 18-hole score.
  - The scorecard should be signed and verified by players in the foursome before being handed in to the teacher.
  - Scores are then posted on the master "scoreboard" for each pair much as would happen in a golf tournament.

- **Stress the rules and strategy of golf, along with appropriate kicking skills to accomplish selected strategies. Also, stress cooperative communication skills among partners and within foursomes.**

INDOOR SOCCER (III)

Purposes:

- To develop the following soccer skills: dribbling, short passes, trapping, head balls, and goalie skills
- To apply math concepts using the wall for creating triangles and rebounds and as another dimension in establishing offensive balance and transition from defense to offense

Assessment Objectives:

- Do students use varied soccer-style kicks to meet different situations?
- To what extent do students fill passing lanes?
- When trapping, do students move their bodies to receive the ball?

Materials:

- 1 soccer ball for each student
- 2 crash mats
- 1 or 2 sets of pinnies

Skill Development:

- See *soccer-related skills* (page 132): dribbling, passing, and trapping.

Activity:

- Divide the class into three or four even teams.
- Set the teams into position as shown in diagram 8.22.
- Place a crash mat on its side at each end of the gym for a goal:
  - The ball must hit the front of the mat for a score.
- Play a round-robin format for 3 minutes or until a goal is scored, then rotate teams.
- Sideline players may pass to either team or shoot and score a goal for either team.
- **Focus on game sense through spatial awareness and positioning to maximize soccer game skills.**

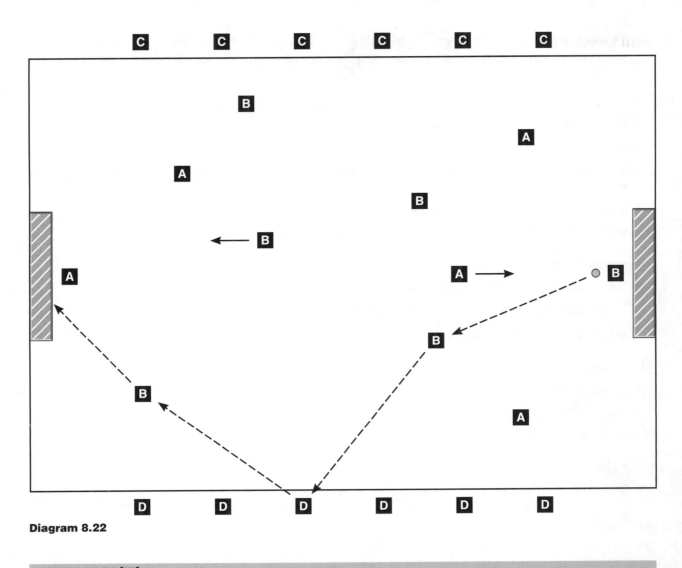

Diagram 8.22

MEDAL PLAY (III)

Purpose:

- To develop the skills of kicking (punting, long kicks, and short kicks) using the rules and strategies of golf

Assessment Objectives:

- Can students use a wide variety of kicking skills to meet a given situation?
- To what extent do students relate the selection of different kicking techniques to the selection of different golf clubs?
- To what extent do students select the appropriate skills to produce proper outcomes?

Materials:

- 1 soccer ball or volleyball per student
- 1 scorecard per 4 students
- 6 cones
- 6 folded mats
- 6 sticks with flags

Skill Development:

- See *football-related skills* (page 131): punting and placekicking.

Activity:

- Divide the class into groups of four players:
  - Fill out a scorecard for each group (see diagram 8.17).
- Set foursomes into position as shown in diagram 8.18 using a shotgun approach (a foursome starts at each hole).
- Explain the rules of golf using *medal play* format:
  - Each player in the foursome tees off by punting her ball from behind the folded mat toward the appropriate cone and flag (this counts as one shot).
  - Players in that foursome decide which shot (punt) is farthest from the hole.
  - Each player then takes another shot, kicking her ball off the ground in order from farthest to nearest to the hole (this counts as her second shot).
  - Players continue in this fashion, playing their own ball until all of the players "hole" their ball (hit the cone and flag).
  - The number of shots taken for each player is counted and recorded for each hole.
  - The foursome moves to the next hole and tees off when the hole is clear.
  - After all six holes have been played, the scores for each hole are tallied and multiplied by three to obtain an 18-hole score.
  - The scorecard should be signed and verified by players in each foursome before being handed in to the teacher.
- **Stress the rules and strategy of golf, along with appropriate kicking skills to accomplish selected strategies.**

SPEEDBALL (III)

Purposes:

- To develop catching/throwing skills (flies and line drives) with round balls and to apply soccer skills to balls on the ground
- To develop team concepts of movement without the ball using triangles and filling lanes for maintenance of court balance
- To relate team movement concepts to court/field games such as basketball and soccer

Assessment Objectives:

- Do students use proper passing techniques to advance a ball above their waists?
- Do students use a variety of soccer techniques to control a ball on the ground?
- To what extent do students attempt to solve problems in playing the ball correctly?

Materials:

- 1 soccer ball for every 2 students
- 1 indoor soccer ball (for indoor game)
- Basketball hoops

- 2 large (6-by-8-foot) exercise mats
- 8 cones
- Pinnies (preferably 2 colors)

Skill Development:

- See *basketball-related skills* (passing) and *soccer-related skills* (passing and trapping) on pages 116 and 134.

Activity:

- Divide the class into two even teams:
  - Have the students on each team count off in consecutive numbers.
- Set the teams into position as shown in diagram 8.23 (each team is against the wall serving as goalies with three players out on the court trying to score).
- The two large exercise mats are propped up on their sides, centered against the end walls of the gym:
  - A 3-point goal is scored for any ball shot through the basketball hoop.
  - A 2-point goal is scored if a ball is kicked and hits the exercise mat.
  - A 1-point goal is scored if a ball is kicked and hits the remaining wall space on the end of the gym below a height of 8 feet (or any natural border in the gym: wood, matting, bleachers, painted line, etc.).
  - Establish a goal area by using cones to create an end line separating goalies from those scoring.
- Explain the team concepts of pushing the ball up court:
  - Review offensive balance using triangles.
  - Review field/court balance by filling lanes.
  - Encourage students to relate strategies to the score; for example, should they be shooting baskets or kicking?
- Play 3-minute games, then switch goalies with those scoring (three from each team at a time).
- Explain the rules:
  - Each game starts with a jump ball. After a goal is scored, play resumes with another jump ball at center court.
  - Basketball rules apply when the ball is being played above the waist, but any time a ball falls below the waist, soccer rules then apply.
  - Defense is played in a basketball/soccer-type fashion.
- If the game is played outside, set up in a soccer format. Score balls thrown into the goal as 1 point, those kicked in as 2 points, and those kicked over the goal or through the uprights as 3 points.
- **Focus on game sense through spatial awareness and passing the ball quickly from player to player.**

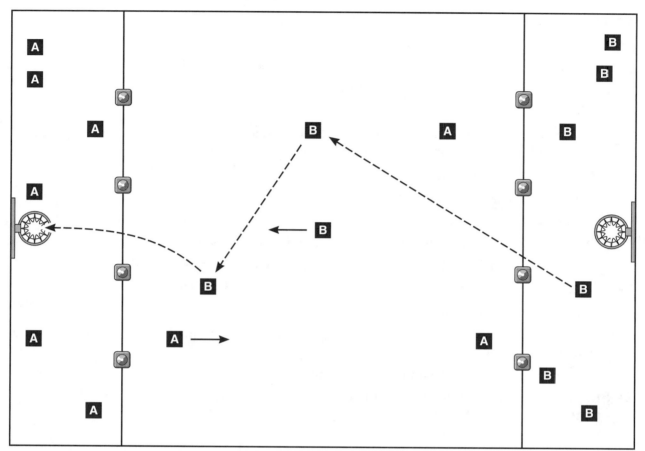

Diagram 8.23

ULTIMATE RUGBY (III)

Purpose:

- To develop the skills of catching/throwing, open-field running, dodging, and kicking on the run

Assessment Objectives:

- Do students display proper hand position in throwing and catching a football?
- While running and dodging, do students plant the outside foot?
- Can students successfully punt while on the run?

Materials:

- 1 football for every 2 students
- Flag belts for every student
- Pinnies (preferably in 3 colors)

Skill Development:

- See *football-related skills* (page 121): catching and passing.

Activity:

- Divide the class into two teams:
  - If the class is large, divide the students into four teams on two fields.
- Set the teams into position as shown in diagram 8.24:
  - Play starts with one team kicking off to the other team (punt).
- The receiving team gets control of the ball and moves it toward its end zone by passing (lateral or overhand) among teammates, kicking the ball, or running the ball.
- A turnover occurs when:
  - a passed or kicked ball is intercepted;
  - a passed ball hits the ground; or
  - a player has his belt pulled off while in possession of the ball.
  - A kicked ball that is dropped is up for grabs, and whoever gets the ball can play it.
- Points are scored when a ball successfully crosses the offensive end line:
  - 2 points for a ball run into the end zone
  - 3 points for a ball kicked through the uprights (football), over a goal (soccer), or between two cones designated as a goal on the end line
  - 6 points for a ball passed and received in the end zone
- **Stress movement without the ball to get open and movement with the ball in the form of dodging, fleeing, and throwing or kicking on the run.**

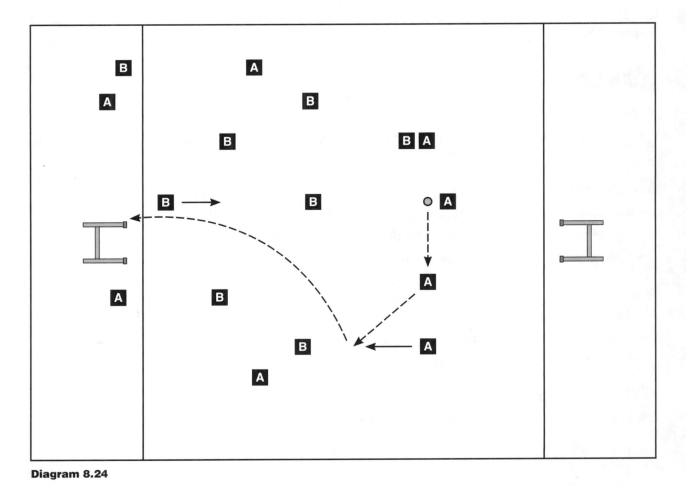

Diagram 8.24

STRIKING

Striking activities challenge students using a variety of lever lengths (arms, bats, rackets, Pillo Polo sticks, hockey sticks, etc.) and different-sized goals or targets. Both aerobic and anaerobic pathways are developed with respect to fitness, while teamwork and cooperative-strategy development take place socially. Activities are listed alphabetically by level of difficulty.

STRIKING SKILLS

BEACH VOLLEYBALL (I)

Purpose:

- To develop striking skills relative to volleyball (i.e., passing, setting, and underhand serving) with application to a game-type activity

Assessment Objectives:

- Do students use their bodies in striking a volleyball instead of just their arms?
- Do students solve problems in selecting appropriate strike techniques for a variety of situations?

Materials:

- 1 volleyball-type ball per student (softer balls, such as "floaters" and "beach balls" would be more appropriate for this lesson)
- 2 volleyball nets

Skill Development:

- See *volleyball-related skills* (page 139): forearm pass, setting, and underhand serve.

Activity:

- Divide the students into four equal teams using two volleyball courts.
- Assign each group to one half of a court and position the group in two or three rows based on numbers:
  - Review a typical volleyball rotation.
- Play games with large beach balls and modified rules:
  - The serve must cleanly pass over the net, but the server can serve from in front of the end line.
  - Balls may be hit an unlimited number of times by players on a team; even twice in a row by the same player (encourage movement and keeping the ball in the air).
  - The ball may be played off overhead obstructions by a team on the same side of its court but may not hit an overhead obstruction and pass over the net.
  - The line is in.
  - A team may only score when it has the serve. Loss of serve results in the other team serving.
  - Team players rotate when winning back the serve.
- Play timed games and rotate teams and courts so students play against different teams.
- **Stress fundamental skills to control the ball and keep it up, as well as movement to the ball.**

BIG-BALL TENNIS (I)

Purpose:

- To develop striking skills while using the hand and arm as a lever: forehand, backhand, overhead, and underhand (ground) strokes with respect to hitting a ball over a net

Assessment Objectives:

- Can students execute forehand and backhand strokes with either hand?
- Can students differentiate between striking for power and striking for accuracy?

Materials:

- 1 PG6-inch to PG8-inch ball for each student
- As many tennis courts as possible

Skill Development:

- See *racket-related skills* (page 137): strokes.

Activity:

- Divide the class into pairs of double partners:
  - Put two pairs on each court.
  - If you have a large class and limited space, then let other students work on skills or act as line judges while they wait their turns to play.
- Students play big-ball tennis much as they would tennis with one exception:
  - Play is initiated with one player serving *underhand* by bouncing and then striking the ball from behind his court's serving box.
  - The serve must land in his opponent's *diagonal serving box* without hitting the net.
  - Tennis rules apply with respect to scoring and strategies.
- **Focus on control with shots, solid contact when striking, anticipation, and decision making with respect to getting in proper position to execute a shot. Also, focus on the strategies involved in playing with a partner and the rules of tennis.**

BOXBALL (I)

Purpose:

- To develop the following striking skills using the hand and arm as a lever: forehand, backhand, and underhand (ground) strokes

Assessment Objectives:

- Can students place the ball accurately in the box using a variety of hand (striking) techniques?
- Are the players in motion without the ball in anticipation of the shot?

Materials:

- 1 PG3-inch ball for each student
- Floor tape to line courts (see diagram 8.25 for dimensions)

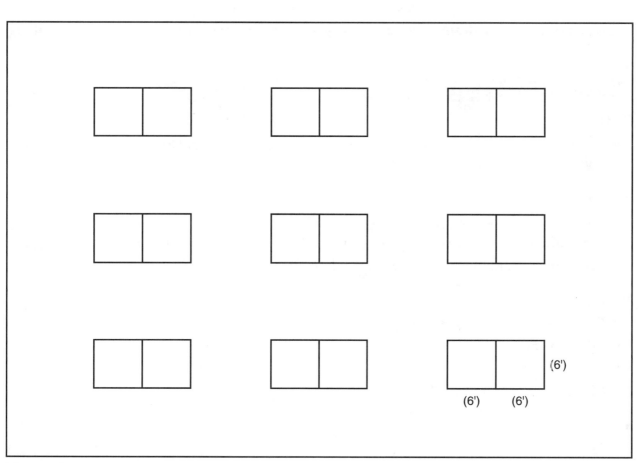

Diagram 8.25

Skill Development:

- See *racket-related skills* (page 137): strokes.

Activity:

- Divide the students into pairs:
  - Put a pair on each court.
  - If you have a large class and limited space, then place three or four students per court and create a rotational system for them so they can participate equally.
- Students play boxball much as they would tennis on their own court, following simple rules that are quite similar to one-wall handball:
  - One player serves *underhand* by bouncing and then striking the ball from behind her court's end line.
  - The serve must land in her opponent's court (on the line is good).
  - Players then volley until one player cannot successfully return her opponent's shot.
  - Points can only be scored when serving. Failure by the server to successfully score on a volley results in loss of serve.
  - 7 points wins a game; a player must win by 2 points.
- Devise a rotational system so that students mix with one another and play a variety of classmates:
  - Players who are waiting to play can serve as line judges.

- Focus on control with shots, solid contact when striking, and anticipation/decision making with respect to getting in proper position to execute a shot.

END-LINE HOCKEY (I)

Purpose:
- To develop striking skills with an extended lever (hockey stick) and to develop goalie catching skills

Assessment Objectives:
- Do students use leverage when striking with a hockey stick?
- Are students in a ready position to receive the ball when participating in a game situation?
- Are students in motion when they are without the ball?

Materials:
- 4 soft, round balls the size of softballs
- 1 floor hockey stick for each student
- 1 set of safety goggles for each student
- 1 baseball glove for every 2 students

Skill Development:
- See *floor-hockey related skills* (page 136): stickhandling.

Activity:
- Divide the class into two even teams.
- Set the teams into position as shown in diagram 8.26.
- Goalies must stay within their designated end zones:
  - They may use any part of their bodies to prevent balls from hitting the wall behind them but are encouraged to use the baseball glove much as an infielder would.
- Build a "neutral zone" between goalie and stick areas—an area where no one is allowed to go. This will greatly reduce the potential for goalies to get hit by a stick.
- All saves are returned to the offensive area by rolling the ball.
- All players not in the end zones must use their hockey sticks to strike the ball.
  - *A* players go in one direction, *B* players in the other.
  - Sticks should remain in contact with the floor.
  - Assess penalties for sticks raised above the waist.
- Play 3-minute games:
  - 1 point is awarded for each goal (hitting the back walls of the gym).
  - Use four balls, and start play by rolling the balls to the offensive team.
- Rotate teams every 3 minutes (goalies to shooters, shooters to goalies).
- **Focus on stick skills, teamwork, and safety.**

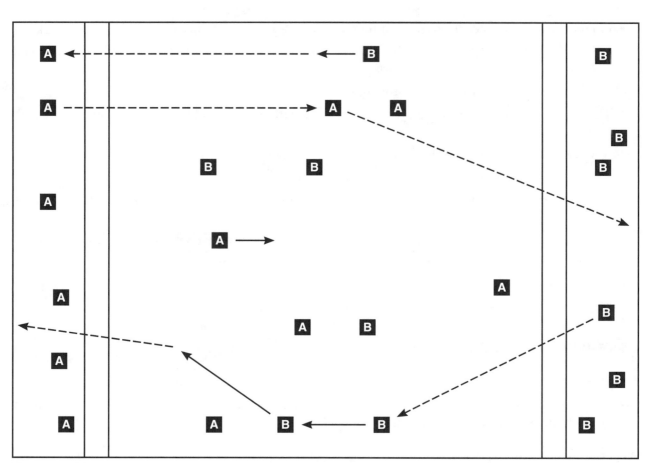

Diagram 8.26

HAND HOCKEY (I)

Purpose:

- To develop the following striking skills: forehand, backhand, overhand, and underhand strokes

Assessment Objectives:

- To what extent do students use their dominant and nondominant hands to move the ball?
- Do students change their centers of gravity and body shape in response to different situations?

Materials:

- 1 sponge and/or soft-type ball for each student
- 8 cones

Skill Development:

- See *racket-related skills* (page 137): strokes.

Activity:

- Divide the class into three even teams.
- Set the teams into position as shown in diagram 8.15 (*A* players in one end zone, *C* players in the other, and *B* players on offense in between the two end zones).

- Goalies must stay within their designated end zones:
  - They may use any part of their bodies (including hands) to prevent balls from hitting the wall behind them.
  - All saves are returned to the offensive area.
- The *B* players must select an appropriate stroke to either pass to a teammate or shoot at the wall behind the end zones:
  - Offensive players are not allowed in the end zones.
  - Offensive players can score at either end of the gym.
  - Offensive players must strike a moving ball; no catching and then hitting is allowed. No kicking is allowed.
- Designate a certain height as acceptable for a goal and count each goal as 1 point:
  - Use balls, and start play by tossing the balls to the offensive team.
- Rotate teams every 3 minutes (Dauer and Pangrazi 1986).
- **Focus on stepping into shots and making solid contact when striking.**

SOCK-OVER (I)

Purpose:

- To develop the following striking skills: overhand and underhand strokes as in serving a volleyball, as well as catching skills

Assessment Objectives:

- Can students serve successfully using both underhand and overhand serves?
- When catching a ball, do students use their bodies as well as their hands?
- Do students move without the ball?

Materials:

- 1 sponge and / or soft-type ball for each student
- 16 cones

Skill Development:

- See *racket-related skills* (strokes) and *volleyball-related skills* (overhead and underhand serves) (pages 137, 142-143).

Activity:

- Divide the class into two teams and four groups.
- Set the teams into position as shown in diagram 8.2.
  - *o* plays in an offensive area and tries to intercept serves from *x* to *X*, serving them to players in the *O* zone. Players score by successfully serving a ball to their end zone and having a teammate catch a fly ball in that zone (only the *X* players and *O* players can score points).
- Catchers must stay within their designated zones, and servers must stay in theirs (all catches are re-served to the appropriate middle zones).
- Use 8 to 12 balls, and start play by tossing the balls to the middle zone.

- Play four quarters, and record score after each quarter:
  - Rotate zones after each quarter.
  - Switch sides at halftime.
- **Focus on making solid contact when serving and on catching technique when catching a moving ball.**

TARGETBALL (I)

Purpose:
- To develop striking skills relative to baseball/softball, as well as throwing/catching skills

Assessment Objectives:
- Can students throw for distance using proper technique?
- Can students throw for accuracy using proper technique?
- When hitting a ball with a bat, can students direct the flight of the ball?
- Do students count on their teammates for help?

Materials:
- 1 Whiffle ball bat for every 3 students
- 1 Whiffle ball for every student
- 12 cones
- 2 large mats
- 1 old tire or inner tube suspended about 4 feet above the floor, against a wall
- 1 large, oversized Whiffle ball bat
- 1 PG4-inch- or PG6-inch-sized rubber ball

Skill Development:
- See *softball-related skills* (pages 128 and 138): hitting, catching, and throwing.

Activity:
- Divide the class into two teams.
- The object of the game is for the "at bat" team to hit the ball and run as many bases as possible before the fielding team throws the ball into the target area (see diagram 8.12). Unlike Transitional Lacrosse, however, which uses a goal, in Targetball a hoop, tire, or other similar target should be suspended to hang at about head level for the throwing team:
  - 1 point is awarded for each base.
  - Bonus points can be added for long hits (hitting a far wall is 5 points, etc.).
- The "fielding" team members try to catch a fly ball (3 points) or field a ground ball, throwing the ball at least once to a teammate who then throws it into the target area. The "fielding" team should also have a catcher who retrieves wild throws, relaying them back to the fielders:
  - When the target is hit, play stops and the next batter is up.
- Everyone on a team gets up, and then teams switch positions.
- **Focus on the fundamental skills of striking and catching/throwing and on the cooperative skill of teamwork.**

FOUR-CORNER HOCKEY (II)

Purpose:

- To develop striking skills with an extended lever (hockey stick)

Assessment Objectives:

- Do students use leverage properly when striking with the hockey stick?
- Do students apply spatial awareness concepts when moving without the ball?
- Do students apply the geometric concept of triangles to create passing lanes and floor balance?

Materials:

- 4 soft, round balls the size of softballs
- 16 cones
- 1 floor hockey stick for each student
- 1 set of safety goggles for each student
- 1 baseball glove, hockey helmet, and safety goggles for each of the 4 goalies
- 4 indoor hockey goals or 4 mats

Skill Development:

- See *floor hockey-related skills* (page 136): stickhandling.

Activity:

- Divide the class into two even teams, then subdivide each team further into two groups.
- Set the teams into position as shown in diagram 8.27:
  - Each team has two diagonally opposing goals to defend and shoot at.
- Goals are either used or formed by turning and standing two mats on their ends:
  - A goal is scored if the ball hits the net inside the goal or the two inner panels of the mat.
  - 1 point is given for each goal.
  - Form a crease by placing four cones around each goal.
  - Only the defensive team is allowed in the crease.
  - Relate the "crease" to other sports (hockey, lacrosse, etc.).
- Explain the team concept of positions for goalies, forwards, backs, and centers:
  - Review offensive balance using triangles.
  - Review field/court balance by filling lanes.
- Play three periods of hockey with instructional rest breaks between periods.
- **Stress game concepts of balance and teamwork.**

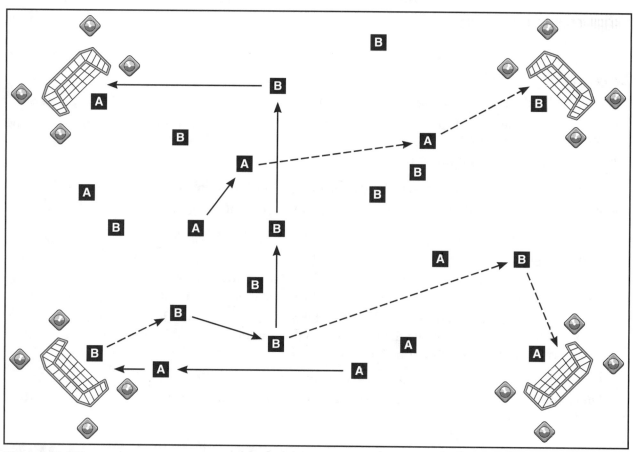

Diagram 8.27

MODIFIED CRICKET (II)

Purpose:

- To develop striking skills relative to baseball/softball, as well as throwing/catching skills

Assessment Objectives:

- When catching a ball, do students adjust their centers of gravity and body shape in response to different situations?
- When hitting a ball, do students properly transfer their weight?
- Do students realize that a thrown ball travels faster than a ball that is carried and/or run from place to place?

Materials:

- 1 Whiffle ball bat for every 3 students
- 1 Whiffle ball for every student
- 26 cones
- 3 large mats
- 1 large, oversized Whiffle ball bat
- 1 PG4-inch- or PG6-inch-sized rubber ball

Skill Development:

- See *softball-related skills* (pages 128 and 138): hitting, catching, and throwing .

Activity:

- Divide the class into two teams (see diagram 8.28).
- The object of the game is for the "at bat" team to protect the wicket (bowling pin) by hitting the pitched ball:
  - The pitch must be bounced.
  - If the bowling pin is knocked down, the batter is out and the next batter is up.
- After striking the ball, the batter runs repeatedly from mat to mat until play is stopped:
  - 1 point is awarded per base (mat).
  - Bonus points can be added for long hits (5 points for hitting off the far wall, etc.).
- The "fielding" team members try to catch a fly ball (3 points) or field a ground ball, throwing the ball at least once to a teammate who then throws it, knocking the bowling pin down:
  - The "fielding" team should also have a catcher who retrieves wild throws and throws back at the bowling pin or relays the ball back to the fielders. When the bowling pin is knocked down, play stops and the next batter is up.
- Everyone gets up, and then teams switch positions.
- **Focus on the fundamental skills of striking, throwing, and catching and on the cooperative skills of teamwork.**

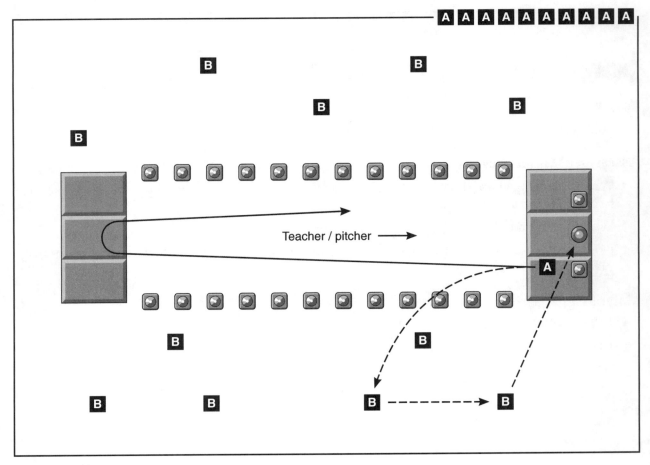

Diagram 8.28

ONE-WALL HANDBALL (II)

Purpose:

- To develop the following striking skills using the hand and arm as a lever: forehand, backhand, and underhand strokes

Assessment Objectives:

- Do students adjust the surface area of their hands to accommodate their shots?
- Do students exhibit good eye-hand coordination when striking the ball?
- Can students anticipate the angle of deflection the ball makes off the wall?

Materials:

- 1 PG3-inch ball for each student
- Floor tape to line courts (see diagram 8.29 for dimensions)

Skill Development:

- See *racket-related skills* (page 137): strokes.

Activity:

- Divide the class into pairs:
  - Put a pair on each court.
  - If you have a large class and limited space, then place three or four students per court and create a rotational system so they can participate equally.
- Students play handball off the wall at their own court using the following simple rules:
  - One player serves *underhand* by bouncing and then striking the ball from behind the court's end line.
  - The serve must hit the wall above a 4-foot horizontal line taped on the wall and land at least 3 feet from the wall (see diagram 8.29) between the serving line and end lines within the boundaries of the court (the line is good).
  - Players then volley until one player cannot successfully return his opponent's shot.
  - Points can only be scored when serving. Failure by the server to successfully score on a volley results in loss of serve.
  - 7 points wins a game; a player must win by 2 points.
- Devise a rotational system so students mix with one another and play a variety of classmates:
  - Players who are waiting to play can serve as line judges.
- **Focus on controlling shots and making solid contact when striking, as well as anticipation and decision making with respect to getting in proper position to execute a shot.**

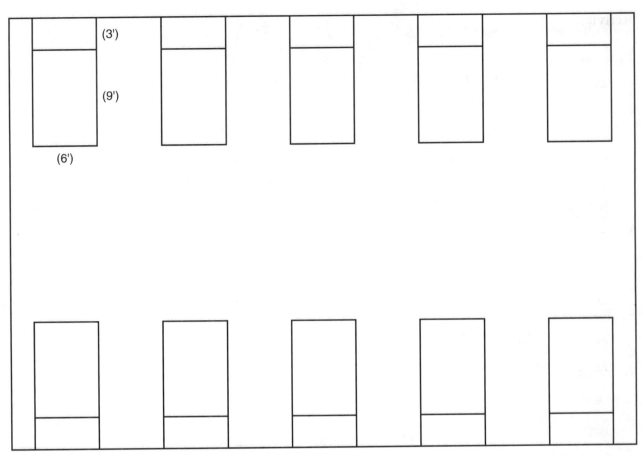

Diagram 8.29

PILLO POLO (II)

Purpose:

- To develop the following striking skills with an extended lever arm (Pillo Polo stick): forehand, backhand, overhand, and underhand strokes

Assessment Objectives:

- Do students realize the effect that lever length has on striking objects?
- Can students use a lever effectively to strike a ball for power and/or accuracy?
- Do students move without the ball to open areas?

Materials:

- 1 sponge and/or soft-type ball for each student
- 1 Pillo Polo stick for each student (preferably 2 colors)
- 8 cones

Skill Development:

- See *racket-related skills* (page 137): strokes.

Activity:

- Divide the class into three even teams.
- Set the teams into position as shown in diagram 8.15, (*A* players in one end zone, *C* players in the other, and *B* players on offense in between the two end zones).
- Goalies must stay within their designated end zones:
  - They may use any part of their bodies (including hands) to prevent balls from hitting the wall behind them.
  - All saves are returned to the offensive area.
- The *B* players must select an appropriate stroke to either pass to a teammate or shoot at the wall behind the end zones:
  - Offensive players are not allowed in the end zones.
  - Offensive players can score at either end of the gym.
  - No kicking is allowed.
- Designate a certain height as acceptable for a goal, and count each goal as 1 point:
  - Use six balls, and start play by tossing the balls to the offensive team.
- Rotate teams every 3 minutes.
- **Focus on stepping into shots and making solid contact while using the correct stroke for the situation.**

PUNCH BALL (II)

Purpose:

- To develop striking skills as well as to develop catching/throwing skills relative to softball/baseball

Assessment Objectives:

- To what extent can students strike balls of varied sizes?
- Can students catch both fly and ground balls?
- Can students throw a ball accurately?

Materials:

- A large gym space
- 4 large mats
- 1 PG-type ball for every student

Skill Development:

- See *softball- related skills* (pages 128 and 138): hitting, catching, and throwing.

Activity:

- Divide the class into two equal teams.
- Set the teams up as denoted in diagram 8.7 using unfolded mats as bases.

- Play starts with the first batter bouncing a PG ball and striking it with her hand:
  - Use a variety of PG-sized balls, and reduce the size each inning.
  - There is no "foul" ball; any contact with the hand puts the ball in play.
  - The batter hits the ball and continues to run the bases in order until called out by the teacher.
  - 1 point is awarded for each base safely reached.
  - The team in the field must get control of the ball and throw the ball to two bases (double play) before throwing the ball home to the catcher, stopping play (the runner is out).
  - After everyone on the first team has been up, the teams switch positions.
- **Stress proper hitting, fielding, and throwing techniques.**

QUADRANT VOLLEYBALL (II)

Purpose:
- To develop striking skills relative to volleyball (i.e., passing, setting, and underhand serving) with application to a game-type activity

Assessment Objectives:
- Do students use the proper volleyball techniques for given situations?
- Are the student's head and feet in alignment with the ball when making contact?

Materials:
- 1 volleyball-type ball per student (softer balls, such as "floaters" and "beach balls" would be more appropriate for this lesson).
- 2 volleyball nets

Skill Development:
- See *volleyball-related skills* (page 139): forearm pass, overhead pass, and underhand serve.

Activity:
- Divide the students into four equal teams.
- Assign each group to one quadrant (see diagram 8.30) and have the students count off numerically within their quadrants.
- Team *A* serves first into any of the other three quadrants. The other three teams (*B, C,* and *D*) work together to take the serve away from *A* by hitting the ball to the floor on *A* team's court:
  - Players on the *A* team keep serving and scoring points until the serve is taken from them.
  - The serve must cleanly pass over the net, but the server can serve from in front of the end line.
  - Players rotate the serve among teammates with each serve in numerical order.
  - Balls may be hit an unlimited number of times by players on a team; even twice in a row by the same player (encourage movement and keeping the ball in the air).
  - The ball may be played off overhead obstructions by a team on the same side of its court but may not hit an overhead obstruction and pass over the net.
  - The line is in.
  - A team may only score when it has the serve. Loss of serve results in another team serving.

- Players rotate courts when changing the serve—*A* to *B*, *B* to *C*, *C* to *D*, and *D* to *A*—so that serves always occur from the same quadrant.
  - 15 points win a game.
- Use a beach ball, "floater," or real volleyball based on the level of skill demonstrated by students in your class.
- **Stress fundamental skills to control the ball and keep it up, as well as movement to the ball.**

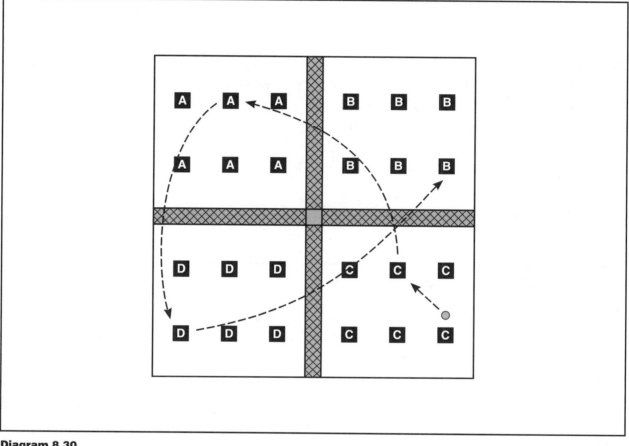

Diagram 8.30

STICKS AND KICKS (II)

Purpose:

- To develop the following striking skills with an extended lever arm (Pillo Polo stick): forehand, backhand, overhand, and underhand strokes; to develop the following soccer skills: dribbling, kicking, trapping, and goalie play

Assessment Objectives:

- Do students use the Pillo Polo stick as a proper lever to increase striking power?
- Do students use a variety of soccer techniques to control the ball?
- Do goalkeepers move their bodies behind their hands?

Materials:

- 6 blue and 6 yellow Pillo Polo sticks
- Modified, rubberized soccer-sized balls
- 2 sets of pinnies
- 1 soccer-sized ball for every student

Skill Development:

- See *racket-related skills* (strokes) and *soccer-related skills* (dribbling, passing, and trapping) (pages 137 and 132).

Activity:

- Divide the class into two teams and further subdivide each team into two groups.
- Set the teams into position as shown in diagram 8.31.
- Goalies must stay within their designated end zones:
  - They may use any part of their bodies (including hands) to prevent balls from hitting the wall behind them (or the end zone line if outdoors).
  - 1 point is given for each goal.
  - All saves are returned to the offensive area away from pressure by throwing or punting the ball.

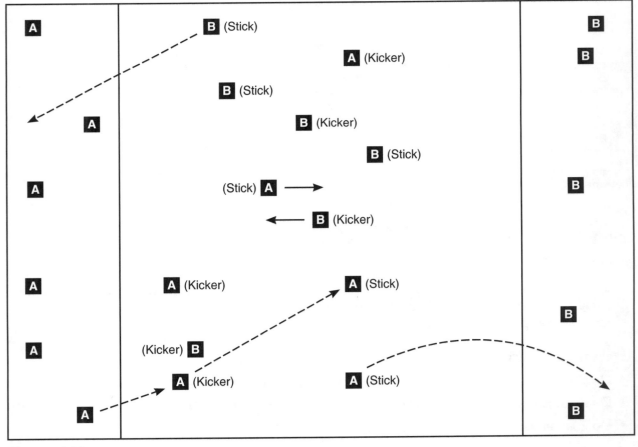

Diagram 8.31

- Half the offensive players on each team have Pillo Polo sticks, and half do not:
    - Those with a stick must strike the ball with it.
    - Those without a stick play soccer.
    - Teamwork and cooperation between the "stickers" and "kickers" should be encouraged.
- After 2 minutes, "stickers" and "kickers" switch roles. After 4 minutes, goalies and offensive players switch places.
- Two balls are used for this game, put into play at the start of the game by tossing them into the offensive area (Rohnke 1989).
- **Focus on stepping into shots and making solid contact when striking, kicking through the ball when kicking, and using proper body position when catching and / or blocking a shot on goal.**

THREE-COURT VOLLEYBALL (II)

Purpose:

- To develop striking skills relative to volleyball (i.e., passing, setting, and underhand serving) with application to a game-type activity

Assessment Objectives:

- Do students use angle shots off walls to enhance the effectiveness of the shot?
- Are students in alignment with the ball when making contact?

Materials:

- 1 volleyball-type ball per student (softer balls, such as "floaters" and "beach balls" would be more appropriate for this lesson)
- 2 volleyball nets

Skill Development:

- See *volleyball-related skills* (page 139): forearm pass, overhead pass, and underhand serve.

Activity:

- Divide the students into three equal teams.
- Assign each group to one triangle (see diagram 8.32) and have the students count off numerically within their triangles.
- Team A serves first into any of the other two triangles. The other two teams (B and C) work together to take the serve away from A by hitting the ball to the floor on the A team's court:
    - Players from team A keep serving and scoring points until the serve is taken from them.
    - The serve must cleanly pass over the net, but the server can serve from in front of the end line.
    - Serves and shots can hit the walls behind courts B and C as in Walleyball.
    - Players rotate the serve among teammates with each serving in numerical order.
    - Balls may be hit an unlimited number of times by players on a team; even twice in a row by the same player (encourage movement and keeping the ball in the air).
    - The ball may be played off overhead obstructions by a team on the same side of its court but may not hit an overhead obstruction and pass over the net.

- The line is in and so are the walls.
- A team may only score when it has the serve. Loss of serve results in another team serving.
- Players rotate courts when changing the serve—*A* to *B*, *B* to *C*, and *C* to *A*—so that serves always occur from the same triangle.
- 15 points win a game.
- Use a beach ball, "floater," or real volleyball based on the level of skill demonstrated by students in your class.
- **Stress fundamental skills for controlling the ball, as well as movement to the ball.**

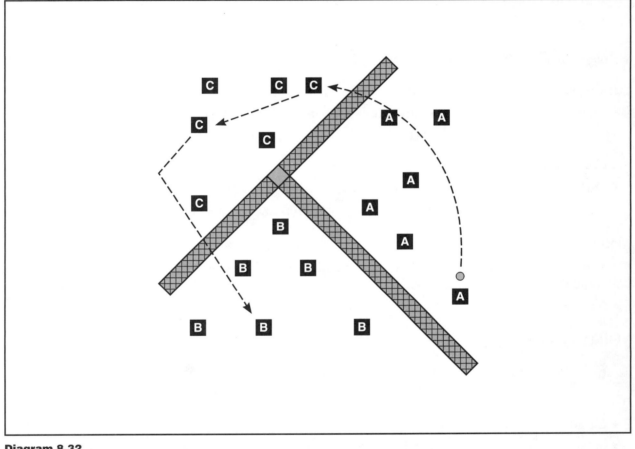

Diagram 8.32

FLOOR HOCKEY (III)

Purpose:

- To develop striking skills with an extended lever (hockey stick)

Assessment Objectives:

- When striking the ball, do students use the leverage of the hockey stick to their advantage?
- Do students use spatial-awareness concepts to maintain proper positioning?

Materials:

- 4 soft, round balls the size of softballs
- 8 cones
- 1 floor hockey stick for each student
- 1 set of safety goggles for each student
- 1 baseball glove, hockey helmet, and safety goggles for each of the 2 goalies
- 2 indoor hockey goals or 2 mats

Skill Development:

- See *floor hockey-related skills* (page 136): stickhandling.

Activity:

- Divide the class into two even teams, then subdivide further into two groups per team.
- Set the teams into position as shown in diagram 8.11 (two groups on a court, two on sideline).
- Use two floor hockey goals, or form goals by turning and standing two mats on their sides:
  - A goal is scored if the ball hits the net inside the goal or the two inner panels of the mat.
  - 1 point is scored for each goal.
  - Form a crease by placing four cones around each goal.
  - Only the defensive team is allowed in the crease.
  - Relate the "crease" to other sports (hockey, lacrosse, etc.).
- Explain the team concepts of positions for goalies, forwards, backs, and centers:
  - Review offensive balance using triangles.
  - Review court/field balance by filling lanes.
- Play 3-minute games, 6-on-6, then switch the "on-court" groups with the "sideline groups."
- **Stress game concepts of court balance and teamwork.**

GARBAGE-CAN BASEBALL (III)

Purpose:

- To develop the skills of striking, catching, and throwing relative to softball/baseball

Assessment Objectives:

- When striking a moving target, do students coordinate hip, shoulder, elbow, and wrist movements to improve accuracy?
- When throwing a ball, do students step in opposition to the throwing hand?
- Do students use proper speed techniques when running bases?

Materials:

- 1 PG4-inch ball for every student
- 1 oversized Whiffle ball bat or broomstick
- 4 large mats
- 1 large garbage can

Skill Development:

- See *softball-related skills* (pages 128 and 138): hitting, throwing, and catching.

Activity:

- Divide the class into two teams.
- Set the teams into position as shown in diagram 8.33:
  - One team is up at bat.
  - The other team spreads out in the field with a base player at each base (mat).
- Basic softball rules apply:
  - Three outs are allowed for each team.
  - The far wall is an automatic home run.
  - After striking the ball, however, the bat must be placed and remain in the garbage can.
- The teacher serves as a pitcher.
- Students waiting to get up must wait in the dugout for safety.
- **Stress the rules of softball and the strategies involved.**

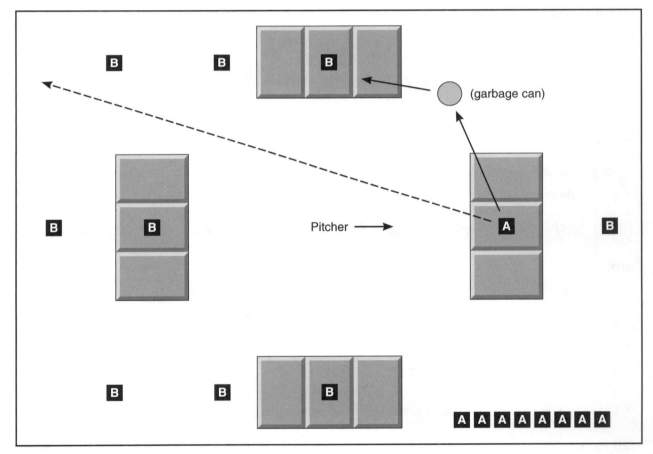

Diagram 8.33

PADDLE TENNIS (III)

Purpose:

- To develop the following striking skills while using a paddle and/or racquetball racket as a lever: forehand, backhand, overhead, and underhand (ground) strokes with respect to hitting a ball over a net

Assessment Objectives:

- Can students use the racket as an extension of their arms?
- Do students use appropriate shots relative to the situation's demand?
- Do students attempt to solve problems when placing a shot?

Materials:

- 1 tennis ball for each student
- As many tennis courts as possible
- 1 paddleball or racquetball racket for each student

Skill Development:

- See *racket-related skills* (page 137): strokes.

Activity:

- Divide the class into pairs of double partners:
  - Put two pairs on each court.
  - If you have a large class and limited space, then let other students work on skills or act as line judges while they wait their turns to play.
- Students play Paddle Tennis much as they would tennis with one exception:
  - Play is initiated with one player serving *underhand* by bouncing and then striking the ball from behind the end line of his court.
  - The serve must land in the *diagonal serving box* on the opponent's side without hitting the net.
  - Tennis rules apply with respect to scoring and strategies.
- **Focus on making solid contact when striking the ball to control shots and on getting in proper position to execute a shot through anticipation and game strategy.**

SOFTBALL (III)

Purpose:

- To develop the skills of striking, catching, and throwing relative to softball/baseball

Assessment Objectives:

- When striking a pitched ball, do students wait for the ball to drop into the strike zone?
- When fielding a ground ball, do students move their feet first?
- Do students exhibit proper foot-speed techniques when running bases?

Materials:

- 1 softball for every student
- 1 softball bat
- 4 bases (mats)
- 1 set of catcher's equipment
- 1 softball mitt (glove) for each student

Skill Development:

- See *softball-related skills* (pages 128 and 138): hitting, catching, and throwing.

Activity:

- Divide the class into two teams:
  - One team is up at bat.
  - The other team is spread out in the field with a base player at each base (mat).
- Basic softball rules apply:
  - Three outs are allowed for each team.
  - The catcher must wear equipment for safety.
  - Throwing the bat is an automatic out.
- The teacher serves as a pitcher.
- Students waiting to get up must wait in the dugout for safety.
- **Stress the rules of softball and the strategies involved.**

VOLLEYBALL (III)

Purpose:

- To develop striking skills relative to volleyball (i.e., passing, setting, and overhand serving) with application to a game-type activity

Assessment Objectives:

- Do students use three hits before passing a ball over the net?
- Do students demonstrate spatial awareness by maintaining court balance?
- Do students apply appropriate techniques for a given situation?

Materials:

- 1 volleyball per student
- 2 volleyball courts

Skill Development:

- See *volleyball-related skills* (page 139): forearm pass, overhead pass, and overhead serve.

Activity:

- Divide the students into four equal teams.
- Assign each group to one half of a court, and position players in two or three rows based on numbers:
  - Review a typical volleyball rotation.
- Play games with a real volleyball and volleyball rules:
  - The serve must cleanly pass over the net.
  - The server must strike the ball from behind the end line of her court.
  - Balls may only be hit three times by players on a team and never twice in a row by the same player.
  - The ball may be played off overhead obstructions by a team on the same side of its court but may not hit an overhead obstruction and pass over the net.
  - The line is in.
  - A team may only score when it has the serve.
  - Loss of serve results in the other team serving.
  - Team players rotate when winning back the serve.
- Play timed games and rotate teams and courts so that students play against different teams.
- **Stress fundamental skills of ball control and movement to the ball:**
  - **Encourage students to use the three hits they are allotted by bumping to the front-center position and then setting to the front corners.**

WALLEYBALL (III)

Purpose:

- To develop striking skills relative to volleyball (i.e., passing, setting, and overhead serving) with application to a game-type activity

Assessment Objectives:

- Do students use appropriate volleyball techniques in a given situation?
- Do students anticipate a ball's deflection off the wall?
- Are students supportive of their teammates?

Materials:

- 1 volleyball-type ball per student (softer balls, such as "floaters," would be appropriate for this lesson)
- 2 volleyball nets
- 3 walls surrounding each of the two courts (see diagram 8.34)

Skill Development:

- See *volleyball-related skills* (page 139): forearm pass, overhead pass, and overhead serve.

Activity:

- Divide the students into four equal teams.
- Assign each group to one half of a court and position players in two or three rows based on numbers:
  - Review a typical volleyball rotation.
- Play games with "floater"-type balls and modified rules:
  - The serve must cleanly pass over the net, but the server can serve from one stride inside the end line.
  - Balls may be hit an unlimited number of times by players on a team; even twice in a row by the same player (encourage movement and keeping the ball in the air).
  - The ball may be played off overhead obstructions by a team on the same side of its court but may not hit an overhead obstruction and pass over the net.
  - The line is in and so are the walls.
  - A team may only score when it has the serve.
  - Loss of serve results in the other team serving.
  - Team players rotate when winning back the serve.
- Play timed games, and rotate teams and courts so students play against different teams.
- **Stress fundamental skills to control the ball and keep it up, as well as movement to the ball.**

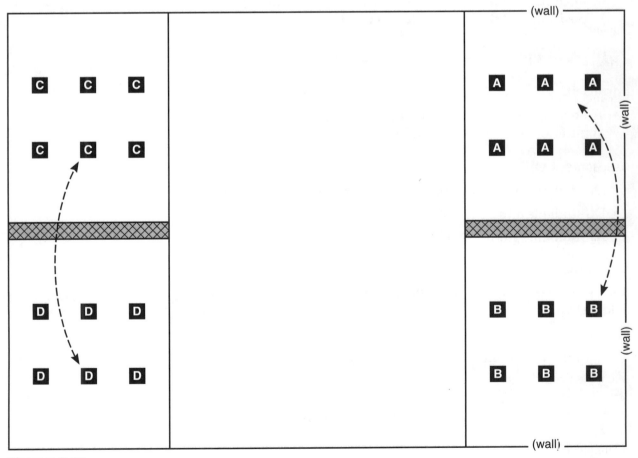

Diagram 8.34

chapter 9

INDIVIDUAL AND PAIRED ACTIVITIES

The *individual and paired activities* in this chapter are designed to be used in the same way as the team activities were in chapter 8. Their design allows for maximum student participation, regardless of skill level, providing ample opportunity for skill development through fun activities that challenge students.

Each *individual/paired activity* is ready to be "inserted" into the modular lesson format (table 3.1) much as we did with the *warm-ups*, *health-related fitness concepts*, *skill-development activities*, and *team activities*. For ease of reference, activities are presented under the general headings of dance, gymnastics/tumbling, obstacle/challenge courses, track and field, and wrestling. Within each of these categories, a number of kinesthetic skills are addressed: rolling/balance/weight transfer (gymnastics/tumbling), jumping and landing (track and field, gymnastics/tumbling), running (track and field), and relationships between body, space, and effort (wrestling, gymnastics/tumbling, and dance).

Using the concept of *assessment objectives*, as presented under each activity in chapter 8, you can develop your own assessment bench-marks for each activity in this chapter. Tie them in with the benchmarks provided in tables 4.4 (page 34) and 4.5 (page 35) or with the benchmarks developed by your staff. For example:

- In *dance*, a sample benchmark might read, "The student HAS performed a variety of simple line, circle, mixer, square, and reel dances."

- In *gymnastics/tumbling*, a sample benchmark might read, "The student HAS designed and performed gymnastic sequences that combine traveling, rolling, balancing, and weight transfer."

- In *obstacle/challenge courses*, a sample benchmark might read, "The student VALUES physical and performance limitations of self and others."

- In *track and field*, a sample benchmark might read, "The student KNOWS principles of training and conditioning for specific physical activities."

- In *wrestling*, a sample benchmark might read, "The student KNOWS how to detect, analyze, and correct errors in personal-movement patterns."

You should, of course, feel free to expand upon these samples to best meet your needs in evaluating student progress.

We have found that by interspersing these *individualized and paired activities* with the *team activities* presented in chapter 8, we best maintain the interest of our students while helping them become well rounded and physically fit. For an example of how this is done, refer to table 2.2.

DANCE

Dance is an excellent activity through which students can develop social skills while integrating repetitive movements to music. We have found that using a progression within the dance unit of first teaching line dances, next

moving to circles and mixers, and finally introducing square and reel dances works well in developing the greatest social interaction with the middle school student. For more of a fitness focus, aerobic dance and step aerobics could be used to challenge students while still keeping within the rhythmic classification of dance. The box below lists resources for ordering dance music tapes and instructor videotapes for many dance activities.

To best clarify, reinforce, and ensure your students' success, try a five-step progression when teaching individual dances (Reitano and Collins 1983):

- Provide verbal cues with teacher demonstration.

- Walk students through basic cues with verbal instruction and teacher demonstration.

- Have students dance to the music while continuing verbal cues with teacher demonstration.

Chime Time Movement Products
One Sportime Way
Atlanta, GA 30340
1-800-477-5075

GOPHER Sport
2929 W. Park Dr.
Owatonna, MN 55060
1-800-533-0446

Greg Larson Sports
P.O. Box 567
Rochester Hills, MI 48309
1-800-950-3320

Palos Sports
12235 S. Harlem Ave.
Palos Heights, IL 60463
1-800-233-5484

Sportime
One Sportime Way
Atlanta, GA 30340
1-800-283-5700

Toledo Physical Education Supply, Inc.
P.O. Box 5618
Toledo, OH 43616
1-800-225-7749

Flaghouse, Inc.
150 N. MacQuesten Pkwy.
Mt. Vernon, NY 10550
1-800-793-7900

Great Lake Sports
P.O. Box 447
Lambertville, MI 48144
1-800-446-2114

Gym Closet
2511 Leach Rd.
Brainerd, MN 56401
1-800-445-8873

Snitz Manufacturing
2096 S. Church St.
East Troy, WI 53120
1-800-558-2224

Things From Bell, Inc.
230 Mechanic St.
Princeton, WI 54968
1-414-642-7337

Wolverine Sports
745 State Circle
Ann Arbor, MI 48106
1-800-521-2832

- Let the students dance with the music.
- Introduce "changes" in basic patterns (e.g., add turns, play "current" music, etc.).

Suggestions for successfully delivering each specific dance are presented by dance formation under separate headings.

Aerobic-dance and *step-aerobic* classes are excellent activities for promoting cardiovascular fitness while developing agility and coordination using rhythmic, music-oriented movements. Structure your classes using easy-to-follow "movements," adding to or modifying each step after eight repetitions (32 beats). Progress from large muscle warm-up activity to aerobic-type movements that incorporate both upper- and lower-body muscles. Next, add upper-body exercises, torso and/or abdominal exercises, and hip and leg exercises, and finish with stretching-type activity. Adding energy, enthusiasm, and appropriate music (118 to 122 beats per minute) will all contribute to making your classes more dynamic.

This type of exercise is also perfect to use as warm-up activity for other types of activities. If your district does not have "step aerobic steps," simply use folded exercise mats with a student working at each end of the mat if necessary.

The following is a list of sources of training/certification programs for aerobic dance and step aerobics. As resources, they can guide you further in developing your classes:

Aerobics and Fitness Association of America (AFAA)
  5250 Ventura Blvd., Ste. 200
  Sherman Oaks, CA 91403

The American College of Sports Medicine (ACSM)
  401 W. Michigan St.
  Indianapolis, IN 46202

International Association of Fitness Professionals (IDEA)
  6190 Cornerstone Court East, Ste. 204
  San Diego, CA 92121

Step Reebok
  100 Technology Center Dr.
  Stroughton, MA 02072
  Francis (1993), Herman (1995), and Smith (1995)

LINE DANCES

Line dances are basically repetitive movements performed to music, requiring little if any social interaction among the students. The number of potential dances is unlimited, and from time to time we even create our own to teach specific dance steps or to use music that the students particularly like. Certain line dances become "in vogue" from time to time, and, when appropriate, we will use those in class as well. Browsing through some of the resources listed on page 216 will help guide you in selecting appropriate line-dance music and patterns to meet your needs. We have presented four diverse, yet representative, line dances to get you started, using country/western, rap, and disco music.

SLAP LEATHER

- Formation: line dance
- Music: "Western Girls" by Marty Stuart

Count	Steps
1-4	2 heel splits (heels out, together, heels out, together)
5-8	**Right** heel out, together, **left** heel out, together
9-12	Repeat 5-8
13-16	**Right** heel tap twice in front, **right** toe tap twice behind **left** foot
17-20	**Right** heel tap front, **right** toe to side, **right** kick behind **left** knee (be sure to slap the **right** foot with the **left** hand), **right** toe side
21-22	Bring **right** foot up to **left** knee and slap **right** foot with **left** hand, 1/4 turn on **left** to your **right** and slap your **right** foot with your **right** hand
23-26	Vine to the **right** with a **left** kick behind the **right** knee and be sure to slap your **left** foot with your **right** hand
27-30	Vine to the **left** with a **right** kick behind the **left** knee and be sure to slap your **right** foot with your **left** hand
31-34	Step back **right**, back **left**, back **right**, **left** kick behind **right** knee (slap **left** foot with **right** hand)
35-38	**Left** step forward, **right** slide to **left**, **left** step forward, stomp **right** beside **left**

--Repeat Dance--

TOOTSIE ROLL

- Formation: line dance
- Music: "Tootsie Roll" by 69 Boyz

Count	Steps
1-8	Step hop **left**, step hop **left**, step hop **right**, step hop **right**
9-16	Step hop **front**, step hop **front**, step hop **back**, step hop **back**
17-24	Slide to the **left**, slide to the **left**
25-32	Slide to the **right**, slide to the **right**
33-40	Repeat 17-24
41-48	Repeat 25-32
49-56	Repeat 1-8
57-64	Repeat 9-16
65-72	Dip to the **left**, dip to the **left**
73-80	Dip to the **right**, dip to the **right**

--Repeat Dance--

ELECTRIC SLIDE

- Formation: line dance
- Music: "Electric Boogie" by Marcia Griffiths

Count	Steps
1-4	4 steps **right** (clap hands on 4th beat)
5-8	4 steps **left** (clap hands on 4th beat)
9-12	Back **right**, back **left**, back **right**, lean back, touch with **left** toe in front
13-16	Lean **forward**, touch **right** toe in back, lean **back**, touch with **left** toe in front
17-20	Step hop with 1/4 **left** turn, 3 steps **right**
21-36	Repeat 5-20
	--Repeat Dance--

MACARENA

- Formation: line dance
- Music: "Macarena" (A. Monge/R. Ruiz-Warner Bros.) by The Countdown Dance Masters

Count	Steps
1	Turn **right** palm down
2	Turn **left** palm down
3	Turn **right** palm up
4	Turn **left** palm up
5	Place **right** palm on **left** shoulder
6	Place **left** palm on **right** shoulder
7	Touch **right** palm to back of head
8	Touch **left** palm to back of head
9	Place **right** palm to **left** hip
10	Place **left** palm to **right** hip
11	Place **right** palm on **right** hip
12	Place **left** palm on **left** hip
13	Shake hips to the **left**
14	Shake hips to the **right**
15	Shake hips to the **left**
16	Clap, jump, and turn 1/4 turn to the **left**
	--Repeat Dance--

CIRCLE AND MIXER DANCES

Circles and *mixers* require more social interaction among students than do line dances because they include holding hands and switching partners. Here are three representative dances that use different music and dance steps.

COTTON EYED JOE (REITANO AND COLLINS 1983)

- Formation: partner dance; double circle facing counterclockwise with the boys on the inside
- Music: "Cotton Eyed Joe" by Al Dean
- Starting position: hands joined together (right/right over girl's shoulder, left/left)

Count	Steps
1-4	2 quick **kicks** forward from the knee with the **left** foot, step in place (left, right, left)
5-8	2 quick **kicks** forward from the knee with the **right** foot, step in place (right, left, right)
9-16	Repeat 1-8
17-20	**"Two step"** starting with the **left** foot (left, together, left, pause)
21-24	**"Two step"** starting with the **right** foot (right, together, right, pause)
25-32	Repeat 17-24
33-36	**"Two step"** straight starting with the **left** foot (left, together, left, pause)
37-40	**"Two step"** with 1/2 turn starting with the **right** foot (right, together, right, pause)
41-44	Repeat 37-40
45-48	Repeat 33-36
	--Repeat Dance--

DOWN ON THE CORNER (REITANO AND COLLINS 1983)

- Formation: partner dance; double circle facing partners, boys on the inside
- Music: "Down on the Corner" by Creedence Clearwater Revival
- Starting position: closed (partners facing each other)

Count	Steps
1-2	**Side touch** counterclockwise
3-4	**Side touch** clockwise
5-8	**Walk** counterclockwise in semi-open position with the hips touching (1, 2, 3, **1/4 turn touch** facing partner, ending in closed position)
9-10	**Side touch** clockwise
11-12	**Side touch** counterclockwise with **1/4 turn** facing clockwise
13-16	Partners **walk** clockwise holding inside hands (1, 2, 3, **turn** to face counterclockwise)
17-18	**Side touch out** while holding inside hands (away from partner)
19-20	**Side touch in** while holding inside hands (toward partner . . . release hands)
21-24	**Walk** away from partner . . . boys into the center, girls out (1, 2, 3, **1/4 turn with clap**)
25-26	**Side touch in** toward partner
27-28	**Side touch out** away from partner
29-32	**Spin** to new partner, ending in closed position (1, 2, 3, **touch** . . . boys follow inside hand, make full turn traveling forward to face next partner . . . girls follow outside hand, make full turn, and travel backward to face next partner)
	--Repeat Dance--

FLIP FLOP MIXER (REITANO AND COLLINS 1983)

- Formation: partner dance; double circle facing partners with the boys on the inside
- Music: "Flip Flop Mixer" by Jack and Helen Todd
- Starting position: closed

Count	Steps
1-4	**Walk backward** (1, 2, 3, pause)
5-8	**Walk** forward **diagonally left** to the next partner (1, 2, 3, pause)

Count	Steps
9-12	Boys extend both hands, palms facing up at waist height . . . girls **slap right hand** to right hand (2 count) then **left hand** to left hand (2 count)
13-16	Repeat 9-12 with the boys slapping the girls' hands
17-20	Bend elbows . . . partners **bump right elbows** 2 times, then **bump left elbows** 2 times
21-24	**Bump right hips** 2 times (2 counts for each bump)
25-28	**Stomp** in place (1, 2, 3, pause)
	--Repeat Dance--

SQUARE AND REEL DANCES

Square and *reel dances* can be used as mixers or to allow students to remain with one partner throughout a dance. It also fosters small-group cooperation because students work in groups of eight. We have presented three dances, progressing from a reel to traditional square with partner to traditional square that mixes partners.

MARCHING THROUGH ESM (REITANO AND COLLINS 1983)

- Formation: reel dance; two lines of four facing each other (boys in one line, girls in the other)
- Music: "Joys of Quebec" by Yankee Ingenuity
- Starting position: closed
- Basic cues:
  - Do-si-dos (8 counts . . . pass right shoulders, backs, left shoulders)
  - Right-hand turn (8 counts . . . partners approach each other, grasp right hands, turn each other clockwise, and walk back home)
  - Seesaw (8 counts . . . pass left shoulders, backs, right shoulders)
  - Left-hand turn (8 counts . . . partners approach each other, grasp left hands, turn each other counterclockwise, and walk back home)
  - Top couple walk (8 counts . . . between the two lines down to the bottom)
  - Weave (8 counts . . . each partner weaves up his or her own line back to the top)
  - Cast off (8 counts . . . partners in the head couple walk away from each other, to the outside of their line, and walk to the bottom, where they rejoin hands to form an arch)
  - Others follow (8 counts . . . each couple casts off following the "head" down to the bottom, joins hands, passes through the arch, and walks back to the starting position of two lines using another 8 counts)

Count	Steps
1-8	**Do-si-do** your partner
9-16	**Right hand** turn your partner
17-24	**Seesaw** your partner
25-32	**Left hand turn** your partner
33-40	**Top couple walk** to the bottom
41-48	**Weave** up own line to top
49-56	Top couple **cast off** . . . lead line to bottom . . . and form arch
57-64	Others go through arch holding hands and return to line as they cast off
65-128	Keep repeating 1-64 with each new head couple until all four couples have gone as a head couple

MAGIC TRUMPET (REITANO AND COLLINS 1983)

- Formation: traditional square with partner
- Music: "Magic Trumpet" by Dick Leger and Patricia Phillips
- Basic cues:
  - Square your set (heads, sides, couples number 1, 2, 3, 4)
  - Bow (to your partner, to your corner)
  - Shuffle step (one step per beat of music . . . feet almost slide on the floor)
  - Circle (right, left, all the way . . . 16 counts; back, 1/2 way . . . 8 counts)
  - Forward and back (8 counts . . . inside hands joined, walk forward 4 steps, back 4 steps)
  - Do-si-dos (8 counts . . . pass right shoulders, backs, left shoulders)
  - Promenade with boys holding palms up and girls palms down (full . . . 16 counts, 1/2 way . . . 8 counts, corner . . . always return to the boy's spot)

Count	Steps
1-4	**Bow** to **partner**
5-8	**Bow** to **corner**
9-24	**Circle left** (all the way)
25-40	**Circle right** (all)
41-48	**Forward and back**
49-56	**Circle left** 1/2 way
57-64	**Forward and back**
65-72	**Circle right** 1/2 way
73-80	**Do-si-do corner**
81-88	**Do-si-do partner**
89-104	**Circle left** (all the way)
105-112	**Do-si-do partner**
113-120	**Promenade partner** 1/2 way
121-128	**Heads forward and back**
129-136	**Sides forward and back**
137-144	**Do-si-do corner**
145-152	**Do-si-do partner**
153-160	**Circle left** 1/2 way
161-168	**Do-si-do corner**
169-176	**Do-si-do partner**
177-192	**Promenade partner** (all the way)
193-200	**Heads forward and back**
201-208	**Heads forward** and **do-si-dos** (with person opposite)
209-216	**Sides forward and back**
217-224	**Sides forward** and **do-si-dos** (with person opposite)
225-230	**Circle left** 1/2 way
231-238	**Circle right** 1/2 way
239-254	**Promenade** your **corner**
255-260	**Heads forward and back**

Count	Steps
261-276	**Heads forward** and **circle left** (all around . . . just four people)
277-284	**Sides forward and back**
285-300	**Sides forward** and **circle left** (all around . . . just four people)
301-308	**Circle left** 1/2 way
309-316	**Circle right** 1/2 way
317-332	**Promenade** your **corner**
333-394	Repeat 193-254
395-472	Repeat 255-332

PEANUTS (REITANO AND COLLINS 1983)

- Formation: traditional square mixing partners
- Music: "Peanuts" by Dick Leger and Patricia Phillips
- New cues:
  - Ladies chain (8 beats . . . 4 steps to opposite boy . . . offer right hand to other chaining girls as they pass right shoulders before joining left hands with opposite boy for 4-step courtesy turn)
  - Chain back same (back to partner)
  - Allemande left (8 beats . . . always left hands . . . walk around corner unless directed differently to end facing partner)
  - Heads promenade 1/2 way (8 beats . . . sides walk in 4 steps, then out 4 as heads walk around to opposite side)
  - Pass by your own (partner . . . promenade the next girl . . . boys always return home)

Count	Steps
1-8	**Head ladies chain**
9-16	**Chain back**
17-24	**Side ladies chain**
25-32	**Chain back**
33-40	**Do-si-do** your **corner**
41-44	**Do-si-do** your **partner**
45-60	**Promenade** your **corner** (all the way)
61-68	**Allemande left** your corner
69-76	**Do-si-do** your **partner**
77-84	**Circle left** 1/2 way
85-92	**Allemande left** your corner
93-100	**Do-si-do** your **partner**
101-108	**Circle left** 1/2 way
109-124	**Promenade** your **corner**
125-132	**Heads forward and back**
133-140	**Head ladies chain**
141-148	**Sides forward and back**
149-156	**Side ladies chain**
157-164	**Allemande left** your corner

Count	Steps
165-172	**Do-si-do** your **partner**
173-180	**Boys promenade** inside
181-188	**Do-si-do** your **partner**
189-252	Repeat 125-188 . . . sides go first
253-260	**Heads promenade** 1/2 way
261-268	**Head ladies chain**
269-276	**Sides promenade** 1/2 way
277-284	**Side ladies chain**
285-292	**Allemande left** your corner
293-308	**Pass by** your partner . . . **promenade the next** girl
309-364	Repeat 253-308 . . . sides go first
365-368	**Bow** to your **partner**

GYMNASTICS/TUMBLING

Although the word *"gymnastics"* often conjures up fond memories of Olga Korbut, Dominique Dawes, or a young Nadia Comaneci, it need not be associated with movements of Olympic caliber being judged by a panel of experts. In its purest form, gymnastics is an activity that teaches students kinesthetic awareness and spatial relationships.

The teaching of gymnastics should include activities that students can take part in throughout the entire school year. A number of low-level gymnastic movements are integrated into the warm-ups and circuits presented in chapter 5; for example, lying on a scooter pulling hand over hand along a horizontal rope or vaulting back and forth over a folded mat. For apparatus experiences, we are forced to teach in a traditional unit format because of the logistics involved in sharing equipment within our district. Our teaching style is anything but traditional, however.

We have found that a big key to success during our gymnastics unit is to provide enough daily activities for students of all body types, thus we can hold their attention and keep them motivated to stay on task. Initially, many middle school students cringe when they hear the words "gymnastics unit." Many factors affect their attitude: fear, poor elementary school experiences, lack of adequate upper-body strength,

and excessive body weight, to name but a few. If not accounted for in program planning, these factors will almost always ensure failure in the unit. As a result, many middle school programs no longer teach gymnastics, which is a disservice to many students, or continue to teach so traditionally that only a small percentage of "body types" succeed—at the exclusion of the masses.

Consider breaking your unit down into individual lessons, as we have done with most of the modular curriculum concepts presented in chapters 6, 7, and 8, and consider using the smaller components of balance, body-space awareness, and coordination activities in an exploratory-movement environment. We think of our gymnastics as more of a *"kinastics"* experience because kinesthetic and gymnastic concepts blend together.

The use of apparatuses as movement-exploration stations within the warm-up segment of class allows students with less-than-perfect gymnastic-type bodies to enjoy gymnastics in a nonthreatening way. For example, in the Upper-Body Strength Circuit (see page 44) one of the stations requires that students vault back and forth over a folded mat, a task easily achieved by all students, yet a task that is gymnastic in origin.

An entry level (Level I) student could place her hands on the mat and vault back and forth over the mat without fear of height, falling, or failing. While gaining confidence and success, she should strive to straighten her knees and keep her feet together. The intermediate student (Level II) could perform cartwheels or a round-off as he passes repeatedly over the mat. The advanced (Level III) student might kick to a momentary handstand with a quarter or half turn off the mat.

Such a station within a warm-up circuit will allow students of varied levels to experience success, thus improving body control and overcoming a fear of movement that involves turn-ing the body upside down. As was mentioned earlier, a tumbling or "kinastics"-type station need not only be used during gymnastics; it could also be used to help students experience movement throughout the year.

Apparatuses can also be used to form obstacle courses that students of all ability levels will find fun and challenging while developing problem-solving skills. This concept will be discussed in greater detail later in this chapter.

SAMPLE GYMNASTICS AND TUMBLING LESSON PLAN

Purpose:

- To develop balance, strength, and problem-solving skills through participation in varied balancing and strength stunts using apparatus and floor exercise movements

Assessment Objectives:

- To what extent can the students balance in a number of positions on the different pieces of apparatus?
- Can the students put a mount, dismount, and two intermediate (Level II) moves into a creative routine?
- Do the students appreciate the amount of strength and courage needed to be a gymnast?

Materials:

- 2 wrestling/gymnastic mat sections
- 4-8 folded tumbling mats
- 2 8-inch crash mats
- 4 4-inch crash mats
- 1 regulation balance beam
- 1 low-level balance beam
- 1 set of rings
- 1 Reuther board

Skill Development:

- Set the gym equipment up as shown in diagram 9.1:
  - One 8-inch crash mat is to be placed under the rings; the other is to be used for teaching the front flips at the wrestling mat area.
  - The 4-inch crash mats are to be placed around and under the regulation balance beam.
  - The folded tumbling mats are to be used with the low balance beam and for teaching handsprings.
  - The Reuther board is to be used for teaching the front flips with the 8-inch crash mat at the wrestling mat area.

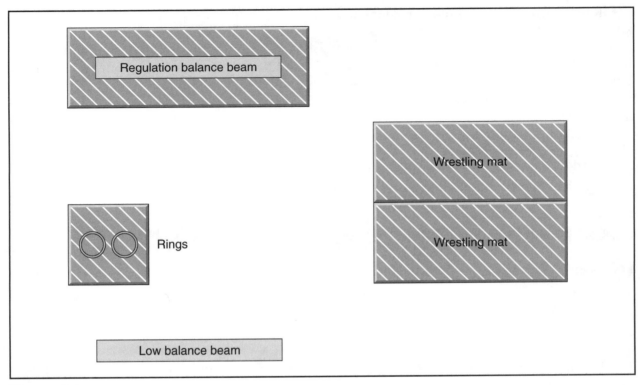

Diagram 9.1

- Review previously taught basic floor exercise travels and balances:
  - Have students work out of a "follow the leader"-type formation.
  - Students who cannot progress through all the skills should repeat those skills they feel comfortable with as the class progresses, allowing all students to work at their level.
  - Skills include:

    forward roll, dive roll, back roll, cartwheel, round-off, forward roll step out, three-point tip up, headstand, frog stand, handstand with roll out, and walk on hands.

Activity:

- Teach new floor exercises and/or independent work:
  - Students may opt to learn a front handspring and a front flip with the teacher on one floor exercise mat.
  - Other students may work on the low beam, performing previously taught skills:

    Press to "V" seat; stand, walk, and turn; knee scale; handstand; and kick dismount out of a knee scale.

  - Other students may tumble using previously taught skills on the other floor exercise mat.
- Teach new balance-beam skills and/or independent work:
  - Students may opt to learn a swing to a straddle seat and turn 360 degrees in the straddle seat on the regulation balance beam with the teacher.
  - Other students may work on the low beam, performing previously taught skills:

    Press to "V" seat; stand, walk, and turn; knee scale; handstand; and kick dismount out of a knee scale.

  - Other students may tumble using previously taught skills on the other floor exercise mat with the exception of front flips.

- Review ring skills and/or independent work:
  - Students may opt to review previously taught ring skills:

    Inverted hang; bird's nest, one-arm cross, and a dislocate dismount under the direct supervision of the teacher.
  - Other students may work on the low beam, performing previously taught skills:

    Press to "V" seat; stand, walk, and turn; knee scale; handstand; and kick dismount out of a knee scale.
  - Other students may tumble using previously taught skills on the other floor exercise mat with the exception of front flips.

Another concept we use to reach students that "breaks from tradition" is to use folded mats as balance beams, vaulting stations, and apparatuses. The possibilities are endless, as we have been shown by our students. For the overweight or unstable students, or for students who fear heights, we use the folded mats (approximately 2 1/2 feet wide) as a modified balance beam. The shape of the beam does not even need to be straight. By using the mats to form the shapes of letters (e.g., *T, H, A,* etc.), students can perform and create a number of routines without falling off the "beam." We have already mentioned using the mats in a warm-up circuit to introduce and teach vaulting. Try having students work in pairs using these mats to create routines or partner pyramids of their own. It is hardly "traditional gymnastics," but students will accept the challenge and surprise you with their creativity!

You will notice in reviewing this sample gymnastics/tumbling plan that previously taught skills are reviewed and new skills are introduced each day. This class format allows students of varied skill to participate at a level of comfort that promotes fitness and safety and allows the instructor to split time at several pieces of apparatus that require spotting.

Table 9.1 provides a listing of appropriate middle school skills for floor exercise, uneven parallel bars, vaulting, rings, parallel bars, side or pommel horse, horizontal bar, and the balance beam. When working with beginners, use folded mats to teach vaulting as well as the low beam to ensure safety while minimizing the fear factor associated with heights. Each skill is further classified by level of difficulty for use in establishing teaching progressions and evaluating students through the portfolio-assessment process outlined in chapter 4. Although your daily classes should follow the outline of

the *sample lesson plan,* the activities you use in the *skill-development* and *activity segments* should be progressive over the two- to three-week time span allotted for this unit. Use the activities listed in table 9.1 to guide you.

OBSTACLE/CHALLENGE COURSES

A logical extension of the gymnastics/tumbling unit is to use apparatuses and mats to create *obstacle/challenge courses.* These courses provide students of all body types with problem-solving experiences while exploring movement. Use the following suggestions to be creative in designing an obstacle/challenge course for your students:

1. Create various-sized walls (heights and widths) by placing mats over side horses and parallel bars. Some of the walls should be easy enough for all students to conquer while others

Table 9.1   Gymnastic/Tumbling Movements by Level

Category/Movement	Entry Level I	Intermediate Level II	Advanced Level III
Balance beam			
• arabesque		X	X
• cartwheel			X
• dip steps	X		
• flying angel		X	X
• forward roll			X
• full 360 degree turn			X
• handstand off			X
• jump to a cross beam straddle		X	
• jump to a straight arm	X		
• knee scale	X		
• pirouette		X	
• round-off			X
• shoulder stand			X
• simple Swiss outside the beam			X
• straddle "L" seat			X
• straddle seat on beam			X
• Swedish fall			X
• "V" seat			X
Horizontal bar			
• back hip circle		X	X
• back upraise		X	X
• cast away	X	X	
• cast to a half pirouette		X	X
• cherry drop	X	X	
• front hip circle	X	X	X
• front swing	X	X	
• front swing to a half turn off	X	X	
• kip up		X	X
• mixed grip kip			X
• rear swing	X	X	
• skin the cat	X		
• straddle inverted hang	X	X	
• travel across bar with mixed grip	X	X	
Parallel bars			
• back upraise		X	X
• backward roll		X	X
• backward swing	X		

Table 9.1 *(continued)*

Category/Movement	Entry Level I	Intermediate Level II	Advanced Level III
• cast to straight arm support		x	
• cast to upper arm hang	x	x	
• dip swing	x	x	
• double leg cut and catch		x	x
• forward roll to straddle seat	x	x	
• forward roll to upper arm hang	x	x	
• forward swing	x		
• front dismount	x	x	x
• front upraise	x	x	
• giant swing			x
• glide kip		x	
• jump to straight arm support	x		
• "L" seat	x	x	x
• rear dismount	x	x	x
• shoulder cross bar	x	x	x
• shoulder stand		x	x
• simple Swiss outside bars	x	x	
• single leg cut and catch	x	x	
• straddle travel	x		
• Stutz to upper arm support		x	x
• swing to straddle seat	x	x	
• upper arm kip		x	x
Rings			
• back lever		x	x
• back upraise		x	x
• backward roll			x
• bird's nest	x		
• dislocates			x
• dislocate off		x	x
• forward roll above rings		x	x
• forward roll to half hang	x		
• forward upraise			x
• front lever			x
• half cross	x	x	
• half lever below rings	x		
• inlocates		x	x
• inverted hang (straight body)	x		
• kip up			x

(continued)

Table 9.1 *(continued)*

Category/Movement	Entry Level I	Intermediate Level II	Advanced Level III
• "L" seat above the rings		X	X
• muscle up	X	X	X
• pendulum swing below rings	X		
• pike inverted hang	X	X	X
• roll backward to a half hang	X	X	
• single leg cut and catch		X	X
• shoulder stand			X
• skin the cat	X		
• straddle cut off		X	X
• straddle "L" seat above the rings		X	X
• straddle off			X
Side or pommel horse			
• double leg circle off			X
• double leg half circle	X	X	
• double leg full circle			X
• feint to a feint	X	X	
• feint to a flank off	X	X	X
• flank vault on end	X	X	
• full scissors		X	X
• half scissors	X	X	
• jump to single leg cut and catch	X	X	
• jump to straight arm support	X		
• reverse scissors		X	X
• simple Swiss	X	X	X
• single leg full circle	X	X	
• travels	X	X	
Tumbling (floor exercise)			
• arabesque	X	X	X
• Arabian dive roll			X
• back handspring			X
• backward roll	X	X	
• backward roll with extension		X	X
• backward roll with extension to handstand			X
• cartwheel	X	X	X
• dive cartwheel			X
• dive roll	X	X	
• forearm stand	X	X	
• forward roll (tuck, straddle, pike)	X	X	

Table 9.1   *(continued)*

Category/Movement	Entry Level I	Intermediate Level II	Advanced Level III
• front somersault			x
• handspring		x	x
• handstand with roll out			x
• headspring		x	x
• headstand	x	x	x
• headstand press to handstand			x
• kip up (snap up)	x	x	x
• "L" seat		x	x
• one-handed cartwheel			x
• round-off		x	x
• shoulder stand	x		
• straddle jump	x	x	
• Swedish fall	x		
• tripod to tip up	x	x	
• "V" seat	x	x	
Uneven parallel bars			
• back hip circle		x	
• cast		x	
• cast away off top bar			x
• cherry drop	x		
• free hip circle			x
• front hip circle			x
• glide kip mount			x
• jump to a straight arm support	x		
• pirouette under bar		x	x
• sole circle			x
• toe on/toe off		x	
Vaulting			
• flank vault	x	x	
• handspring			x
• handspring to 1/4 turn off		x	x
• headspring		x	x
• squat on—jump to feet	x		
• squat on—stoop through		x	x
• squat vault	x	x	
• straddle vault	x	x	x
• wolf vault	x	x	

should challenge even the most advanced students.

2. Use balance beams for walking above (balance) or scaling below (strength) in a "sloth"-like manner.

3. Ropes can be used for swinging, scaling walls, or pulling one's body weight while lying on a scooter.

4. Mats can be used for forming tunnels and mazes or for tumbling and crawling.

5. Cones and hoops add color, create excitement, and aid in controlling traffic flow. Another method for controlling flow patterns is to use a "shotgun" start, much like a golf tournament, in which five or six students start at different obstacles and go through the course at the same time.

Although diagram 9.2 provides an example of a basic obstacle course, be creative in forming your own, meeting the unique needs and abilities of your students.

TRACK AND FIELD

Like *gymnastics/tumbling* activities, many components of *track and field* should be taught throughout the year. Running, throwing, and jumping are three of the most natural movements students make in a variety of warm-up, game, and sport activities. As teachers, we can help students more fully develop these movements if we approach these movements as skills. In the case of throwing and jumping, we often spend time on mechanics through drill work. Running, however, is often taken for granted—the "either you have it or you don't" attitude. Nothing could be a bigger mistake, because speed is a skill and, as such, should be taught and maximized for every student through warm-up activities (Speed Dynamics 1 and 2, Orbiter, etc.) and game activities.

Although we have addressed speed in some of our warm-up activities and team games, track and field is the logical place to address speed in greater detail. Speed is central to all track and field events. In fact, speed is universal to gauging performance in almost every

sport. Since speed is a skill, it can be taught and developed by targeting four primary concepts: neurological efficiency, skill acquisition, increased strength and power, and improved aerobic capacity (Gorney 1995); we have focused on these concepts throughout the suggested yearly curriculum in this book. More specifically, there are five main focuses for the runner to concern himself with, the single most critical objective being reduced time on the ground (and in the air) for each stride taken. This objective is accomplished through improved stride length and stride frequency resulting in a maximum velocity.

Several mechanical cues can maximize your students' running abilities, whether on a track, court, or field:

- Acceleration is best achieved with a forward-leaning body and high knees. The shins and feet fire back as the body gradually comes to a sprint, with body height and stride length gradually increasing as well.

- *Maximum velocity* can only be sustained for 2 to 3 seconds before the student settles into the mechanics of *speed maintenance*:

  - Body position: Teach students to run with a tight stomach, flat back, and tall posture. This position is initiated with a deep breath and maintained by holding the breath for prolonged periods. The time students hold their breath will vary from student to student and distance to distance, but the principle is the same—the more stable the musculature of the upper body, the less unwanted movement. The key here is to get students focused on proper body position.

  - Recovery: This phase will minimize time spent in the air. Students only increase or maintain speed when pulling back against the ground, so they will want to get the legs back to the ground as quickly as possible. "Toe up . . . heel up . . . knee up" is an easy teaching cue to remember and use. The recovery leg should have the ankle stepping over the opposite knee, using the tibialis anterior (toe up), not the hamstring, making the ankle the most important joint in recovery mechanics.

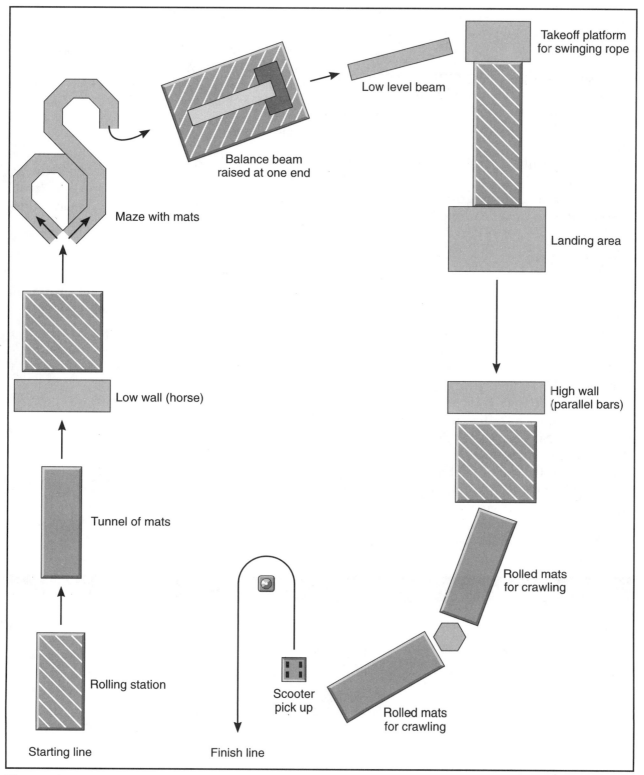

Takeoff platform
for swinging rope

Low level beam

Balance beam
raised at one end

Maze with mats

Landing area

Low wall (horse)

High wall
(parallel bars)

Tunnel of mats

Rolled mats
for crawling

Rolling station

Scooter
pick up

Rolled mats
for crawling

Starting line   Finish line

Diagram 9.2

– Ground preparation: Minimize contact time with the ground, reducing the *braking* effect and, instead, pulling back against the ground, propelling the body forward. Combined with recovery mechanics, ground preparation will maximize and/or maintain velocity through improved stride lengths and frequencies.

- Arm action: The arm action should balance leg action by driving the elbows back, recovering elastically with the thumbs up.

These mechanics can be practiced and drilled through the *speed-dynamics drills* presented as warm-up activities in chapter 5, as well as through some of the partner warm-ups (Pull or Push Your Own Weight, etc.). Plyometrics relay races, agility drills, obstacle courses, and many game-type activities will all promote speed if verbal cues are reinforced through a variety of lesson activities on a yearlong basis.

TRACK ACTIVITIES

Similar to the gymnastics/tumbling unit, the track and field unit provides a variety of activities that will appeal to students of all body types, shapes, and personalities. The shot-putter's physique is different from that of a hurdler. A big key to having a successful unit is to provide enough daily activities for students of all body types. As with the *sample gymnastics/ tumbling lesson plan*, review previously taught skills and introduce new ones each day.

By keeping the running challenges fun and creative, you will get more out of your students, and, in turn, they will get more out of the experiences. Table 9.2 lists the activities we use throughout our track and field classes. With the exception

of the one-mile, 880-yard and 440-yard runs, all the other runs are of a short, sprint-type nature, ideal for helping students focus on the previously presented speed development cues. Also, there are eight relay races that challenge students to cooperate as well as run.

Relay Races

We have included five rather traditional relays (the 4-by-25 through 4-by-440 relays), but, by using a little creativity, you will help motivate students even more. Three easy relay variations we use include:

1. The *uneven relay*, that incorporates strategies and cooperative skills:
   - Divide your entire class into teams of approximately 10 students.
   - Set them on the track, and require them to cover a given distance as a team (quarter mile, for example) in a relay format.
   - Let the students decide the best way to achieve their goal based on their team members.
   - Some students may run farther than others based on body type, running ability, and so on.
   - The team goal is to run one lap as fast as possible.

Table 9.2 Track and Field Activities		
Field activities		
• discus	• long jump	• softball throw
• high jump	• shot put	• triple jump
Running activities		
• 50-yard dash	• hurdles	• 4 x 220 relay
• 75-yard dash	• one-mile run	• 4 x 440 relay
• 100-yard dash	• 4 x 25 relay	• gender relays
• 200-yard dash	• 4 x 50 relay	• race across nations
• 440-yard dash	• 4 x 100 relay	• uneven relay
• 880-yard dash		

- This race can easily accommodate up to 40 students in a single race by using four teams.

2. *Gender relays* can be juggled to have girls race girls, boys race against boys, and/or mix teams (two girls, two boys) for coed competition.

3. *Race across nations* is an activity that integrates well on an interdisciplinary level and affords your department positive schoolwide exposure:

   - Have the students run 5 minutes (or longer) each class period and log their distances.

   - The total school population can pool the distances to run from Los Angeles to New York, Barcelona to Moscow, through Asia, across Africa, or any other route spanning the globe:

     - This can also be done competitively, racing one grade level against another.

   - Such an event makes every student important as part of the overall team.

     - Post the results weekly on a prominently displayed map, possibly in the cafeteria, to showcase progress.

   - Ask social studies teachers to get involved, integrating geography lessons with the locales passed through in the "race."

   - In the mornings, on the public address system, update the school's progress by mentioning the current location, giving a brief geographic description of it.

Distance versus *sprint* techniques vary, and the race across nations is a perfect time to introduce distance techniques, pacing, the mental aspects of distance running, and such fitness concepts as target heart rate and caloric expenditure. Build on a progression of distances from sprints up to the one-mile run. During distance training, introduce interval training concepts, fartlek training, and team relays and hills, using a cross-country format.

Hurdles

Hurdling should be incorporated into the sprint section of your lessons, progressing from folded mats to hurdles placed on grass. Running on the grass will be much less threatening than running on the track, and three flights of hurdles, four lanes wide, can easily be set up on half a football field as illustrated in diagram 9.3.

FIELD EVENT ACTIVITIES

Field events can easily be worked into your track and field lesson plan, providing students with a variety of diverse, safe teaching stations (refer to diagram 9.3). Many of these events such as shot put, discus, and softball throw (which we liken to throwing the javelin) will attract different students from those attracted to the running events, both motivating them and keeping them involved in your lessons.

High Jump

The *high jump* is unique in that it is somewhat gymnastic in nature, having a certain level of fear and elements of visible failure that must be overcome. When teaching it, start the bar at a level low enough so that virtually every student can succeed. Using a round bar and padding it with foam or rolled towels will also help to eliminate the fear factor some students face when jumping.

Teach jumping techniques (scissors and western roll) that minimize risk to the neck and back during landing, and save the more advanced "flopping" techniques for the more advanced students. Emphasize the approach, takeoff, clearance, and landing phases of jumping. Caution: The teacher should always be present when students are using the high jump station.

Long and Triple Jumps

Long and *triple jumping* give students the chance to combine speed (sprint techniques) with jumping. These jumps are relatively safe, and the teaching station is easy to administer because students can cooperate by judging one another's accomplishments.

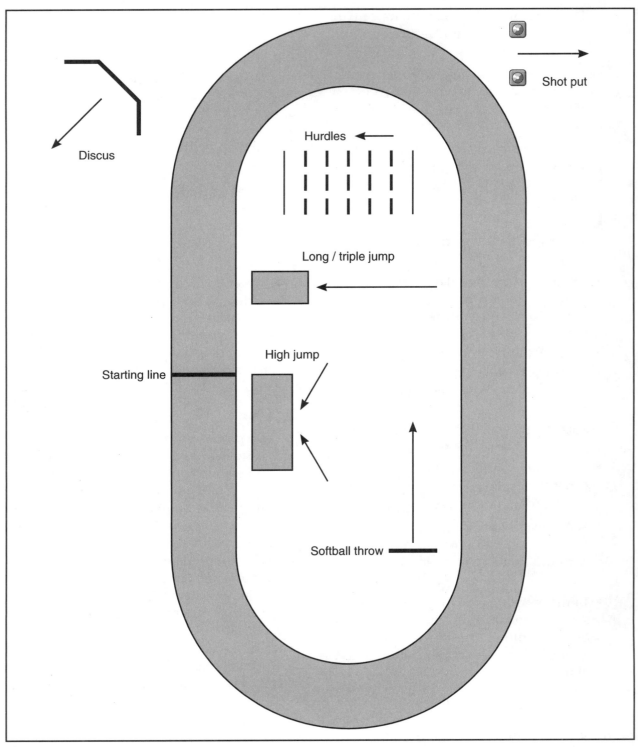

Diagram 9.3

As with the high jump, stress the approach, takeoff, flight, and landing aspects of the events when teaching the mechanics. Teach the long jump before the triple jump because the long jump is not only easier for students but is also the third phase of the triple jump. Teach the triple jump in segments, as a hop, step, and jump. Start without a run, then have students verbalize the progression as they do it—"Hop . . . Step . . . Jump"—and finally put it all together with a run.

Shot Put

The *shot put* station should be placed in an area that provides safety for the nonthrowing students and where the repeated landing of the "shot" will not damage a field (indentations) needed for running activities. As illustrated in diagram 9.3, provide cones for students to wait behind about 10 feet from the throwing student. A simple safety rule is to have the next student in line retrieve the shot and then enter the throwing area, alleviating the possibility of one student accidentally dropping the shot put on another while handing it to him.

Six- to eight-pound shot puts are appropriate for this age group because their joints and musculature will safely support and control such a weight. Teach mechanics in a progression that includes footwork; coordination of leg, torso, and arm actions; release; and follow-through.

This is another station in which students should be able to cooperate and self-govern their own activity after initial instruction.

Discus

The *discus* station can be run in identical fashion to the shot put, with the exception that we place the nonthrowing students behind a baseball backstop for safety. Use home plate to throw from and the first- and third-base lines as limits for the throwing area. A junior high or women's size discus (one kilo) is most appropriate for middle school students because many of them have small hands and will have greater success with the smaller, lighter discus.

Teach mechanics in a progressive manner, including grip; release; and the coordination of leg, torso, and arm action. At this level it is not necessary to teach a "spin" unless working with a very athletic, elite student.

Softball Throw

We use the *softball throw* as an added activity station and discuss its likeness to throwing a javelin. It is a unique throwing event in that it combines sprinting speed with a throwing motion, that requires transitional footwork between the two phases. Use this event as yet another method of teaching biomechanical principles relative to an applied activity.

Track and field lessons can be successfully taught following a class plan similar to *the gymnastics/tumbling plan*, in which new concepts are introduced daily, balanced by a variety of independent student activity.

SAMPLE TRACK AND FIELD LESSON PLAN

Purpose:

- To develop a proficiency and competence in the skills of jumping (high and hurdles), sprinting, and shot putting

Assessment Objectives:

- To what extent do students select to participate in events that will be successful for their body types?
- Can students maintain a heart rate in their respective target zone for a prolonged period of time?
- Can students perform proper jumping and throwing techniques for a given activity?

Materials:

- 2 crash mats, 6-8 exercise mats
- 2 high jump standards, 1 cross bar
- 6 hurdles
- 12 cones

- 1 discus
- 6-8 softballs
- 2 stopwatches
- 1 shot put

Skill Development:

- Set up the equipment as shown in diagram 9.3
- Have the students race across nations for 5 minutes:
  - Have the students take their pulse rates at the end of the 5-minute period and compare their findings with their heart rate zone.
  - Remind students to note their distances and record them when returning to the locker room after class.
- Teach the fundamentals of shot put:
  - Foot position
  - Hand and arm position
  - Use of legs and torso to generate power and throwing force
  - Extension at release
- Teach the fundamentals of high jumping:
  - Approach (steps and angle)
  - Takeoff (leg and arm functions)
  - Various jumping styles (scissors and western roll)
- Verbally review the previously taught skills of dash starts:
  - Hand-to-foot relationship
  - Weight distribution and hip position
  - First step and arm drive
- Verbally review the previously taught skills of hurdling:
  - Focus on one hurdle at a time
  - Opposite arm and leg relationships for counterbalance during the hurdle phase
  - The difference between, and importance of, hurdling versus jumping

Activity:

- Provide students with individual work time at stations of their choice:
  - Dashes—let the students challenge one another using dashes of various distances and applying the previously taught start and sprint principles (25, 50, 75, 100 yards) during independent work time
  - Hurdles using four lanes of three flights
  - High jump
  - Shot put

As with the *gymnastics/tumbling sample plan*, you will notice that each day a previously taught skill is reviewed and one or two new skills are introduced to challenge students. This class format allows students of varied body types to participate in varied activities at a level of comfort that both promotes fitness and is safe. As the teacher, you can then supervise a particular activity based on safety or student need.

WRESTLING

Wrestling is one of the oldest and most natural of the individual sport activities. It challenges students to think quickly in an ever-changing environment through the use of mind and body. As students learn to move, counter, and recounter, they can be likened to pawns in a game of "movable chess," developing speed, strength, balance, and spatial awareness. Keep your focus on teaching movement, and dispel the image many students and parents have of wrestling, which is what they see on television as "pro wrestling."

Our curriculum uses *"determination"* games so that students can be competitive when learning the physical skills of wrestling without the added fear of failure. Although many students need to learn the harsh lesson of how to accept failure without pointing the finger at teammates, our approach minimizes singling students out to be pinned in front of their peers. The games teach wrestling skills as well as good human attributes, namely determination, perseverance, and problem solving.

All these activities involve 1-on-1, pure and basic human competition. To make your classes easier for you, more successful for the student, and safer from the point of liability, we offer two suggestions: (1) weigh all your students and allow students to select their own partners based on weight; and (2) match students with respect to the aggressiveness of their personalities. Do not underestimate this last suggestion because mismatched students (timid versus aggressive) will not benefit from wrestling each other. Remember that our goal

This is an excellent time to also teach students about *abduction avoidance* through self-awareness/self-defense experiences. The focus of these lessons should be on awareness and body control. Through the presentation of different potentially dangerous scenarios that require split-second problem solving and serve to heighten student awareness, you can relate education to real life.

Drill students in a line formation using basic karate, judo, and jujitsu skills, that can be taught as a coed activity. Speed and the targeting of appropriate body parts for "strikes" should be emphasized, not strength. Involve your local police department in these lessons because avoidance, not conflict, should be the first rule of defense.

as teachers is to use wrestling as a means for teaching movement, not to make wrestlers out of our students.

A typical wrestling class should consist of approximately 10 to 12 minutes of strenuous exercise focusing on the primary muscles used in wrestling. Any of the *fitness circuits* presented in chapter 5 would be appropriate. The warm-up period should be followed by a stretching session, paying particular attention to muscles in the neck and shoulder areas. Follow stretching with a review of previously taught skills and the demonstration of new moves. Individual wrestling skills are categorized and presented in table 9.3. Situation wrestling, which is a combination of drilling and live wrestling while applying problem-solving skills, should culminate with wrestling game/challenge activities.

The purpose of these wrestling challenges is twofold. First, they conclude the wrestling class on a fun, positive note. Second, they develop qualities found not only in a good wrestler (mentioned earlier in this section) but also in a good person. Try using a different challenge activity each class period as a means of closure. Lessons will be learned and self-esteem preserved, and your lesson will conclude in a fun atmosphere.

Table 9.3 Wrestling Skills

Breakdowns	Pinning combinations
• cross face • half nelson and wrist ride • near side bar arm and tight waist • tight waist and far arm • three quarter nelson • waist and far ankle	• bar arm and half nelson • cradle series • double bar arms • half nelson • three quarter nelson
Escapes and reversals	**Takedowns**
• hip roll • inside stand • outside stand • Peterson • sit out and turn (in/out) • switch	• crank • double leg • duck under • fireman's carry • hip toss • single leg • stance and setup • tie up

ONE-LEGGED CHICKEN FIGHTS

Purpose:

- This activity challenges problem-solving skills and balance. There is no team concept because everyone is on his or her own.

Materials:

- A well-matted floor area

Activity:

- Have each student find a space on the matted area and balance on one foot while holding the other foot at all times.
- On the command "Go," the students hop in a variety of directions trying to bump, push, and/ or pull other students off balance while retaining their own balance.
- A student is considered out of the activity when she lets go of her foot or touches the floor with more than one body part.
- To maximize safety:
  - Remind students how to fall safely.
  - Encourage them to get off the mat quickly when they are eliminated.
  - Divide your class into weight divisions so large students are not participating with smaller students.

FOOTBALL DETERMINATION

Purpose:

- This challenge activity not only develops a sense of determination, it also uses the breakdowns, pinning combinations, and escapes taught as wrestling skills. It is a goal-oriented challenge and can be played either on an individual basis with students paired by weight or as a team concept.

Materials:

- A well-matted floor area
- 1 football

Activity:

- Students set up as illustrated in diagram 9.4, with the football centered between the end lines.
- Two groups of students assume the referee position on the end lines as illustrated. When set, the teacher blows a whistle, and the person in the bottom position tries to get to the football, grasping it with both hands, thus scoring a point.
- The person on top uses wrestling skills to prevent the bottom person from succeeding.
- 30 seconds are allowed for each match; then the students switch places, and the same pairs go again.
- For safety, be sure to match students by weight and personality as mentioned earlier in this section.

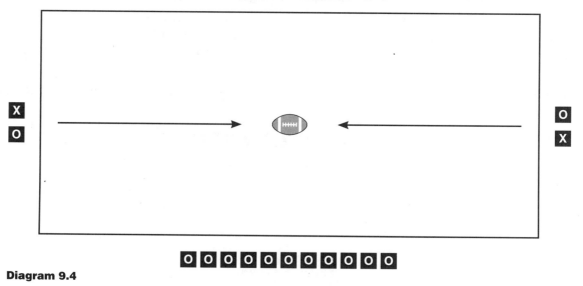

Diagram 9.4

GRIP AND RIP

Purpose:

- This activity uses grip strength and balance to help students learn when to apply an offensive movement and when to counter.

Materials:

- A well-matted floor area
- 1 large *"Physio-type"* ball, 3 to 4 feet in diameter

Activity:

- Two opponents, paired by weight, grip the large ball while kneeling on the mats.
- On the whistle, each student tries to tear the ball loose from the other student's grasp, using moves and countermoves to throw the opponent off balance.
- For safety:
  - Have the students turn their heads to the side and place them against the ball when setting up and throughout the competition.
  - Students should start and remain on their knees.
  - Limit contests to 30 seconds in duration.

PUSH BALL

Purpose:

- This activity is much like Grip and Rip in that it requires offsetting the balance through moves and countermoves. It also takes into consideration the factors of power and momentum.

Materials:

- A well-matted floor area
- 1 large *"Physio-type"* ball, 3 to 4 feet in diameter

Activity:

- Set the students up as illustrated in diagram 9.5, again pairing students by weight.
- Students start much as they did in Grip and Rip, with the heads turned and placed on the ball, kneeling and gripping the oversized ball from opposite sides. On the whistle, the students attempt to push the ball into their opponents' end zone using power, momentum, and balance to overcome the resistance from their partners.
- Limit matches to 30 seconds, and stress the safety factors of head placement and the kneeling position.

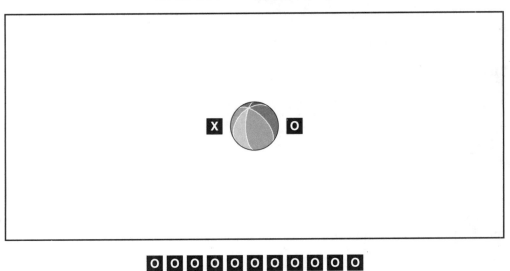

Diagram 9.5

THE HUMAN KNOT

Purpose:

- This activity, that challenges grip strength and perseverance, may be tried in two-person groups or as a team activity.

Materials:

- A well-matted floor area

Activity:

- One group of students sits on the matted area as shown in diagram 9.6; the students form a circle and join themselves together by hooking arms or joining hands.

- The opposing group members, remaining on their knees, try to separate the arms/hands of the first group and are timed until they complete the task.

- For safety:

  - Make sure students pull or push joints in their natural direction.

  - If grabbing fingers to separate hands, at least four fingers must be grabbed (bending one finger back is not allowed).

- After one group has had the offensive, switch groups and repeat the challenge.

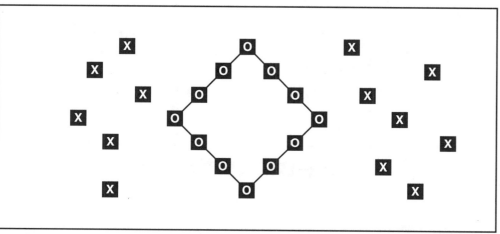

Diagram 9.6

BREAKTHROUGH AND CONQUER

Purpose:

- This challenge combines those elements used in Push Ball and Football Determination, much like on the popular television show *American Gladiators*.

Materials:

- A well-matted floor area

- 1 large *"Physio-type"* ball, 3 to 4 feet in diameter

Activity:

- Arrange the students as illustrated in diagram 9.7. Designate two students as "gladiators" (and for added fun, assign them appropriate names—believe us, the students will help you in this respect).

- On the "Go" signal, a student starts a two-part challenge, being allowed 15 seconds at each station:
  - Station 1 is much like Push Ball in that the student must push both the giant ball and the gladiator over the designated boundary lines. Whether successful or not, the challenger then moves on to station 2 after 15 seconds while the gladiator remains in place until changed by the teacher.
  - Station 2 is much like Football Determination in that the student tries to push or pull the gladiator out of the designated box, while the gladiator uses wrestling moves to remain inside the box for the 15 seconds.
- If using a team format, score 10 points for each station in which the student successfully overcomes the gladiator. If scoring on an individual basis, the gladiator remains in the game until beaten.
- For safety, be sure to pair individuals by body size and personality.

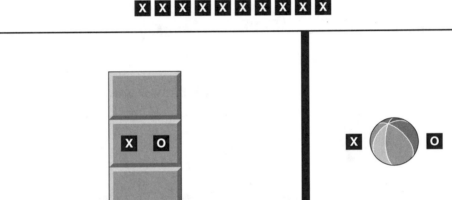

Diagram 9.7

PLATFORM WRESTLING

Purpose:
- This challenge is based on the sumo wrestling concept in Japan and uses many of the wrestling skills taught in class.

Materials:
- A well-matted floor area
- 2-3 exercise mats measuring 4-by-6-feet in size

Activity:
- Pair students by weight on each of the 4-by-6-foot wrestling mats, as shown in diagram 9.8, and have them start in a referee's position (kneeling).
- On the command "Go," they proceed to wrestle until one partner knocks her opponent off the 4-by-6-foot mat, thus becoming the winner.
- These matches are without time limits.

- The winner retains the right to wrestle again, and many choose either the "up" or "down" position.

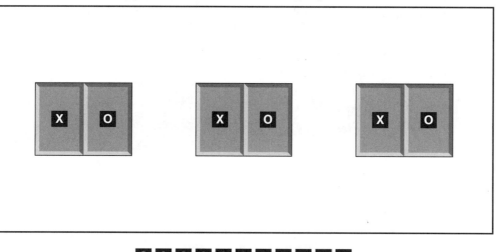

Diagram 9.8

TAKE THE PIN

Purpose:

- This challenge is an excellent activity to use before your takedown drills once proper foot and hand position for a takedown has been taught.

Materials:

- A well-matted floor area
- 1 bowling pin

Activity:

- Divide the students into two teams, and position them as illustrated in diagram 9.9.
  - The pairing of students by weight for this activity is not necessary because there is no contact between players.

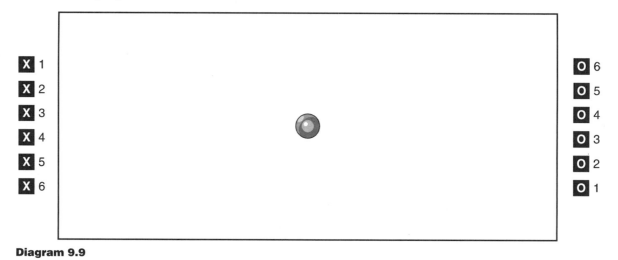

Diagram 9.9

- – Success in this activity is based on reaction time and thinking.

- – Each student needs to receive a number and remain in a standing position.

- The teacher calls out a number, and each student with that number sprints out onto the mat, trying to "take the pin." The student uses head and hand fakes along with foot movement to outmaneuver his opponent, taking the pin and sprinting back across his end line before he is tagged.

- This game is quite similar to *"steal the bacon"* except that the emphasis is placed on using wrestling techniques to outperform the opponent.

musical references

"Western Girls" by Marty Stuart, from the Marty Party Hit Pack Album © 1995 by MCI Records, Universal City, CA 91608

"Tootsie Roll" by 69 Boyz, from the Quad Album © 1990 by Downlow Records, 715 N. Ferncreek Ave., Orlando, FL 32803

"Electric Boogie" by Marcia Griffiths, from the Carousel Album © 1990 Island Records, 14 E. 4th St., New York, NY 10012

"Macarena" (A. Monge / R. Ruiz-Warner Bros.) by The Countdown Dance Masters, from the Macarena Tropical Disco Album © 1996 Madacy Entertainment Group, Inc., P.O. Box 1445, St. Laurent, Quebec, Canada H4L 4Z1

"Cotton Eyed Joe" by Al Dean, from the K-202-A Album © 1967 Age Productions, Nashville, TN

"Down on the Corner" by Creedence Clearwater Revival, from the Willy and the Poorboys Album © by Fantasy Records, Willowdale, Ontario, Canada

"Flip Flop Mixer" by Jack and Helen Todd, from the #15016 Album © by Grenn, Batch, OH 44210

"Joys of Quebec" by Yankee Ingenuity, from the Kitchen Junket Album © 1977 by Alcazar, Inc. Distributed by Silo, Inc., P.O. Box 429, Waterbury, VT 05676

"Magic Trumpet" by Dick Leger and Patricia Phillips, from Square Dancing: The American Way Album (K4061) © 1981 by Kimbo Educational, Long Branch, NJ 07740

"Peanuts" by Dick Leger and Patricia Phillips, from Square Dancing: The American Way Album (K4061) © 1981 by Kimbo Educational, Long Branch, NJ 07740

references

American Heart Association. 1994. *Heart and stroke facts*. Dallas: AHA National Center.

AS&S (Advanced Safety and Standards). June 6-10, 1994. Project Adventure Workshop. Brattleboro, VT.

Block, M., and E. Vogler. 1994. Inclusion in regular physical education: The research base. *Journal of Physical Education, Recreation & Dance* 65(1): 40-44.

Brandt, R. 1992. On outcome-based education: A conversation with Bill Spady. *Educational Leadership* 50(4): 66-70.

Chu, D., and R. Panariello. 1988. Jumping into plyometrics. *NSCA Journal* 10(3): 73.

Chu, D., and R. Panariello. 1989a. Jumping into plyometrics. *NSCA Journal* 11(5): 82.

Chu, D., and R. Panariello. 1989b. Jumping into plyometrics. *NSCA Journal* 11(6): 86.

Cooper Institute for Aerobics Research. 1994. *The Prudential FITNESSGRAM test administration manual*. Dallas: Cooper Institute for Aerobics Research.

Corbin, C. 1987. Physical fitness in the K-12 curriculum: Some defensible solutions to perennial problems. *Journal of Physical Education, Recreation & Dance* 58(7): 49-54.

Dauer, V., and R. Pangrazi. 1986. *Dynamic physical education for elementary school children*. New York: Macmillan.

Francis, L. 1993. Teaching step training. *Journal of Physical Education, Recreation & Dance* 64(3): 26-30.

Franck, M., G. Graham, H. Lawson, T. Loughrey, R. Ritson, M. Sanborn, and V. Seefeldt (Outcomes Committee of NASPE). 1992. *Outcomes of quality physical education programs*. Reston, VA: National Association for Sport and Physical Education.

Fulmer, R. 1994. *Secondary portfolios*. Ticonderoga, NY: Edlink.

Gorney, J. 1995. Teaching speed in physical education. October 27, Superintendent's Conference Day Presentation at East Syracuse, NY.

Heitmann, H., and M. Kneer. 1976. *Physical education instructional techniques: An individualized humanistic approach*. Englewood Cliffs, NJ: Prentice Hall.

Herman, S. 1995. A step circuit program. *Strategies* 8(4): 16-20.

Hopple, C. 1995. *Teaching for outcomes in elementary physical education*. Champaign, IL: Human Kinetics.

Humphrey, J. 1990. *Integration of physical education in the elementary school curriculum*. Springfield, IL: Charles C Thomas.

Mc Swegin, P., C. Pemberton, C. Petray, and S. Going. 1989. *Physical best: The AAHPERD guide to physical fitness education and assessment*. Reston, VA: American Alliance for Health, Physical Education, Recreation and Dance.

Miller, A., J. Cheffers, and V. Whitcomb. 1974. *Physical education: Teaching human movement in the elementary schools*. Englewood Cliffs, NJ: Prentice Hall.

Pate, R., J. Ross, C. Dotson, and G. Gilbert. 1985. The national children and youth fitness study: A comparison with the 1980 AAHPERD norms. *Journal of Physical Education, Recreation & Dance* 56(l): 70-76.

Reitano, L., and H. Collins. 1983. *Dancing: Lines to circles to squares.* East Syracuse, NY: East Syracuse-Minoa Central School.

Rohnke, K. 1989. *Cowtails and cobras II.* Dubuque, IA: Kendall/Hunt.

Ross, J., and G. Gilbert. 1985. The national children and youth fitness study: A summary of findings. *Journal of Physical Education, Recreation & Dance* 56(1): 45-50.

Sherrill, C. 1994. Least restrictive environment and total inclusion philosophies: Critical analysis. *Palaestra* 10: 25-35.

Smith, T. 1985. Selling physical education. *Journal of Physical Education, Recreation & Dance* 56(6): 66-67.

Smith, T. 1994. High school fitness units: Teaching lifetime skills. *Journal of Physical Education, Recreation & Dance* 65(5): 69-72.

Smith, T. 1995. Keys to success in teaching dance aerobics. *Dance Teacher Now* 17(2): 77-81.

Smith, T. 1996. Off-season vertical jump training for junior high volleyball players. *Strength and Conditioning* 18(2): 24-28.

Smith, T. 1997. Authentic assessment: Using a portfolio card in physical education. *Journal of Physical Education, Recreation & Dance* 68(4): 46-52.

Smith, T., and N. Cestaro. 1992. Saving future generations—the role of physical education. *Journal of Physical Education, Recreation & Dance* 63(8): 75-79.

Smith, T., and N. Cestaro. 1995. Teaching health/fitness concepts to elementary students—a modular strategy. *Journal of Physical Education, Recreation & Dance* 66(4): 69-72.

Smith, T., M. Powell, and P. Belodoff. 1992. Control the line, control the game! *NSCA Journal* 14(6): 65-67.

Spady, W. 1988. Organizing for results: The basis of authentic restructuring and reform. *Educational Leadership* 46(2): 4-8.

State Education Department. 1986. *Physical education syllabus grades K-12.* Albany, NY: The University of the State of New York.

State Education Department. 1991. *A new compact for learning.* Albany, NY: The University of the State of New York.

index

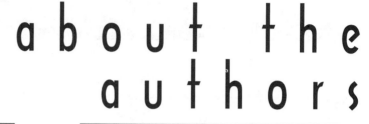

about the authors

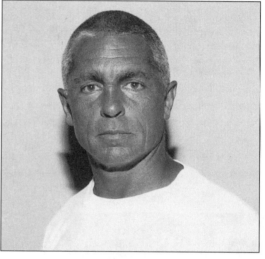

Timothy Smith has been a physical education teacher, volleyball coach, and lacrosse coach within the East Syracuse-Minoa Public School System in East Syracuse, New York, since 1991, but his physical education and fitness experience goes back much further. He has also been an adjunct faculty member in Adelphi University's Department of Physical Education and Human Performance Sciences, director of Adelphi University's Adult Fitness Program, an exercise physiologist in private practice, and a general partner in a physical therapy and sports medicine practice.

Smith has written many articles on fitness-related topics for publications such as the *Journal of Physical Education, Recreation and Dance (JOPERD), American Fitness,* and *Fitness Management.* He has been a member of the National Strength and Conditioning Association since 1987. Smith earned his MEd in applied physiology from Columbia University. He is a resident of Manlius, New York.

Nicholas Cestaro has been a physical education teacher since 1971, working with children in kindergarten through high school. Since 1985 he has taught physical education at Kinne Street Elementary School in East Syracuse, New York. From 1974 to 1988 he also had coaching responsibilities in five sports at the junior high level. He was presented with the Teacher of Excellence Award in 1990 by the East-Syracuse-Minoa School District faculty and board of education.

Cestaro has been a master teacher in conjunction with Syracuse University since 1988. He has written articles for *JOPERD* and spoken at the New York State Physical Education Conference. He earned a bachelor's degree in education and a graduate degree in health education from SUNY at Cortland. Cestaro makes his home in Fayetteville, New York.

More guides to middle school fitness and skills

Teaching Sport Concepts and Skills
A Tactical Games Approach

INCLUDES 169 LESSONS

Linda L. Griffin
Stephen A. Mitchell
Judith L. Oslin

Make the transition from teaching skills to teaching how to use those skills in a game! This book introduces a tactical approach that allows students to first develop an overall sense of the sport, then take a problem-solving approach to mastering skills. Then, when they understand why each skill is important, students can apply the skills effectively during game play.

Each of the 169 lesson plans includes a tactical problem, a lesson focus, objectives, appropriate games, problem-solving questions, and practice tasks. Separate chapters provide guidelines for assessing game performance and implementing the tactical approach.

1997 • Paper • 248 pp
Item BGRI0478 • ISBN 0-88011-478-9
$19.00 ($28.50 Canadian)

TEACHING MIDDLE SCHOOL PHYSICAL EDUCATION

A Blueprint for Developing an Exemplary Program

BONNIE S. MOHNSEN

Create a program that addresses the specific needs and capabilities of middle school students! This comprehensive guide is packed with exciting ideas and proven strategies for

- selecting instructional units,
- integrating with other subject areas,
- developing unit and lesson plans,
- assessing and grading students,
- motivating students,
- demonstrating positive teaching behaviors,
- selecting teaching styles and strategies,
- choosing instructional materials, and
- incorporating technology effectively.

Includes sample programs for sixth, seventh, and eighth grade.

1997 • Paper • 360 pp
Item BMOH0513 • ISBN 0-88011-513-0
$27.00 ($39.95 Canadian)

To request more information or to place your order, U.S. customers call **TOLL FREE 1-800-747-4457**. Customers outside the U.S. place your order using the appropriate telephone number/address shown in the front of this book.

Human Kinetics
The Information Leader in Physical Activity
http://www.humankinetics.com/

Prices subject to change.